DAILY LIFE DURING

THE INDIAN WARS

Recent Titles in
The Greenwood Press Daily Life Through History Series

Ancient Egyptians, Second Edition
Bob Brier and Hoyt Hobbs

Civilians in Wartime Latin America: From the Wars
of Independence to the Central American Civil Wars
Pedro Santoni, editor

Science and Technology in Modern European Life
Guillaume de Syon

Cooking in Europe, 1650–1850
Ivan P. Day

Victorian England, Second Edition
Sally Mitchell

The Ancient Greeks, Second Edition
Robert Garland

Chaucer's England, Second Edition
Jeffrey L. Forgeng and Will McLean

The Holocaust, Second Edition
Eve Nussbaum Soumerai and Carol D. Schulz

Civil War in America, Second Edition
Dorothy Denneen Volo and James M. Volo

Elizabethan England, Second Edition
Jeffrey L. Forgeng

The New Americans: Immigration since 1965
Christoph Strobel

The Inuit
Pamela R. Stern

DAILY LIFE DURING

THE INDIAN WARS

CLARISSA W. CONFER

The Greenwood Press Daily Life Through History Series

 GREENWOOD

AN IMPRINT OF ABC-CLIO, LLC
Santa Barbara, California • Denver, Colorado • Oxford, England

Library of Congress Cataloging-in-Publication Data

Confer, Clarissa W., 1965–

    Daily life during the Indian Wars / Clarissa W. Confer.

        p. cm. —(The Greenwood Press daily life through history series)

    Includes bibliographical references and index.

    ISBN 978-0-313-36454-9 (hard copy : alk. paper)—ISBN 978-0-313-36455-6 (ebook) 1. Indians of North America—Wars—Social aspects. 2. United States—Territorial expansion—Social aspects. 3. Frontier and pioneer life—United States. 4. War and society—United States. I. Title.

    E81.C59   2011

    973.2—dc22   2010039387

ISBN: 978-0-313-36454-9

EISBN: 978-0-313-36455-6

15   14   13   12   11   1   2   3   4   5

This book is also available on the World Wide Web as an eBook. Visit www.abc-clio.com for details.

Greenwood
An Imprint of ABC-CLIO, LLC

ABC-CLIO, LLC
130 Cremona Drive, P.O. Box 1911
Santa Barbara, California 93116-1911

This book is printed on acid-free paper ∞

Manufactured in the United States of America

—For John and Denali who give so much encouragement and
support and happily visit historic sites.

CONTENTS

PREFACE

This book covers a large scope of time and place in examining daily life during the Indian Wars. The study of war could be endless; however, here the focus is on the series of conflicts between Native American nations or tribes and the Euro-American forces of the various governments who claimed possession of the region of the United States. From the 1600s through 1900 Indians fought armies representing various colonies, France, Britain, and the United States. Countless individuals fought and often died in struggles with individual settlers that are outside the story presented here. Also, native groups routinely contested each other for access to territory, resources, and prestige, but that is a separate subject.

The idea of war is a familiar concept to most readers. Causes, combatants, and outcomes vary but violence, bloodshed, and death reverberate through the centuries of warfare. The focus of the history of wars is usually on the soldiers and the battles they fought. However, that is viewing war in a vacuum. The reality is that societies fight wars, engage in epic struggles for dominance or survival, and exist through the experience. An understanding of daily life in the wars must include a comprehension of the native groups affected, including culture, economic strategies, social organization, and the political pressures and decision making that led them to conflict. The majority of people in a warring society do not fight.

Women, children, and older men experience war as support staff, advisors, healers, and in dozens of other roles that rarely take them onto a field of conflict. The daily life of wars is their story too, the unfolding of years, often decades, spent in conflict with strangers, and how that affected society.

The book moves chronologically from the 1600s to the late 1800s and generally geographically from east to west. The first pitched battles between British settlers and indigenous peoples occurred in the two earliest areas of settlement—New England and Virginia. The Powhatan, Pequot, and Wampanoag peoples felt the power and danger of European expansion in the 17th century. As disease and conflict forced these groups from their homelands the same pattern of Euro-American expansion and native displacement continued westward. In the 18th century, the French and British involved the natives in their imperial struggle for control of the continent's interior. Soon after that was settled the Indians had to contend with the newly formed government of the United States. The race westward to the Mississippi was on, and leaders like Tecumseh and Black Hawk fought hard to hold their peoples' place in the world.

American land hunger and desire for resources soon pushed settlement west of the Rockies and engaged hundreds of other tribes in the fight for their homelands. From lesser known Indian groups like the Pomo and Modoc to the famous Navajo, Comanche, and Lakota, nearly all 19th century indigenous people would find their lifestyles threatened. The natural and perhaps only realistic response to the impending peril was warfare. Those groups who thrived on conflict, like the Lakota and Apache, may have fared better than those who did not, but by 1890 all had experienced military defeat and had submitted to reservation life, where they were stripped of their weapons and forbidden to fight. The last conflict between the 19th-century U.S. Army and native peoples ended in the deaths of nearly 200 Lakota men, women, and children on the frozen banks of Wounded Knee Creek in South Dakota.

The voices of native peoples are hard to hear, especially in the early years of our history. With no written languages, the indigenous peoples left little record that the dominant Euro-American culture respected or preserved. Throughout this book the available primary sources have been used and quotes included to help the reader move back into the past inhabited by a people for whom the conflicts were a source of daily terror, of worry, of sadness. Dozens of pictures have been included to breathe life into a text about real people. Not surprisingly, few pictures preserved an image of native life. The majority of the existing illustrative record comes from the non-native point of view. As photography became more widely available after the Civil War, some native leaders sat for stiffly posed studio portraits. Others, like the famous Crazy Horse, are visible to us only through contemporaries' descriptions. Women and children generally faded first from the historic record and left even less retrievable evidence of their lives.

Some of the locations where the Indian Wars took place are devoid of historical reference while others, especially in the West, remain in a condition the combatants would recognize. The opportunities are there. To walk along the Big Hole River among skeleton tipis imagining the terror as the cavalry charged the sleeping camp, to hide behind the wagon boxes at Fort Phil Kearny, or stand in the cemetery at Wounded Knee, is to truly feel daily life in the Indian Wars.

CHRONOLOGY

17th Century

1607	Powhatan assist Jamestown settlers
1608	Iroquois meet Champlain
1613	Pocahontas captured by the English
1616–1619	Smallpox ravages coastal New England
1621	Pilgrims and Wampanoags share Thanksgiving
1622	Powhatan attack Jamestown settlers
1636–1637	Pequot War
1644	Opechancanough attacks Virginia settlements
1649	Iroquois defeat Huron
1675	King Philip's War
1675	Bacon's Rebellion

18th Century

1712	Tuscarora War
1715	Yamasee War
1754	French and Indian War breaks out

1763	French abandon native allies
1763–1765	Pontiac's War (Rebellion)
1776	Cherokees fight Americans
1777	Shawnee leader Cornstalk killed
1777	Oneida aid Washington at Valley Forge
1777	Iroquois League divides during American Revolution
1791	Blue Jacket leads confederacy to defeat U.S. General Harmer
1792	Blue Jacket leads confederacy to defeat U.S. General St. Clair
1794	Native confederacy defeated by Wayne at Fallen Timbers

19th Century

1811	Tecumseh builds a native alliance
1813	Tecumseh defeated at Battle of the Thames
1813	Red Stick Creeks fight Americans
1817–1818	First Seminole War
1830	Indian Removal Act
1832	Black Hawk War
1832–1838	Removal of Five Southeastern Nations
1835–1842	Second Seminole War
1849	Pomo Massacre
1851	Fort Laramie Treaty
1855	Grattan Incident
1855	Blue Water Massacre
1860	Apache Wars: Mangas Coloradas abused by whites, vows revenge
1861	Apache Wars: Cochise captured, family murdered
1861–1865	Civil War in Indian Territory
1862–1864	Dakota War
1863	Apache Wars: Mangas Coloradas murdered
1864	Navajo Long Walk
1864	Sand Creek Massacre

1864	Adobe Walls battle
1866	Powder River War
1867	Wagon Box Fight
1868	Washita Massacre
1868	Medicine Lodge Treaty
1871	Apache Wars: Camp Grant Massacre
1871	Apache Wars: Cochise surrenders
1872–1873	Modoc War
1874	Red River War
1874	Custer discovers gold in Black Hills
1876	Dull Knife Fight
1876	Battle at Rosebud
1876	Battle at Greasy Grass (Little Big Horn)
1876	Battle at Slim Buttes
1877	Crazy Horse surrenders, is killed
1877	Sitting Bull to Canada
1877	Nez Perce Flight
1878	Satanta dies in prison
1881	Sitting Bull surrenders to reservation
1884	Apache Wars: Geronimo surrenders
1885	Apache Wars: Geronimo breaks out of reservation
1886	Apache Wars: Geronimo surrenders
1887	Dawes Act results in the loss of 60 percent of Indian land
1890	Ghost Dance
1890	Sitting Bull's murder
1890	Wounded Knee Massacre

1

EARLY COLONIAL WARS

COLONIAL WARS

Most Americans are familiar with what we refer to as the "founding" of our country. From an early age we are regaled with tales of the stern yet brave Pilgrims who came to the shores of North America seeking freedom. These hardy souls crossed the terrifying Atlantic Ocean in an old and leaky ship, the *Mayflower*. After surviving that journey, they set about to create a new life on the virgin shores of a new continent. Or was it virgin? Usually the Pilgrim story expands to include a nice vignette of the first Thanksgiving which was shared with a few noble savages remaining on the periphery of the story of America. Occasionally, Americans remember the other English colony which was established at Jamestown 13 years before the Pilgrims arrived. This too is a story of endurance and determination against frightful odds and it too includes the noble and this time beautiful savage in the form of Pocahontas. If we pay any attention to the stories we will notice that natives appear only briefly, in small numbers, and on the periphery of the English experience. The reality of course was quite different.

Anglo settlers stumbled into a world inhabited by many thousands of native people. The forces unleashed by the 15th-century connection between the continents of the world had already altered the lifestyle of native America. Disease, and to a lesser extent trade and technology, changed native lives forever. It did not, however, destroy them entirely. So European colonists disembarked onto an inhabited continent populated by a diversity of people. Many of these people would be forced into direct contact with the new arrivals, and for many that contact would be in the form of warfare. The 17th century brought a nearly constant state of warfare to native peoples living east of the Mississippi River.

Native Warfare

Warfare was not unknown to native people. Europeans did not invent and import conflict of arms. Almost all the people of the world will take up weapons to defend themselves, their loved ones, and their homeland. Few cultures can be said to have no experience of war at all. Experience with and commitment to warfare varied among the peoples of the Eastern Woodlands. Some like the Iroquois seemingly designed their entire culture around violence, while others like the various Algonquian groups fought when they had to but spent more time on other pursuits. The arrival of the new settlers would change that ratio. The coming of Europeans meant more native time and resources would have to be spent engaged in warfare.

It is important to remember that although war drastically altered the lives of Native Americans, in many ways their life remained the same for some time after the coming of the Europeans. Violence and the threat of it lurked in the background and frequently broke to the forefront during the colonial period. But like any people engaged in a struggle, the Native Americans of what is now the eastern United States had to continue their daily lifestyle as best they could. They might be able to go weeks, months, perhaps even years in between active warfare against whites. During that period they tried their best to practice their traditional lifeways. For the majority of people spread along the coasts of eastern North America that was an Eastern Woodlands lifestyle.

EASTERN WOODLANDS CULTURE

Historians and anthropologists use the term Eastern Woodlands tradition to refer to the cultural adaptation that allowed people to live so successfully in eastern North America. The name refers to the most striking characteristic of the East—massive forests. The Eastern Woodlands in the centuries before European arrival were heavily forested. Dense old-growth forest boasting huge ancient specimens blanketed the land. Northeastern natives lived among dark woods with few openings except those they made themselves. Arriving Europeans claimed that a squirrel could travel from the Atlantic Ocean to the Mississippi River without ever setting foot on the ground. In the mid-Atlantic region mostly deciduous species like oak, maple, and hickory predominated while coniferous fir, pine, and spruce intermixed as the woods spread northward to the Arctic. In addition the area is rich in water resources. Thousands of rivers, streams, and small creeks bisect the land, many following the north-south alignment of the mountains, providing migration routes for humans and animals. The flowing water feeds lakes, ponds, and wetlands which in turn support a wide variety of aquatic life. The Northeast is among the richest temperate regions, supporting hundreds of species of mammals, birds, fish, and reptiles in addition to abundant plant life. The bountiful variety of plants and animals translated into rich food resources for humans.

Economic Life

The Woodlands tradition has been described as probably the most distinctive, the most completely indigenous culture ever to exist in eastern North America. Woodland Culture is generally recognized by characteristics such as the exploitation of local resources, widespread use of pottery, supplemental agriculture, and elaborate mortuary customs. Europeans encountered natives living in what anthropologists refer to as the Late Woodland period which began about 1200 CE. The lifestyle appeared primitive to European observers. Native Americans had no domesticated animals so all of their protein came from wild game. Males hunted in the vast forests surrounding their villages. Since these people relied so heavily on forest animals, they altered the forest through burning to create better habitat and ease of travel and hunting. White-tailed deer were a critical species for Woodland peoples. They also hunted bear, squirrel, rabbit, and turkey with bows, traps, and snares. Protein also came from fish caught with lines, traps, and nets. All this hunting seemed barbaric to Europeans, but there is one aspect which they could recognize. The native peoples of the East were farmers.

Native Americans of the East shaped their culture around a few main crops. The triad of maize, beans, and squash became the focus of subsistence for many groups. These three crops worked well together, with beans returning nitrogen to the soil which had been absorbed by growing corn. Still, fields could be played out within a decade of consistent farming. There were many more varieties of these foods than we currently utilize today, but they played a similar role in diets. Corn proved to be a major staple in Woodland life. Cornmeal kept well and provided a stable food supply for lean winter months. Nearly every group in the Northeast that could grow maize did so. Indians ate it nearly daily, as corn cakes, corn bread, corn porridge, corn soup, and a brew made with parched corn. Some of the meals they enjoyed are still around today. For example, boiled beans and corn is what we call succotash. Washing corn with wood ash loosened the hulls and created hominy, still prepared today. Berries—fresh, cooked, and dried, added flavor to their meals, as did spices such as wild onions, ginger, and maple sugar.

Because they exploited such a variety of food sources, Eastern Woodlands people were fairly mobile, described as being semi-nomadic. This lifestyle dictated portable, comfortable housing and they chose the wigwam style. Four saplings bent into the center quickly created a frame over which were placed long strips of bark sewn together. An inside lining of swamp grass both insulated and absorbed moisture while animal skins hanging at the one low entrance blocked cold air. There was no furniture in this portable dwelling, but fir branches covered with skins acted as beds to insulate sleepers from the cold earth. A constantly burning fire in the middle kept the whole place fairly warm. This well-designed dwelling was common throughout the Algonquian culture area.

Algonquians, and indeed all Woodlands people, enjoyed a fairly stable, comfortable lifestyle in the years before contact. Into this relative prosperity and constancy arrived Europeans. The first permanent English settlement was established on the James River in Virginia in 1607. Jamestown remains a settlement to this day. This tiny outpost of the British Empire faced extensive challenges that threatened its very existence, but persevered and survived only because of two critical factors. One was the continued support of England in the form of money, supplies, and colonists, and the other was support from Native Americans. Indian support came both willingly in the form of trade and gifts and unwillingly as a result of violence. There is little doubt that the English colony would not have survived if they had not been able to seize food supplies, game animals, and land from the local inhabitants.

SOUTHEAST

The small ships *Susan Constant*, *Godspeed*, and *Discovery* crossed the Atlantic and deposited their human cargo on the shores of the

James River in May 1607. One hundred and four Englishmen had landed in a world they knew little about. Both the natural and human world seemed very foreign to them, but they would have to figure out both in order to survive. Although this new world appeared as wilderness to the English, it was in fact rich in both resources and human culture. The particular spot that came to be known as Jamestown was empty when the ships arrived which revealed the semi-nomadic behavior of the local Algonquian Indians.

Social and Economic Organization

We refer to the Algonquians of Tidewater Virginia as the Powhatan, a name taken from the dominant village in the 17th century. The Powhatan lived in a region that can be roughly described as the coastal plain of today's Virginia. They controlled about 6,000 square miles of land, laid out 100 miles east to west and 100 miles north to south. To the east lay the Atlantic Ocean and to the west resided territorial rivals, the Siouan-speaking Monacan and Mannahoac tribes. Although the Powhatan could not expand much farther, by the 17th century their numbers had been reduced by disease to only 14,000, which fit comfortably within their boundaries. The land is bisected by numerous large rivers, including the Potomac, the Rappahannock, the York, and the James, as well as countless small streams and creeks. Not surprisingly, water provided the easiest form of travel. The climate is fairly mild, providing bountiful natural resources. The native people pursued a varied economic strategy of hunting, fishing, gathering, and farming with clear gender divisions for each activity. They located their communal villages near waterways for easy access to water and fishing. Men left the villages, particularly in the fall, on extended hunting trips, primarily for white-tailed deer. Women farmed fields of corn, beans, and squash located near the villages. The agriculture was slash-and-burn with new fields carved out of nearby forests. Once a field was exhausted, planting moved to a new patch of forest while the old area recovered. Women usually constructed new dwellings near the new fields for their convenience. So entire settlements sort of sprawled around the Tidewater.

Political Organization

The Powhatan differed from northern tribes mostly in their political organization. By the European contact period, the Powhatan had a chiefdom level leadership. One paramount leader attempted to control foreign policy and warfare and collect tribute from other groups within his sphere of influence. Social distinctions existed within the tribe. Chiefs, or *werowances*, who could be male or female, and their families could be distinguished by their dress. At important events they wore long, fringed buckskin mantles with multiple necklaces of pearls and copper and shell beads. They controlled large quantities of food which they could dispense to others. The leading families were paid great deference. They gave orders and had servants to cook, serve, and dress them. Only these highest ranking males received special burials and had access to sacred temples. Thus the Virginia Indians shared more aspects of the ancient Mississippian system centered on wealth, privilege, and religion than did Northern Woodlands groups.

With rank and power came responsibility. So when the pale, hairy Englishmen stepped off the ships in the spring of 1607 it was the problem of the paramount chief of the area, Powhatan. His personal name was Wahunsenacawh but when he became *mamananatowick*, or paramount chief, he took the name Powhatan from the village of his birth. Powhatan led a somewhat disparate collection of tributary villages. He came to power somewhere between the 1550s and 1580s, by inheriting six chiefdoms and then expanding his holdings either by intimidation or military conquest. By 1607 Powhatan claimed power over all the peoples of the coastal plain except the Chickahominy, and even they were paying certain duties to Powhatan. This somewhat unified group of territories was called Tsenacomoco by its occupants. Many of its composite parts retained considerable autonomy and some cultural differences while maintaining a political alliance with the larger group. Unified aggression was one of the main achievements of this coalition.

The chief's capital town of Werowocomoco always maintained the largest force of warriors. To remain the overall leader, Powhatan had to be able to both defend his people, and squash any rebellion quickly. Tribes collected under his mantle of protection paid annual tributes. They paid in corn, furs, and the only real item of material value, pure copper ore. Powhatan held a monopoly on copper and used it as gifts and payments to subject tribes for military service. Tribute wealth could be redistributed in order to maintain the alliances. The organization was run by a hierarchy of rulers called *werowances* (*weroansquas* if they were female), or "commanders." Werowances of villages deferred to district leaders, who deferred to Powhatan. Naturally, many of these werowances were relatives of the overall chief. As an important man, Powhatan had many wives and thus a large extended family. His daughter Pocahontas, seemingly an only child according to English history, was but one of his many children. In addition to werowances, priests, esteemed warriors, and elders also held a special place in the Powhatan community. It was in fact a fairly stratified society. The elite were set off by their clothing, housing, behavior, burial practices, and other aspects of daily culture. When Europeans came they recognized a society divided by wealth and status. For example, Powhatan had large tracts of land reserved specifically for him for hunting or planting as well as the necessary labor to produce crops, not unlike European royalty. The social and political system that governed Tidewater Virginia had been developing for centuries and everyone knew their part in it.

In 1607 new players in the game arrived with no place in the Powhatan chiefdom. These Europeans would have to be fit into the existing world of the Algonquian Indians. The Indians of Virginia already had experience with Europeans. They knew of earlier Spanish

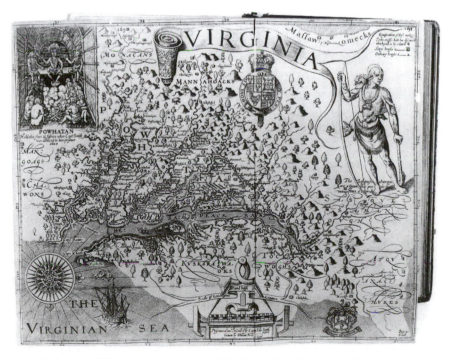

A 1606 map of Virginia as described by John Smith. It includes a drawing of a native man and a depiction of Powhatan. (Library of Congress)

and English expeditions to the New World. In fact, it appears that they wiped out the Chesapeake tribe, which may have harbored English survivors from the Lost Colony at Roanoke. Now the Indians had to decide if the latest newcomers were allies who received protection and support or enemies to be routed. To a great extent the English made that decision for the Indians. The behavior of the newcomers appeared far more like enemies than friends. They stole Powhatan food, dug up graves, and behaved violently. The Jamestown colonists really gave the local indigenous people little opportunity to classify them as allies. If you were not friends you were enemies, and enemies were soon at war.

Gender Divisions

Virginia Indian males grew up in a world that encouraged and practically glorified fighting. Since they lived in a hunting society, they learned early what it took to dominate and kill. Boys were trained from a young age in archery. Mothers normally withheld breakfast from their sons until the boys had successfully shot an arrow into an object thrown in the air. They progressed to hunting trips with their father in the hope of qualifying for initiation to manhood by the time they were 10 to 15. Real men were proficient, rugged, and courageous. A man's ability in warfare was an important mark of his status in society. Those who encountered them characterized the Virginia Indians as proud and aggressive. They were encouraged to recite accounts of their exploits as hunters and warriors, especially in public. A great deal of time at festivities was given over to stories of amazing feats showcasing incredible bravery. Powhatan leaders frequently rewarded men for their skills. So the men that took on the English in warfare in the early 17th century were confident of their skills.

Warfare

Powhatan warriors had experienced but did not possess the technology of the English. Not only did they not possess firearms, or any metal tools, as other indigenous peoples, but stone was a relatively rare commodity in the coastal plain. Sometimes arrowheads had to be made from oyster shells or wild turkey spurs. However, the Powhatan warriors were experts with their long bows. Their heads were shaved on the right side to avoid tangling their hair in bowstrings, and they were quite deadly shots. The bows were strong enough to shoot 40 yards close to target and 120 yards plus with some accuracy. They could pierce English wooden shields more easily than the English pistols could. Bows could not match the power of English muskets, but they could be reloaded and fired much faster than these primitive guns.

The English reported that the Powhatan painted and dressed themselves for battle, engaging in elaborate rituals of singing and dancing before forming ranks and advancing steadily toward the enemy. Frontal assaults were not unknown but the Indians also employed guerrilla tactics. Eyewitnesses described Indians as creeping on all fours like bears with their bows in their mouths. The Virginia Indians had already learned that the Europeans favored pitched battle, and so they relied more often on stealth and surprise. They also adapted to the use of new weapons and worked hard to obtain firearms and modify their tactics to use them most effectively.

The Powhatan war was a long-term conflict ebbing and flowing between the Virginia colonists and the native inhabitants. Powhatan had evaluated the English for nearly a decade after their arrival knowing he could either use or destroy them. He traded with them, suffered their thefts, and even sent his daughter Pocahontas to their village as an ambassador. Powhatan tried several avenues of diplomacy. After his brother captured the strongest English leader, John Smith, Powhatan chose to hold a ceremony in which he probably appointed Smith as a *werowance* for the new subsidiary white tribe. The "English tribe" was to pay tribute of two cannons, a grindstone, and military aid if ever Powhatan should require it. (In a later ceremony the English tried to anoint Powhatan as a vassal of James I. The Indian chief refused to kneel before the people he regarded as *his* vassals, who were bringing him presents to show their subservience.)

Why tolerate these obnoxious newcomers at all? The Powhatan chiefdom was a fairly volatile political entity. The paramount chief guarded constantly against rivals, against any one group gaining too much strength. Although the English could not seem to feed themselves, they did have amazing new technology. These new guns could make a great difference in the balance of power in Virginia so Powhatan wanted to make sure those guns were on his side. Accordingly, he suffered the English until it became apparent that they would be the ruin of his realm.

The English had clearly upset the somewhat fragile balance of the Powhatan chiefdom. The initial settlement at Jamestown proved to be of little consequence. The inhabitants were weak and barely able to survive. However, the English kept arriving by ship, worsening the hardship at Jamestown. In 1609 John Smith sent recent arrivals out to be "self-sufficient." Some groups burned villages and robbed graves, while others demanded to be "sold" complete villages with ripening fields of corn. This behavior caused the Powhatans to kill half of the newly arrived English and to encircle Jamestown bringing on the famous "starving time" which drove the colony to the brink of extinction. Yet, the English kept coming until their numbers stabilized and grew. The new settlers had a nearly insatiable desire for land. They continued to expand, claiming more and more of the Powhatan realm. They hunted the deer out of the woods, allowed livestock to destroy Indian crops, and reacted violently in most encounters with the Indians. As time passed the Powhatan leadership realized that these Europeans posed a serious threat to their continued autonomy.

The Virginia Indian Wars continued sporadically. As Europeans raided native cornfields the Indians had to defend their food supply. The tide began to turn to the English, newly supplied with armor that proved effective against warriors with few stone arrowheads. Likewise, fighting in open fields favored Europeans rather than native tactics. Most important, the Powhatans had to fight cautiously to preserve their manpower while the English were constantly resupplied by ship. The early years of conflict reached a peak when the English captured Powhatan's daughter Pocahontas and held her for a huge ransom. This maneuver placed Powhatan in a terrible position. If he could not protect and control his own family's safety, he had little authority as a paramount chief. On the other hand, to pay extortion money to the newcomers would further embolden them in their constant demands on his people. The stalemate ended a year later with both sides claiming victory as Pocahontas, now Anglicized as Rebecca, was married off to a prominent colonist many years her senior. Thus sacrificed for diplomacy, Pocahontas entered the history books for eternity. Her own story ended tragically three years later when she died of smallpox far from her beloved Powhatan homeland.

The Powhatan chiefdom continued to lose their best land to the English. The imminent tobacco boom exacerbated the struggle for viable land. The leader Powhatan spent the last years of his life in a deteriorating relationship with the Europeans who had arrived only ten years earlier. After Powhatan died in 1618 his warrior brother Opechancanough assumed power. The Indians' fight was not over. Opechancanough welcomed the chance to challenge the English. He had already tricked them into attacking and weakening the only tribe not within the Powhatan domain, the Chickahominy. Opechancanough nursed resentment of the English and carefully plotted his revenge. Although the English still died at an amazing rate, their numbers had become considerable. The Indians needed the element of surprise on their side in order to offset English strength in numbers and technology.

Society's Decline

Opechancanough planned a devastating blow that would teach the intruders a lesson. On March 22, 1622, hundreds of Powhatan warriors entered settlements and farms and killed the inhabitants. In some ways, this was not a traditional native raid because women and children were killed—the English merited a special class of enemy. It was traditional however, in the execution: hit hard, hurt the enemy, and then leave to allow the enemy to withdraw. Except the shaken English did not withdraw, despite heavy losses. Instead they turned to vicious retaliation and trickery. Indian cornfields went up in flames, destroying the year's crop and forcing warriors to clear new fields farther in the backcountry. The English poisoned and scalped hundreds of Indians at a time and accelerated their destruction of Indian villages. The settlers expressed their intentions to "root out the Indians from being a people." Opechancanough's resistance had come at a very high price. The Powhatan people for the first time in a century faced insecurity and starvation.

The Powhatan had lost a distinct advantage in the power struggle with the invaders and now spent more of their time hiding their fields and food supply than fighting. Both sides took every opportunity to strike a blow at the other, and the days of Pocahontas' diplomacy seemed a distant memory. The Indians lost access to 300,000 acres of their coastal land when the English built a six-mile-long palisade. In a worse separation from their land, Indian captives taken in skirmishes became slaves in the Caribbean never to return. In one generation the proud Powhatan had lost their dominance. The hundred-year-old Opechancanough tried to make a last attempt to drive out the invaders who had ruined his people's lives.

In 1644 he coordinated an attack which killed 500 English. From an Indian point of view, this was a great success as it killed even more people than the multiple attacks of 1622. However, the English numbers had grown considerably in the intervening decades, and the latest losses sparked vicious retaliation. After several strikes at nearby Indians the Virginia legislature sent a force to capture Opechancanough. Guards killed the aged and feeble leader of the Powhatan people. With the murder of the great warrior the Powhatan chiefdom died. No future Indian ruler would have autonomous power in Virginia. The Indians lost access to their homeland, and within 40 years of the arrival of English ship at Jamestown had been assigned to reservations. The Virginia Indian Wars had been fast and brutal. Aided by the ravages of disease, the English had been able to subjugate a powerful chiefdom in less than half a century.

NEW ENGLAND

As the Pilgrims landed on the rocky New England coast in 1620 they desperately sought an appropriate village site. They were poorly supplied in the face of a building New England winter, so the task seemed quite difficult. In fact, they had arrived in an area of considerable natural abundance. Native groups enjoyed a comfortable living by utilizing the diversity of natural resources along the northeast coast. People like the Wampanoag could choose from a wide range of food sources. They could collect fish and shellfish along the rocky coastline, grow crops in fertile fields along the river valleys, or hunt and gather in the vast inland forests. The Indians routinely burned the underbrush of the forests to keep them open, easy to travel through, and inviting to game animals. The woods held mature oak, hickory, and chestnut trees which were heavy with nuts in the fall and provided firewood and timber year-round. Sheets of chestnut bark covered their homes in the summer, while chestnut wood fires kept them warm in the winter. Furs from forest animals protected people in the winter, while their meat provided critical protein. The Wampanoag, as did other Northeast dwellers, carved out a very successful adaptation to the northeastern landscape.

The Pilgrims and Plymouth Colony occupy a critical position in American history. They stand as a personification of the ideological roots of the American Republic. It should not surprise us then that their warfare with native peoples is regarded as one of the most important events in early American history. The Pequot War of 1636–1637 was the first serious conflict between English and Indian, though certainly not the last. The Puritan success brought long-term effects for English colonization. Historians generally feel that this victory over the Pequot established English hegemony over the Indians of southern New England and paved the way for English colonial expansion. Quite a feat indeed. The consequences for the defeated Pequot would of course also be far-reaching.

PEQUOT SOCIETY

Pequot people were Algonquian speakers and shared a similar culture to many other indigenous groups in the Northeast. By the early 17th century they lived along the Connecticut River Valley. Their territory began near what is now New London, Connecticut, and ran northward between today's Connecticut and Thames rivers, then east to today's Connecticut/Rhode Island border and south to the coast. Before the arrival of Europeans the Pequot were expanding their territory, and had recently gained the eastern end of Long Island. It's not as though these were empty lands just there for the taking, so Pequot expansion came at a cost to someone else. The Pequot thus had plentiful and recent experience in territorial warfare.

Economic Life

When not expanding, the tribe lived a fairly typical Woodlands lifestyle. Sachems, or principal chiefs, oversaw matters of war and diplomacy in consultation with highly ranked men. Men hunted the forests for white-tailed deer, bear, raccoon, opossum, eastern cottontail, gray squirrel, porcupine, gray fox, and weasel. Muskrat and beaver could be trapped in the numerous waterways. These inland waters yielded a wide variety of fish as well as waterfowl such as loons, geese, brandts, and numerous ducks. The proximity of the ocean further enhanced the variety of the Pequot diet. A wide range of oceangoing fish including sturgeon, sheepshead, sandbar shark, skate, and the oddly named sea robin could be easily caught. The distinct flavor and high fat content of gray and harbor seals enlivened an otherwise typical Woodlands diet. Scallops, clams, oysters, mussels, whelks, and other shellfish took the Pequot meals toward the gourmet.

While the men hunted, fished, trapped, netted, and speared the protein portion of meals, women gathered and harvested a wide range of plant materials. Fruits we might think of as treats including fresh strawberries, blueberries, blackberries, elderberries, and currents added flavor to many dishes. More flavor came from walnuts, acorns, hickory nuts, and chestnuts which could be dried or roasted and used throughout the year. Other wild plants served as flavorings or greens, but the main source of plants came from cultivated fields. Pequot women worked the agricultural fields and controlled their produce. The North American triad of corn, beans, and squash remained a crucial part of the 17th-century New England diet. One other crop, tobacco, was planted purely for ceremonial use and, due to its connection to male dominated ceremonies, it was cultivated only by men.

Pequot fields would have been located in fertile floodplains to take advantage of the best soils. To minimize energy expense and for pure convenience, settlements would have been located near the fields, at least in the critical growing season. After the harvest time, residence patterns could be more dispersed. A typical Pequot village may have contained 10 to 20 houses. It was probably not fortified, and many people may have lived on their own outside of town. Villages were occupied primarily in the summer when their inhabitants made only short trips to fish or gather plants. Who could pass up the chance to harvest lobsters when they were in season? Once the crops so critical to their food supply were safely harvested and stored, residents were free to move around. Families moved inland to the protection and rich hunting territories of the great woods. After the long New England winter, members of the tribe looked forward to fishing and fowling camps which provided a welcome change in their diet. They would return to their summer villages to plant and start the cycle anew. This general seasonal pattern continued harmoniously for generations until Europeans arrived to upset the balance.

Warfare and Disease

European arrival brought many changes and, in some ways, two distinct types of war. One was a near hopeless struggle against imported diseases, while the other was more conventional military style warfare. The first warfare did the most damage. It was a great assistance to the English settlers, one that they believed was an act of God, that native New Englanders fell victim to a wave of deadly diseases before the English colonists even arrived on the shores of the New World. Native North America had some diseases but no immunity to pathogens from the Old World. The list of illnesses that could destroy native populations seemed endless—smallpox, measles, malaria, yellow fever, chickenpox, whooping cough, scarlet fever, diphtheria, plague, cholera, poliomyelitis, and others. It would take only one outbreak of one of these maladies to decimate a village. However, southern New England suffered recurring bouts over three years from 1616 to 1619. European observers referred to the waves of deadly disease as "plague." Experts do not agree as to the specific nature of this infection; it could have actually been bubonic plague or possibly smallpox, hepatitis A, or yellow fever. For three years the coast of New England lost incredible numbers of indigenous people, but the Pequot were spared. However, in 1633, smallpox raged through the native population and struck the Pequot squarely. Smallpox is a particularly gruesome way to die. People become horribly disfigured and suffer in great pain as their skin disintegrates. This struck Indians with no warning, no known cause, and no known remedy. The suffering of individuals was only part of the experience. Elders, medicine men, and family members all had to watch helplessly as their loved ones died. A feeling of rage and vulnerability gripped everyone.

Modern readers may perhaps not believe the incredible losses attributed to 17th-century epidemics. Conservative estimates refer to a 55 percent loss while others believe a 95 percent loss to be accurate. The Pequot counted about 13,000 souls before contact, but by 1637 they could claim only 3,000 individuals. That would give them a 77 percent mortality rate.

Society's Decline

As the Pequot faced what might have been their greatest challenge they were in a terrible state of flux. The arrival and continuing growth of the English colony in their region presented enormous challenges. At their very height, in their greatest strength, the Pequot would have had their hands full. The Englishmen possessed considerable advantages in technology, communication, organization, and sheer numbers. It would have taken all the resources and leadership skills of the Pequot nation to deal with this new power. However, the Pequot were far from at their best. The epidemic of 1633 wreaked havoc with the Pequot community. A 77 percent mortality rate had obvious consequences. There were fewer men to serve as warriors in the upcoming conflict with the English. Similarly, there were fewer men to hunt and fish to provide protein for the people, and fewer women to harvest, gather, store, and prepare food. So even those who survived would have faced serious challenges in obtaining enough food. The incredible reduction in manpower played out in areas of defense, protection, homebuilding, and nearly every physical aspect of daily life. Less tangible would have been losses to community and leadership. As leaders, advisors, and elders died, suddenly a power and knowledge vacuum appeared in Pequot life. Gone were the experience and wisdom to deal with an unknown threat. The entire Pequot way of life was badly shaken. How to continue "being Pequot" if so much of your culture and lifestyle had disappeared?

An English observer left us some sense of the tragedy in the Pequot nation.

But contrary wise in short time after the hand of God fell heavily upon them [the Indians], with such a mortall storake, that they died in heapes, as they lay in their houses and living; [sic] that were able to shift for themselves would runne away, & let them dy, and let there Carkases ly above the ground without burial. For in a place where many inhabited, there had been but one left alive, to tell what became of the rest, the livinge being (as it seems) not able to bury the dead, they were left for Crowes, Kites, and vermin to pray upon. And the bones and skulls upon, the severall places of their habitations, made such a spectacle after my coming into those partes, that as I travailed in that Forest, nere the Massachusetts, it seemed to mee a new found Golgotha.[1]

Such horror and dislocation would have left any community ill-prepared for another challenge.

Yet the Pequot did face a tremendous challenge hard on the heels of their 1633 epidemic. The Pequot War of 1636–1637 did not burst full-blown and unexpected upon the native landscape. Rather it was in some ways a culmination of a tumultuous period of constant change initiated by the arrival of Europeans. When Europeans arrived in the Northeast, both the English settlers and the explorers who came before them, they drastically altered the political landscape. Aside from the obvious impacts of European diseases, contact with the culture of the Old World brought significant challenges to the political, economic, religious, and social concepts of Native Americans. The intrusion of a capitalist, Christian, patriarchal society required considerable adjustment by the Indians.

In the early 17th century, the Pequot lived in 15 villages in what is now southeastern Connecticut. Prior to the ravages of imported diseases, they were a proud, confident, and expanding people. In the late 1620s, the Pequot were expanding their territory and trade networks, traveling as far west as Hartford, Connecticut, and also east onto Long Island and Block Island. In the midst of this Pequot progress arrived the Europeans. The first recorded contact between the two groups came in 1632. The English and the Dutch both had interests in southern New England, and both recognized the Connecticut River as a key to further expansion and trade. The Pequot soon found themselves with aggressive Europeans in their midst. At Wethersfield, Connecticut, the English established Pyquaq and then they built Fort Saybrook at the mouth of the Connecticut River. Migrants from Massachusetts Bay swelled towns in the Connecticut Valley, pushing ever closer to Pequot territory.

Such continued pressure from the newcomers might have been quite enough for the Pequot to deal with. However native politics and power struggles did not end because of the new threat from across the ocean. Instead the injection of new forms of trade usually magnified traditional native rivalries. Despite their successful long-term adaptation to the environment of southern New England, native peoples lived in a world that was constantly adjusting and changing. A delicate balance of power had to be maintained between the various tribal groups. These neighbors tended to be rivals who competed for land and resources. If none gained a distinct advantage over another, relative harmony could be achieved. There would always be some jostling for position, small skirmishes, and perhaps a few brief but intense wars. Real change would come, however, with the injection of new elements that threatened to severely upset the traditional power balance in southern New England.

The change was of course brought by Europeans. In particular, the system of trade introduced by Europeans altered the process, and the value of the native trading pattern. As indigenous people were drawn into the European designed and controlled trade network, they altered some and magnified other long-standing practices. In New England much of the change focused around the medium. All Europeans in the New World sought a tradable commodity that they could ship to the Old World. Debts and obligations had to be paid off and justification for the expense and danger of colonization had to be found in transportable valuables. So items that Europeans deemed valuable quickly became desirable. On the native side, the Pequot and their neighbors competed for access to the European trade goods they valued. Such access brought wealth and prestige so sachems competed to extend their influence and to assert control over their neighbors in order to consolidate their position in the new economy.

Economic Life

In southern New England the new economy was initially established by the Dutch. The Dutch brought few settlers but quickly set up trading networks from strategic posts in the Connecticut and Hudson River Valleys. Fur was the commodity of choice and Indians were the hunters. Pequot men did not have to learn new skills but simply intensified their hunting activities. Within a few years the Pequot became the dominant Indian power in the region through their trade in furs. In order to obtain more furs the Pequot set up a tributary system. After defeating neighbors in battle, the Pequot then demanded payment in order to receive future protection. Some of the tributary villages were along the coast and on Long Island. From these areas the Pequot received tribute in wampum. Wampum are beads cut from the white or purple shells of small whelks and then drilled and threaded into decorative strings and belts. Wampum existed before Europeans and was traded from the coast into the interior to be used in ceremonial belts by high status individuals. However, the wampum industry developed rapidly in the 1620s using European tools and trading networks. Its greater availability brought widespread use among more people and it gained the status of currency throughout the region. Interior tribes with no access to the raw materials to make wampum eagerly traded resources from their region. The Pequot greatly benefited from this increased status of wampum as they directly controlled wampum trade from the coast. The wampum they received from tributary villages could be used to buy furs to be traded to the Dutch or to buy European goods directly.

The rapid development of such a desirable commodity naturally sparked rivalries in the area. The Pequot and the Narragansett tribes competed to control the flow of wampum, just as the Dutch and English competed for the trade. Southern New England quickly became a hotbed of shifting rivalries and cutthroat competition. In the mid-1630s the Pequot took on the neighboring Narragansett in an attempt to dominate the region. On top of the stress of war the smallpox epidemic of 1633 hit the region. The Pequot were summarily reduced to a mere 3,000 people from their former number of 13,000. In an unfortunate turn for the Pequot, their Narragansett rivals escaped the devastation of the epidemic. Tributary tribes quickly abandoned the weakened Pequot in favor of the still powerful Narragansett. Even the well-known Mohegan sachem Uncas wavered in his alliance to the Pequot sachem Sassacus, his own brother-in-law.

Overall, the early 1630s were a time of tremendous upheaval for the Pequot people. As their leaders scrambled to adjust to changing conditions brought by Europeans' entrance into their world, people wondered what to make of their new existence. They continued their seasonal cycle of migration and resource exploitation. Many aspects of life continued: people fell in love, gave birth, taught their children traditional ways, and mourned the loss of relatives. Yet even everyday life had a brittle edge. Men traveled more, hunting and trading as part of the new economy. With so many deaths due to disease and increased conflict, women struggled to maintain the proper rituals. No one could be sure anymore that the next generation would enjoy the same life as their ancestors. The rapid changes made everyone nervous.

Pequot leaders had to adjust to new players in the age-old balance of power in the region, and it was not always easy to make the right choices. When the Dutch tried to cut the Pequot out of their monopoly on wampum trade a natural native reaction was to attack the Dutch trading house at Hartford in 1634. However, they did not expect the brutal Dutch retaliation. The Europeans seized the top Pequot sachem Tatobem, held him for ransom, then killed him anyway. Treachery was not unknown in native life, but this quick brutality sent ripples through the Pequot nation. The Pequot were stung by the Dutch treatment and in their weakened state needed assistance from a powerful ally. They chose the new colony of Massachusetts Bay. This turned out to be something of a deal with the devil. The confident Puritans demanded payment of wampum, fur, and land in the Connecticut River Valley merely to keep the peace and broker a brief truce with the rival Narragansetts. The cost of dealing with Europeans continued to climb.

PEQUOT WAR OF 1636–1637

Continued relations between the Pequot and Europeans revealed the distance in understanding between the two cultures. After the brutal murder of their sachem by the Dutch, the Pequot naturally sought vengeance. To the Indians, all white men looked the same, and they took their revenge on a white Englishman named John Stone. Stone was an unsavory character little loved by the Puritans, yet they demanded the surrender of his killers. The Pequot asserted their right to vengeance, the justification being that Stone had abducted two Indians, and noted that most of the attackers were now dead. English concepts of justice were not satisfied, and the altercation provided a convenient excuse for flexing their power over the declining Pequot. The officials of the Massachusetts Bay Colony demanded that the Pequot pay heavy tribute and force their tributary tribes to turn over the murderers. The Pequot found that their former power in the region was now a liability as they were blamed for every altercation between any Indians and Europeans. Rival groups were quick to spread rumors about the supposed aggression of the Pequot. Clashes could only increase as more and more Englishman poured in to settle in the Connecticut Valley. It was not a question of whether the English would make war against the Pequot, but which group of settlers would strike the first blow in their quest to claim more Indian land.

Pequot leaders were aware of the growing tensions between their people and the English. Since their primary responsibility was to safeguard their people, they sought every advantage they could find for the upcoming struggle. This meant seeking alliance with their formal rivals, the Narragansett. The premier Pequot sachem, Sassacus, sent two leaders to the Narragansett with a message of partnership against the English. They proposed a plan of guerrilla warfare against English settlements. Their warning—that if the Pequot were destroyed by the English the Narragansett would not be far behind, proved to be prescient. The Narragansett leaders were torn between the veracity of the Pequot argument and their long-standing hatred of the messengers. Apparently, the influence of Roger Williams, who had an excellent relationship with the Narragansett, swung the tribe to the side of the English. And so the Narragansett made the fateful decision to reject a pan-Indian alliance in favor of a European affiliation. The Pequot would face the English alone.

In 1636, 90 men from Massachusetts set out on a punitive expedition against the Indians of Block Island with orders to kill the men of the tribe, enslave the women and children, and take possession of the island. Unable to find any combatants, the English contented themselves with burning a village and returning to the mainland. Once there they marched into Pequot territory. The Pequot leaders saw little point in engaging this well-armed force and so slipped away without combat. This frustrated the Massachusetts men who had been looking for a fight, but as they returned to the safety of Massachusetts Bay they left the Connecticut settlers at the mercy of Pequot wrath. Warriors quickly converged on Fort Saybrook at the mouth of the Connecticut River. They held the small garrison under siege for nine months. A siege produced relatively few casualties for the Indian forces; however, it did disrupt the flow of native life.

While warriors trapped the English in the fort they could not be on hunting or fishing forays or moving with their families among resource sites. The increased frequency of warfare in southern New England affected all native peoples, disrupting their normal patterns and reducing their overall strength.

Pequot warriors sought revenge where they could. In April 1637, a group attacked the English village of Wethersfield, killing nine people and taking two girls as prisoners. The young girls were quickly traded away when it was realized they could not make gunpowder. This incident reveals the rationale of Pequot leaders. After only a few decades of contact with Europeans their men had already become dependent on firearms to wage any type of successful warfare. This produced an extreme vulnerability since native peoples could not manufacture the gunpowder or ammunition that the weapons required. The idea that young girls could manufacture weaponry shows a lack of understanding of the role of technology and warfare in European society. The English saw this only as a brutal attack by uncivilized savages who needed to be destroyed. The settlers of Massachusetts and Connecticut used this relatively minor Pequot aggression as an excuse to begin a war of extermination.

Political and Social Organization

On May 26, 1637, John Mason and John Underhill led English volunteers along with 500 Indian allies toward Pequot territory. They had convinced Pequot rivals to assist them in defeating their mutual enemy. The 500 warriors came from Uncas, the Mohegan-Pequot who had continually challenged Sassacus for power, and from the Narragansett and Eastern Niantic tribes. Too late would these tribes realize that all Indian peoples had a common enemy in Europeans. Their traditional rivalries as well as considerations of the new power situation motivated native leaders, but many would be appalled at English behavior. Mason and Underhill chose not to face the Pequot army directly and risk defeat. Instead they took a circuitous route through the region ensuring complete surprise when they arrived at the fortified Pequot town at Mystic River. Mystic is often referred to as a Pequot fort. It was the type of fortified village Algonquians built; however, it was not a fort in the European sense that it would be manned by the military. This was a village of wigwams sheltering women and children and old men since all the fighting men were away. English leader John Mason did not hesitate to attack civilians. This was a new style of warfare but the Europeans had already used it against Native Americans at Mabila in the 16th century. He ordered the village to be burned and set up two rings of soldiers to cut down any Pequots fleeing the conflagration. The English in the first ring effectively did their bloody job, but many of the Indian allies in the outer ring left when they realized what was being done. Of the several hundred Pequots at home in the village, only five survived the attack. It took only an hour to slaughter the people and by then the Pequot army arrived too late. Their horror and demoralization can only be imagined.

The most shocking eyewitness account comes from the Puritans.

Captain Mason entering into a wigwam, brought out a firebrand, after he had wounded many in the house. Then he set fire . . . and burnt all in the space of half an hour. Many courageous fellows were unwilling to come out, and fought most desperately through the Palisades, so as they

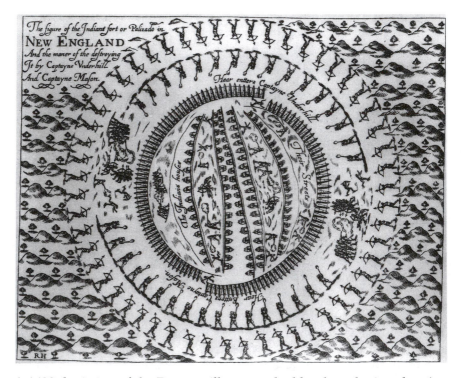

A 1638 depiction of the Pequot village attacked by the colonists showing the inner ring of soldiers and outer line of Indian warriors. (Library of Congress)

were scorched and burnt with a very flame, and were deprived of their arms . . . and so perished valiantly. Many were burned in the fort, both men, women, and children. Others forced out, and came in troops to the Indians, 20 and 30 at a time, which our soldiers received and entertained with the point of the sword. Down fell men, women, and children. . . . It is reported by themselves, that there were about 400 souls in this fort, and not about five of them escaped out of our hands. Great and doleful was the bloody site to the view of young soldiers and never had been a war to see so many souls lying gasping on the ground, so thick in some places, but that you could hardly pass along.[2]

The horror of Mystic fort was not even the end of Pequot suffering. The English and their allies pursued the Pequot people wherever they went. The sachem Sassacus took 40 men and fled to the Mohawk tribe seeking refuge. All of that party were killed by the Mohawk who regarded that as a way to gain favor with the English. Others were pursued relentlessly throughout their homeland, as explained by one Puritan account.

"And in the war, which we made against them [the Pequot], God's hand from heaven was so manifested that a very few of our men in a short time pursued through the wilderness, slew, and took prisoners about 1,400 of them, even all they could find, to the great terror and amazement of all the Indians to this day."[3] Many Pequots were captured, executed, or killed in skirmishes. Those who were captured could be enslaved. Some were sent into chattel slavery in Bermuda or the West Indies, unlikely to survive and certain never to see their homeland again. Others faced perhaps greater humiliation if not suffering as they were enslaved to other Indians. Colonists and Indian leaders allied with the English–Uncas, Narragansett sachem Miantonomo, and Niantic leader Ninigret received "gifts" of Pequot captives.

End of the Pequot Nation

After the Pequot War, which is more properly called genocide, the few remaining leaders were forced to sign the Treaty of Hartford in 1638. Its most humiliating provision was that the Pequot nation was officially dissolved and colonial authorities soon outlawed even the use of the name Pequot. Here was the group that the English described as "rich and potent" in 1627 and a "stately warlike people" in 1634 now reduced to non-entities. Those who helped to bring about the Pequot demise soon found the rewards were less than they had expected. Uncas gained status with the

English although that was primarily because he ceded tributary lands to Connecticut. The powerful Narragansett sachem Miantonomo was promised the Pequot hunting grounds but quickly found that Connecticut and the Mohegan had already usurped them. He would come to realize too late that the English could not be trusted.

New England natives paid a high price for the arrival of Europeans. They did not fare poorly because of inherent weaknesses but rather because the threat was a novel one. No indigenous group had previously dealt with the waves of imported diseases combined with the tactics and technology of Europeans. It took time to adapt to new styles of warfare and particularly to the goals of the new enemy. Complete defeat, possession of structures, and total control over conquered territory characterized European versus native conflict. Native groups were both resourceful and resilient, and soon learned to adapt to the new demands brought by the invasion. As the invaders' settlements marched westward, each independent indigenous group had to come to terms with their arrival. Although they often displayed the same weaknesses and repeated the same mistakes, native peoples also learned lessons from what had befallen previous groups.

We have seen that by the mid-17th century two major indigenous groups had become embroiled in European settlement to their detriment. The primarily English colonization of the Eastern Seaboard had expanded rapidly in a few decades and changed native life forever. The wars, which were the natural response of powerful people to an invasion, had devastated the native community. They could no longer follow their traditional pattern of life. Seasonal movement to support a hunting and gathering economy became impossible with the loss of land. Political structures, religious police systems, and social networks all failed in the face of rapid depopulation and fragmentation. The story is sad enough yet the tragedy was magnified in repetition. The Powhatan and the Pequot were the two major groups in their regions for which we have the most documentation. However, their tragedy was repeated on varying scales throughout eastern North America. Tribe after tribe had to deal with the expanding Europeans.

1675 WARS

By the end of the 17th century the English had come to dominate much of the land east of the Appalachian Mountains. Despite their unparalleled access to land and control of resources, the newcomers still regarded native inhabitants as a threat. In 1675 the last major Indian conflicts of the century further destroyed native autonomy. Settlers in New England and Virginia once again acted in fear and greed to strike out at neighboring Indians.

The aggression of Virginia settlers toward native peoples had not abated since the Powhatan wars. In their destruction of the Powhatan chiefdom the English had sown the seeds of their own fear. The removal of a strong, coercive native authority left a power vacuum in the region which naturally attracted other groups. Undefeated tribes like the Susquehannock who could still put thousands of warriors in the field gravitated toward the rich lands of Virginia. The English had, of course, not destroyed *all* native people, and refugees from various tribes came together in new groups. These newly formed coalitions sought to exploit the current climate of opportunity which often involved trading war captives for guns in a continuous cycle of violence. All the power struggles made the settlers increasingly nervous, and increasingly willing to regard all natives as enemies.

In 1675 the volatile situation came to a head in what is commonly referred to as Bacon's Rebellion. Fearful, greedy settlers whose allotted land stretched into the Indian frontier clamored for the removal of all native people. When colonial officials refused, they took matters into their own hands and began a race war. Unable or unwilling to differentiate between different Indian peoples, Virginia settlers simply attacked any natives. The resulting terror swept through the region sparking waves of violence. No Indian people felt safe when whites approached. Strikes and retaliations continued throughout the year, catching up the powerful Susque-hannock as well as smaller friendlier groups. Finding peaceful, settled native towns easier to attack, Bacon led his men against Virginia's tributary tribe, the Pamunkey. The queen of the Pamun-keys led her people to refuge in the Great Dragon Swamp, ordering them to flee and survive as best they could when discovered by the Virginian militias. The spate of violence against native peoples ended with the death of Nathaniel Bacon, but the damage had been done. By the end of the 17th century the Tidewater region had been wiped clean of autonomous native groups capable of resisting white expansion. Tribes to the west would have to deal with the ceaseless land hunger of Europeans.

1675 also marked the end of meaningful native resistance in New England. Historians often remark on the relative peace that followed the Pequot War. An entire indigenous nation was nearly wiped out so further resistance would have to wait. The following 30 years were still full of tension and violence although Europeans and Indians continued to trade with one another. Tribes in the region which had helped the English destroy the Pequot regarded their new allies uneasily. Europeans showed an unsettling propensity to turn quickly on friends they no longer found useful. The Narragansett found themselves in precisely that position. The New England colonies continued to insist on Narragansett subservience and land transfers. Soon all the tribe had gained by helping to defeat the Pequot had been lost. The United Colonies (Massachusetts Bay, Connecticut, Plymouth, and New Haven) sanctioned the murder of the Narragansett chief Miantonomo by the Mohegan.

Wampanoag Resistance

Another major New England tribe had had enough of the English. The Wampanoag, led by the revered chief Massasoit, had been among the first to befriend Plymouth Colony. From the first Thanksgiving to his death in 1661 Massasoit had held the peace with these newcomers to his land. However the second generations of both groups had less patience with each other. Wamsutta succeeded his father as chief of the Wampanoag while more and more colonists expanded onto Wampanoag land. Officials at Plymouth summoned the chief they called Alexander to a meeting at gunpoint. The young man fell ill and soon died and many of his people believed he'd been poisoned. His brother Metacom, or Philip, came to power blaming the English for his brother's death. Metacom resented the changes the English had brought to his homeland. Just a generation before, under his father's rule, the Wampanoag had been the dominant power in the region. They earned a good living fishing, hunting, gathering, and trading. By 1675 they had lost access to many of their best economic resources and white livestock destroyed their fields. The bold colonists presumed power and superiority over the Wampanoag.

Although frequently blamed for it, Philip did not plan the war that broke out in 1675. An Indian Christian named John Sassamon died after reporting to the colonial authorities that Philip was preparing for war. The resulting execution of his supposed murderers escalated violence to the point that Philip—with only limited power among his people—could not restrain angry young warriors. The Wampanoag could put only 300 warriors against the English colonies' militias of at least 10,000 men armed with flintlocks. Before tackling the Wampanoag the English shrewdly forced the Narragansett to support them. The English war against the Wampanoag then commenced and spread quickly. Frontier settlers panicked and fled to fortified towns. As in so many other wars the English used violence against Indians indiscriminately. Armed men frequently terrorized "praying Indians" as they called native Christian converts living near Puritan settlements. Just as they had in Virginia, whites struck out at the closest, most conveniently located Indians no matter their affiliation. This naturally brought many valuable allies to Philip's side. It was the closest New England Indians would come to united resistance to European invasion.

Tribal Rivalry

Amazingly, it was not their technology or their numbers that allowed the English to defeat Philip and his forces. Philip fell at the hands of Native Americans. The English convinced the Mohawk in New York to attack Philip when he headquartered in the region. The Mohawk aggression deprived Philip of any breathing room, and sent him reeling back to New England to face overwhelming Puritan forces. Things went badly from then on. A mix of English and Indians captured Philip's wife and nine-year-old son. The authorities decided it would be more Christianly to sell them into slavery in the Caribbean than to kill them. Nearly all Indians who were captured or surrendered were promptly sold into slavery. Indian leaders were killed. Philip himself was shot by a Christian Indian leading the English to Philip's camp. The English reserved their worst brutality for the man they believed masterminded the war. Philip's body was quartered and hung upon four trees. His hand went to his killer. Philip's head was prominently displayed on a pike in the Plymouth watchtower for decades.

Society's Decline

A devastating double blow of disease and warfare emptied New England of much of its native population in the 17th century. Indigenous groups were weakened and scattered by the nearly constant trauma. Elders—who would have provided a stabilizing influence and passed on valuable knowledge—had often been taken by disease, while many warriors and hunters—whose role was to sustain and protect the people—fell victim to the constant violence.

Chief Metacom tried to preserve the Wampanoag title
to New England in the conflict known as King Philip's
War. A copy of an engraving
by Paul Revere. (Library of
Congress)

It became very difficult to maintain cultural traditions including religious beliefs, social behaviors, and traditional resource exploitation. This does not mean that native peoples disappeared from the region; however, the distribution and structure of indigenous life was greatly altered and never regained its pre-contact form.

To some extent, encounters in New England and Virginia had set a pattern in what would become an ongoing saga of expanding European colonization. The continuing onslaught of European expansion remained a negative force for indigenous people. However, to simply dismiss the years of conflict as a total win for the newcomers and a total loss for the natives would be a mistake. As the invaders spread across the continent they continued to encounter distinct native groups. Each encounter was unique and the outcome unknown. Moreover, dominance by Europeans did not occur immediately. There was often a considerable period of adjustment, often a period of mutual reliance and cooperation. Historian Richard White coined the term "middle ground" to describe the interaction between Europeans and the natives in whose homeland they had arrived. He was speaking of the Great Lakes region but some level of attraction and accommodation can be found throughout the eastern United States.

By the mid-18th century Europeans had been in North America for almost 150 years. It was clear that they had come to stay. Unlike the Spanish conquistadors, the French and English imposed their culture on the new land as they spread outward from their first tentative settlements. However permanent the occupation appeared, the Europeans were not invincible or even self-sufficient. They relied heavily on trade networks across the Atlantic Ocean and remained tied to the European powers through economy, religion, and culture.

Native Resilience

Native people constituted one of the most important factors in the success of the newcomers. Indian peoples' lives had been drastically altered by the invasion of non-natives, but they had not been destroyed. Disease, warfare, and displacement had taken a devastating toll on indigenous populations, but they remained a unique people. They adapted, adjusted, and coped with the seemingly constantly changing circumstances of their lives, but they were not destroyed or changed into Europeans. One key to their resilience was their value to the invaders. As European colonists depended on their mother country for trade, support, and governance, so too did they rely on native people. The earliest settlers—like those at Plymouth and Jamestown—were the most obviously dependent for their survival on the superiorly prepared natives. However, several generations later whites remained beholden to Indians as trading partners, military allies, and sources of labor and land. These dependencies were no trivial matters, especially in a period of imperial struggles to gain superior claims to American lands.

It is tempting to look back on 17th-century Indians and project their future loss of sovereignty and autonomy onto them. Contemporary settlers made no such mistake. A 1758 woodcut from a Philadelphia periodical shows the understanding colonists had of natives' position in the new power struggle in the eastern United States. It shows an Indian choosing between two offerings–one from the French and the other from the British. Of course the British offered only goodness and peace, indicated by the Bible and a bolt of cloth, while the French greed is borne out by the money and weapons they proffer. British propaganda aside, the image reveals the status accorded to Indians by their contemporaries. They had choices; they had the free will to choose their desire.

As the colonial period progressed, natives would find it increasingly difficult to exercise their free will. The pressures of increased immigration from Europe meant more competition for resources. Consider that the land held a fixed bounty—of mammals, fish, birds, trees, edible plants—that could not be substantially increased by the will of man. Certain human practices, such as intentional burning, might create more favorable conditions for desirable species but could not drastically change the available amounts of necessary resources. As European immigrants flooded the continent, it was inevitable that the newcomers would compete with indigenous people for resources and it was equally likely that warfare would result. To a great extent, the warfare that plagued the 18th century was a continuous conflict over access to the necessities of life.

MID-ATLANTIC

The region of the mid-Atlantic was the next contested area after the Eastern Seaboard between natives and Europeans. The area was home to two distinct cultural groups which complicated their response to the upheavals of colonization and subsequent warfare. It is important to remember that indigenous peoples living in nearby territories rarely cooperated and generally regarded each other as a larger threat than the new arrivals. Centuries of conflict confirmed that opinion. Algonquian and Iroquoian speakers had been in contact for a millennia before the whites arrived. Since they lived in the same Eastern Woodlands the two groups shared several basic similarities. Both formed their society along matrilineal descent with women responsible for farming and gathering while men hunted and fished. Groups relied on agriculture to varying degrees, but all farmed to some extent. In this way they both shared and competed with the new European culture in their midst.

Economic Life

Conflict in a literal sense did not encompass only pitched battles. After European arrival the daily lives of many natives were fraught with conflict. One of the most frequent causes of the ongoing quarrels was differences in the use of the land. Both Europeans and northeastern Indians were farmers; however the European economy also included livestock. The English practice imported to the New World was of letting their cattle and hogs wander freely. In America they rarely had herders, so the beasts were unsupervised. The animals naturally sought out the unfenced Indian cornfields. This was a source of nearly constant friction between natives and newcomers. The results could be heated exchanges, court cases, or outright violence. Even if the issue did not come to blows, it had a constant effect on the daily lives of the local people. On any day Indian women could rise to find their carefully tended crops destroyed by marauding livestock. This added both to the uncertainty of the food supply and to the tension among the human population.

Natives in the eastern region found themselves in a completely changed world by the 1700s. The arrival of Europeans had brought upheaval, challenges, and incredible loss. They fought on a daily basis to maintain traditional ways and practices. Many of the people died from direct warfare, disease, and changed circumstances. Those who survived struggled to adapt, to create an altered sense of themselves as Indians, to maintain their hold on the land they once shared only with other natives.

NOTES

1. Thomas Morton, 1637, quoted in Laurence M. Hauptman and James Wherry, eds., *The Pequots in Southern New England: The Fall and Rise of an American Indian Nation*. Norman: University of Oklahoma Press, 1990, 47.

2. Charles Orr, ed., *History of the Pequot War*. Cleveland, OH: Helman-Taylor Co., 1897, 73.

3. Alden Vaughan, ed., *The Puritan Tradition in America, 1620–1730*. New York: W. W. Norton, 1979, 66.

2

EARLY NATIONAL WARS

By the 1700s, Europeans had been in eastern North America for a hundred years. They had come in relative weakness but had exploited both the land and the native people in order to be successful. In ever-increasing numbers the newcomers spread out across the land, changing the world in their image. As they pushed inland from their first settlements along the coast they encountered different native groups. Some of these groups would present far greater challenges to white dominance than they had yet experienced. A century of warfare was about to unfold.

NATIVE WARFARE

Native people were used to living with both overt and covert tensions. Europeans did not bring warfare to the tribes of the mid-Atlantic. For centuries the Iroquoian peoples had been living in fortified villages. For example, the Huron built large, palisaded settlements that protected the enormous longhouses that housed numerous related families. They fought frequently over territory and resources including human populations. The famed Iroquois League was founded in response to this nearly constant state of violence. Tribes living in central New York fought so frequently that it led to population loss, dwindling food supply, and destruction of villages. Their unique approach to the problem was the creation of what we call the Iroquois League. Five nations—Seneca, Cayuga, Onondaga, Oneida, and Mohawk—agreed to internal peace. The creation of a virtual longhouse or home in which each nation held a particular family position ensured peace and stability for the members of the Iroquois League. The lack of conflict at home allowed the Iroquois to turn their considerable skill at warfare outward toward their enemies. In this way they became both feared and respected throughout the Northeast.

TUSCARORA AND YAMASEE WARS

The changing makeup of the Iroquois League reflects the state of flux that plagued Indian communities throughout the areas of European contact. As primarily British colonists expanded deeper into the interior, they continued to engage distinct native nations. The upheaval created by Anglo intrusion wreaked havoc among communities, many of which were uprooted from their homelands. One prominent tribe, the Tuscarora, migrated from the Carolinas to New York to enter the protection of the Iroquois League. The Tuscaroras who occupied North Carolina's Tidewater region had been pressed by the continual land hunger of settlers. In 1711 they chose to fight back. The Tuscarora had been fairly protected from the first hundred years of European settlement because they lived inland. However, they were not protected from the onslaught of disease. As European settlers pushed westward, epidemic diseases preceded them. In the early 18th century, outbreaks of smallpox devastated Tuscarora communities. None of their traditional treatments, not sweat baths, not prayers, not offerings, stopped the suffering and death. Everyone noticed that the diseases came with Europeans and seemed not to touch them.

The spark to the Tuscarora War was the settlement of New Bern in 1710 by German and Swiss colonists. After capturing and roasting to death a land speculator who was caught scouting in their homeland, Tuscaroras attacked the new settlement returning with booty, prisoners, and scalps. Suddenly the frontier was aflame and Tuscaroras were engaged on all sides. Not only did they need to fight the whites, but also their traditional enemies among over one dozen Algonquain tribes. The hostile tribes were funded and equipped by British colonists who promised spoils of trade goods, cattle, and Tuscarora captives. Tuscarora warriors fought hard for two years defending their forts until they could fight no more. The combination of white and native hostility proved too much for the tribe. They paid a high price for their defiance when 1,000 captives were sold as slaves. With so many of their people dead or captured and the English colonists still in place, the Tuscarora had few choices. Most of the survivors moved northward where they found, at least for a time, a new home in the Iroquois League. Even with the departure of the Tuscaroras, the native-white violence in the Carolinas was far from over.

Economic Life

The Carolinas had from their inception pursued an aggressive policy toward native residents of their newly claimed colony. If the native people could be of some use they would be tolerated— otherwise they would be exterminated. The first Europeans settled along the coast at what is now Charleston, South Carolina, in 1670 and proceeded to expand inland. Conceived purely as a profit-making venture, the Carolina colony sought any means to prosperity, including trade. Local Indians in the Carolinas have long hunted white-tailed deer both for meat and skin. Now they found Carolina traders would buy all that they could bring in. In an escalation of the hunt, Europeans provided guns for easier procurement of prey. This practice was also applied to the slave trade. Merchants armed their allies who captured other Indians to be sold as slaves. The Carolina tribes were quickly enmeshed in the lucrative and violent trading of deerskin and Indian slaves. In 1701, one human being was traded for one gun. The increasing level of violence destabilized the region and brought nearly constant warfare to inhabitants. Daily life for those not allied with the British colonists quickly became a nightmare of uncertainty, stress, and often death. Many groups fled the region seeking to escape the violence. Much of northern Florida was depopulated in response to this new economy. Those within the system also found themselves increasingly squeezed by their dependency on British traders. By one estimate the Indians were so in debt that every adult male owed two years of labor to white traders.

Tensions had been mounting for years. Hunters were finding it increasingly difficult to bring in the meat necessary to feed their families. They could not break the cycle of debt that required them to spend more and more days in the woods away from their families in order to meet their obligations to white traders. The system of trade was designed and run by non-Indians and clearly favored whites. As abuses piled up, southern natives could not continue to tolerate the situation. The Tuscarora War had not depopulated the Carolinas, nor seriously hampered the natives' ability to make war. It had, however, reduced the number of Indians available for the slave trade so that tribes previously allied with whites now feared enslavement by them. Other changes corroded the relationship between natives and whites. Traders frequently married into the tribes in order to gain the many advantages of being in a kinship network. A host of problems followed inter-racial marriages, stemming primarily from differing expectations of the role of women in society. Englishmen had trouble honoring or even understanding the status of women in a matrilineal society. The men resorted to violence against women which tore apart the social fabric of native communities. Frustrated and irritated the Yamasee chose to make a preemptive strike.

Political Organization

In 1715 Carolina traders meeting with Yamasee leaders were killed and one was roasted for three days: war was on. Although the Yamasee began the war it was in fact a confederation of native groups that struck back at whites. Years of abuse, including theft, beatings, rape, and debt, motivated members of at least 10 tribes to risk hostilities to fight for their economy. Warriors from the Cherokee, Yuchi, Catawba, and Apalachee tribes and others struck at settlements, forts, and trading posts. The first year of the war went well for the Indian coalition forces. As the South erupted in flame, men and supplies from North Carolina, Virginia, New England, and England arrived to beat back the Indians. Violence raged for two years with many Indian victories. They destroyed most of the plantations sprouting in South Carolina and nearly took Charleston. Hundreds of white colonists died and the rest were terrorized. Of course, there was considerable cost too as normal patterns of life were disrupted by the ongoing raids. Eventually the native coalition crumbled when the Cherokee switched sides. In 1717, the Carolinians forced a peace settlement. The natives had inflicted serious population losses and areas lay empty for decades, but would eventually be rebuilt. Unfortunately the same was not true for many members of the Indian confederation. Several of the tribes involved in the hostilities soon became extinct, pushed to the brink by a combination of violence and disease. Those who remained coalesced into survivors groups that crossed traditional tribal boundaries.

When the Tuscarora fled the chaos of colonial aggression in the Southeast, they went to a region about to face its own upheavals and periods of warfare. They joined the Iroquois League, which along with other native groups in the Northeast was about to enter a different phase of European warfare. Up to this point natives had clashed either directly with colonists or with native groups acting as colonial allies. Many of the conflicts appeared spontaneous, haphazard, and brief. They took a considerable toll on native groups by disrupting residence patterns and economic pursuits and stressing leadership. However, they did not reflect the immense power or perseverance of a European empire. That was about to change.

Northeastern America in the 17th and 18th centuries was a desirable acquisition in the race to establish colonial empires. The three great colonial powers in the Americas—England, France, Spain— jockeyed for territory and power in several areas. The Northeast, and in particular the Ohio Valley, was one of the most contentious. The struggle for empire engaged native groups and forever altered their lives.

Settlement Patterns

The indigenous settlement patterns of the Northeast in some ways matched the European invasion patterns. An arc of Algonquian speakers stretched along the coast and across the far north, wrapped around a core of Iroquoian speakers, much as the French wrapped around the English colonies. The Algonquian speakers, like the Pequot and Powhatan, were the first to encounter the English who arrived from the ocean. The French, who settled the interior, had more contact with Iroquoian speakers like the Huron. The various native groups, primarily acting out of their own interests, were about to become entangled in the colonial competition and aspirations of European Empires.

As the 18th century unfolded, Native Americans in the Northeast faced their greatest challenge from European settlement. Paradoxically, some of the native Nations were reaching the peak of their power, although at the cost of other native groups. In the early 1700s, the main power broker in the Northeast was the Iroquois League. The Five Nations, and then six after 1726, had maintained unity in the face of European expansion. Iroquois leaders had developed a successful approach to the competing demands of rival European powers. It essentially boiled down to telling everybody what they wanted to hear. In 1701 a set of treaties known as the Grand

Settlement seemed to set the stage for peace. The Iroquois signed treaties in Montréal with the French in which they promised to remain neutral in any subsequent European wars. In exchange for this the French allowed Iroquois to hunt on lands north of the Great Lakes and trade at Fort Detroit. Meanwhile Iroquois representatives met at Albany with the English and polished the "Covenant Chain." This symbolic chain bound the Iroquois and English in friendship. It was a long-running fiction that often proved useful to the Iroquois. Any renewal or strengthening of the chain required considerable presents of manufactured goods to Iroquois leaders. Of course neither the French nor the English knew of the promises the Iroquois made to their rivals.

Political Organization

The Iroquois played a profitable, if dangerous, game with the European powers. Sometimes it reached comic proportions. The English heaped presents of trade goods, arms, ammunition, and other supplies on their Iroquois friends during Queen Anne's War. The Iroquois dutifully sent hundreds of warriors to join the British expedition invading Canada, only to sabotage them by delaying tactics and passing intelligence to the enemy. Even in peace the Iroquois found a way to profit by controlling the smuggling trade between the colonists of the rival empires. Their access to firearms strengthened their military power and allowed them to defeat longtime rivals like the Cherokee. The situation was not ideal. It certainly would have better had the Europeans not come at all, but the Iroquois had managed to craft a fairly successful adjustment strategy to the realities of invasion. Native peoples were dealing with a changing landscape on their own terms and in their own best interest.

Not everyone appreciated the Iroquois' new strategy, however. As the Iroquois sought to meet the needs of the European powers they changed the face of native relationships. The English and French both wanted one native group to speak for all. They had long sought a single power with which they could deal on issues of war and land cessions. As the Iroquois tried to meet their allies' needs, they tried to expand their power and influence far beyond its traditional base. They began claiming the authority to sell land far beyond the Iroquois homeland. That meant they attempted to control the destinies of a wide variety of non–Iroquois League peoples, such as the Delaware, Wyandot,

Shawnee, Miami, and others. The considerable Iroquois military might forced many tribes to acquiesce to the League's demands no matter what the cost. One of the most famous cases was the 1737 Walking Purchase. Pennsylvania colluded with the Iroquois League to force the Delaware people off of their lands in eastern Pennsylvania. These three-quarter-million acres near the Lehigh and Delaware rivers were in no way the province of the Iroquois League, yet the chiefs forced the Delaware to acquiesce to the Penn's fraudulent claims. The Delaware reluctantly removed to the Susquehanna River region, but their treatment at the hands of the Iroquois remained a serious point of contention. In similar style the Iroquois earned the enmity of other groups like the Shawnee. By the 1750s many of the displaced, disgruntled native groups had reestablished themselves in the Ohio country purposely beyond the expected reach of the Iroquois League. As the Iroquois League gained unprecedented power, it also faced growing resistance.

FRENCH AND INDIAN WAR

The period of the late 17th and early 18th centuries was one of great change for all peoples. Representatives of both European empires sought to expand and strengthen their claims in the interior Northeast. All the conflicting forces—native rivalries, European rivalries, colonial aspirations—came together on the western frontier in the mid-1750s. The ensuing struggle for power in this region of the Ohio River Valley has been called the War that Made America. It has long had other names: the French and Indian War, the Seven Years War, the Great War for Empire. All of those reflect a Eurocentric view. For native peoples it would be one of their last chances to challenge Europeans for dominance in the eastern United States This was a war to exert influence, a war to maintain homelands, a war for survival. The desirable land so hotly contested between France and Great Britain was of course the homeland of many thousands of indigenous people who would not give it up without a struggle.

Social Organization

The daily lives of native peoples in the Ohio country had been in turmoil for some time. So many of them had not been original residents of the area but instead had relocated to the region. The growth of European settlement in the 17th century had made life impossible for many native peoples living east of the Allegheny Mountains.

The ravages of epidemic diseases left many groups without a viable population. The core elements of leadership, security, economic pursuits, and spiritual guidance that a community requires often could not be sustained in the face of devastating population loss. Remnant populations of the same loosely affiliated tribal groups could re-form to create new settlements that contained a critical mass. As the Delaware were repeatedly pushed westward in Pennsylvania, they came to reside in the Ohio country. This relocation had the added benefit of removing them from the authority of the Iroquois League, or so they hoped. Some Iroquois even tried this approach, becoming known as Mingoes, ethnically Iroquois but politically independent. Shawnee, Kickapoo, and Miami were their new neighbors in the region.

The Iroquois themselves had experienced a lot of social upheaval. The creation of the League hundreds of years before had permitted the original five Iroquois nations to turn their considerable energy and talent for warfare outward. They had become formidable enemies to natives and whites alike. Their name was feared throughout the Northeast and they were infamous for their complex and excruciating torture of captives. This reputation brought them respect, security, and economic success, but it came at a cost. Constant warfare took a toll on the community. Men and boys left the villages for long periods while on the warpath. Iroquois society already had a matrilineal structure, but the nearly constant absence of males put additional strain on women. And, of course, many men never came home. The combination of warfare and disease pushed the Iroquois population ever downward. In order to maintain their strength and dominance the Iroquois practiced a clever strategy of adopting many war captives. Enemy warriors made poor candidates, but women and children could be adopted and integrated into society fairly easily. The adoption of hundreds of captives helped boost the Iroquois population but also altered society with the introduction of outsiders into their midst.

Economic Life

The lands of the Ohio country were not so different from their homelands so people could re-create their lives. There was, however, one important difference. All the native peoples were now dependent on European trade goods. What had begun as luxury goods had now become indispensable. Firearms were now critical to native success. Metal weapons, tools, cooking utensils, and other manufactured goods now played a vital role in daily life. So life had changed drastically. Access to trade goods was the limiting factor in life, and natives had to seek out and protect their connection to traders.

Indians now moved their villages in accord with the dictates of European economics, not due to any rhythm of nature. Where traders were, Indians would be. When the French founded Detroit in 1701 bands of Wyandot, Ottawa, Ojibwa, Pottawatomie, Mesquakie, Miami, and others moved to the area. The Delaware moved to a town on the Allegheny River they called Kittanning. The Miami created a large village, Pickawillany, whose sole purpose appeared to be trade. In addition to the Shawnee and Delaware, groups from the St. Lawrence Valley and Wisconsin migrated to the Ohio country. Many different ethnic groups, traditional enemies, resided in uneasy peace because of their dependence on access to European trade goods. The transformations sweeping through Indian country changed the patterns of daily life as relocated natives scrambled to continue meeting their daily needs. In the Allegheny plateau region various groups came together bringing both older cultural traits and new adaptations. These disparate native groups eventually adopted a regional identity, a sense of "Ohio Indian country." They created new bonds where none existed before and prepared to defend their new lifestyle.

It seemed to Indian peoples that the ground was shifting under them. European invasion pushed them out of their traditional homelands. They relocated and established new homes. Europeans introduced them to trade goods which they came to accept and depend on. Then the European powers tried to deny them access to the very things they introduced. They tried to use the Indians as pawns in their games of power.

One of the first examples of this came in 1749 when the officials of New France decided to manifest their vague claims to the lands of the Ohio Valley. Under the authority of the King of France, an expedition led by Joseph de Cèleron de Blainville traveled through Indian country. It carried leaden plates inscribed with the French claim to the region. They buried them at strategic locations such as the head of streams flowing to the Ohio River.

What were the local Indians to make of the strange conduct of French troops near their villages? They might be amused or intrigued at a formal ceremony conducted in the language they could not understand. More likely, they would be suspicious of the intentions of the nearly 300 armed Frenchmen who had arrived.

LAN 1749 DV REGNE DE LOVIS XV ROY DE
FRANCE NOVS CELORON COMMANDANT DVN DE
TACHEMENT ENVOIE PAR MONSIEVR LE M DE LA
GALISSONIERE COMMANDANT GENERAL DE LA
NOVVELLE FRANCE POVR RETABLIR LA TRANQVILLITI
DANS QVELQVES VILLAGES SAUVAGES DE CES CANTON
AVONS ENTERRE CETTE PLAQVE A L'ENTREE DE LA
PRES DE LA RIVIERE OYO AVTREMENT BELLE
RIVIERE POVR MONVMENT DV RENOVVELLEMENT DE
POSSESSION QVE NOVS AVONS PRIS DE LA DITTE
RIVIERE OYO ET DE TOVTES CELLES QVI Y TOMBE
ET DE TOVES LES TERRES DES DEVX COTES IVSQVE
AVX SOVRCES DES DITTES RIVIES AINSI QVEN ONT
IOVY OV DV IOVIR LES PRECEDENTS ROYS DE FRANCE
ET QVILS SISONT MAINTENVS PAR LES ARMES ET
PAR LES TRAITTES SPECIALEMENT PAR CEVX DE
RISVVICK DVTRCHT ET DAIX LA CHPELLE

The lead plates the French buried in the Ohio country served as "a monument of renewal of possessions, which we have taken of the said river Ohio, and of all those which fall into it, and of all the lands on both sides." (Ohio Historical Society)

One of the Frenchmen, Joncaire, had a Seneca mother and spoke Iroquois well, but even he did not allay suspicion. The French encountered many empty villages as chiefs chose to put their people out of direct contact with the French expedition. Better safe than sorry, as it did not appear that this group came to trade.

Far from offering trade, the French officials sought to restrict trade. They had the audacity to tell the independent Indians of the Ohio country that they could not trade with the British. The French had long maintained diplomatic ties with the natives of the area. These had been won and later strengthened by the proper protocol, involving feasts, speeches, and liberal distribution of presents. Now the French arrived making demands. When the French arrived in villages and found English traders there they reacted strongly by demanding that the natives drive out the "intruders." French officials insisted that native peoples must refuse to deal with any English colonials.

Political Considerations

This was asking a great deal. First it violated the sovereignty of native groups. They had the right to decide who received hospitality in their villages. The proclamation from the French King "I will not endure the English on my land" grossly misstated the ownership situation in the Ohio country. Just as importantly, the demand fringed on native economic welfare, on their ability to protect their best interests. The plain truth was that English goods were better quality than those of the French. They also came at better prices. Did the French expect the Indians to make poor bargains out of some sense of loyalty to a king across the water? This contradicted the intelligence and long experience of native traders. However, the French delegation delivering this ultimatum was armed. Some chiefs who had not sought to avoid the French visit acquiesced, at least for the moment. Yellow Eyes, sub-chief of a village near present-day Franklin, Pennsylvania, affirmed that his village would send away the English and trade no more with them. For this correct attitude he received a knife, tomahawk, and other gifts. Few on either side of the exchange expected compliance with the French edict. Other villages challenged the expedition more openly. In the native democracies each chief had to take the measure of his followers and decide on the appropriate reaction to the Europeans.

As the French approached Logstown, a large mixed-nation village, they saw their flag flying along with the British flag. The assembled Shawnee, Delaware, Seneca, and Cayuga did little to welcome the intruders. Chief Monakaduto responded directly to the French emissaries. Since the Indians needed access to powder, lead, and blankets they could not turn away English traders unless the French were prepared to guarantee their supplies. Thus turning the tables on the Europeans, the chief at Logstown willingly received their presents. Shawnee at Sinioto went even further in asserting their independence from the French. They fired on the French flag. The might of Shawnee warriors caused the French to tone down their message to Shawnee chief Cornstalk. Instead of demanding that the Shawnee drive out English traders, the French representatives suggested that the English were dangerous to the natives. Cornstalk made it clear that the Shawnee feared neither English nor French and would trade with whomever they liked. Furthermore he gave the French one day to get out of his territory.

The chief of another large trading town, Pickawillany, was even more forceful in his rejection of French demands. The French had attempted to claim and reclaim control the Ohio country but the natives had their own ideas.

The English traders, whose presence in the Ohio country so infuriated the French, represented another power player in the region—colonists. Pennsylvania traders like George Croghan moved quickly to secure a foothold in the lucrative Indian trade. They took risks in pushing west that often paid off handsomely. These independent traders with their inexpensive, accessible goods posed a threat to French interests. However, an even greater challenge loomed. The rapidly growing colony of Virginia had set its sights on the Ohio country. The actions of the Ohio company in collusion with the Virginia governor touched off one of the greatest wars on the American continent. The tensions building in the Ohio Indian country exploded in 1754. Although essentially set up by Euro-American rivalries, the violence originated by native hands.

When young George Washington blundered toward the Forks of the Ohio, he represented the aspirations of the Virginians who naïvely thought to challenge the French claim to the region. Equally naïvely they enlisted the aid of native warriors whose interests and agenda they neither asked about nor understood. Tanaghrisson, or the Half King, sparked an international war as he buried his hatchet in the skull of the French commander Jumonville. The ensuing war inflamed the frontier from the Ohio Valley to the Canadian Maritimes. Thousands of native warriors fought during the conflict and tens of thousands of their family members dealt with the deprivations and uncertainty and fear that war brought.

Native Defense of the Ohio Country

The best aspect of the war was that natives *chose* to participate. Their actions stemmed from desires for revenge and interests in maintaining trade relations with one side or the other. Most of the fighting focused on non-native targets, frequently French or English forts. The battles at Oswego, Lake George, and Montréal targeted European property. Native warriors could mostly decide to fight in the assaults of their choice. And they did fight for their own rewards. Warriors frequently frustrated Euro-American allies as they stopped an offensive to collect captives, scalps, and property— their rewards of battle. Or they might return home after a skirmish in order to properly mourn their dead. These actions revealed the autonomy of the natives involved in the war.

The war was not fought entirely on native terms, however, and new circumstances brought new challenges. Sometimes the new forces at work directly opposed traditional beliefs. William

Johnson, an Irish Indian trader who established close ties with the Mohawk, set into motion one such situation. He convinced his adopted Mohawk kin to fight for the British cause and led them to challenge the French near Lake George, New York. The inevitable clash with the French forces brought a major surprise. In the early seconds of the skirmish that was to be called the "bloody morning scout" Canadian Mohawks recognized their New York brethren in the opposing forces and called out a warning. Although their chief, Theyanoguin, was shot dead, the rest of the New York Mohawks had enough time to retreat. The Mohawk now realized that the price of their alliance with the British would be a bloody confrontation with their Canadian relatives. The shedding of blood by kin was a serious affront to the concept of the Iroquois League. It was not one the Mohawk were willing to make. At the conclusion of the battle the New York Mohawks gathered their captives and went home.

This was not the last time that the interests and traditions of Native Americans would come into direct conflict with those of Euro-Americans during the war. At one level Indians and non-Indians could share compatible goals. Native peoples needed European access to goods, particularly guns and ammunition, and could often find common cause against a mutual enemy. However, the somewhat superficial bonds often broke down in the face of distinct cultural differences. Some whites took their Indian allies as they found them, recognizing to some extent that natives fought for their own goals. These men were few and far between. More often, military men accepted native alliances with preconceived concepts of how allies should behave. This attitude often led to disaster.

Native Warfare Traditions

Europeans may have thought they controlled the war but that concept repeatedly ran up against the realities of Indian behavior. Native conventions continued to shape the conflict. French major general Louis-Joseph Montcalm arrived in Canada prepared to fight a traditional war against his English enemy. With few French troops he needed Indian allies who had already been recruited to the cause by his predecessor. Montcalm refused to accept, or understand the interests of, sovereign Indian nations engaging in this conflict. He was disgusted and appalled by the native tradition of taking captives for adoption and torture which he witnessed after their victory over the British at Oswego. In an effort to stop what he regarded as savage behavior, Montcalm paid his own allies in trade goods and brandy for the return of enemy captives. This inexplicable behavior by a white man convinced the natives that captives had value beyond their own traditions. As a result, nearly 2,000 warriors from 33 native nations came to Montréal to fight for the Frenchman who paid them to return the spoils of war! After a successful assault on Fort William Henry, made possible by Indian warriors, Montcalm offered the conquered British more honor and respect than his own Indian allies. When they realized they were to be denied their traditional reward for fighting, the Indian warriors took what they believed they had earned. In a fast, furious attack native leaders ignored the Frenchman's protests and took the prisoners, trophies, and plunder they had fought for. This so-called "massacre" effectively ended native cooperation with the French. The loss of her Indian allies cost New France dearly, and thus 1758 marked a turning point in the French and Indian War.

Britain prevailed in the long struggle Americans call the French and Indian War. At least on paper this was a major victory. The Treaty of Paris stripped France of her North American possessions. Theoretically it granted Britain undisputed possession of the land between the Atlantic Ocean and Mississippi River. Native Americans, however, had other ideas. No native delegates were represented at the treaty talks, nor were their interests mentioned in the settlement document. The Europeans conveniently forgot the valuable assistance of natives on both sides. If they thought the Indians were going to accept defeat dictated by European diplomats they were very mistaken.

PONTIAC'S WAR

The various tribes who fought in the war did not feel defeated. Native peoples had lost an important ally and supplier of manufactured goods when France left America, but that was a setback not a defeat. Despite the ravages of smallpox, thousands of warriors could still take the field and remained in possession of much frontier territory. The idea that they should suddenly forfeit their sovereignty to the British because of a piece of paper signed in Paris was preposterous. The Delaware chief, Netawatwees, was shocked by the terms of the Treaty of Paris. He said the English "was grown too powerfull & seemd as if they would be too Strong for God himself."[1] In a foolish move, the British cut back on the gift giving which was an integral part of Indian diplomacy. Arrogant British commanders displayed further disregard for Indian traditions

Indian leaders had to deal with often unsympathetic British officers like Colonel Henry Bouquet after the British won control of the Ohio country from the French. (Ohio Historical Society)

by demanding the return of captives—many of whom had been adopted into the tribes. By exhibiting a callous disregard for the traditions and power of the native residents the mighty British Empire would find itself stymied by the determined resistance of various tribes in the Ohio Valley.

Historians have called Pontiac's War one of the most successful campaigns fought by the Indian peoples of eastern North America.

They base this on the fact that every major British fort west of the Allegheny Mountains had been captured by the Indians with the exception of Detroit and Niagara, and those held only after much bloodshed. Natives used an intriguing combination of cunning strategy and guerrilla warfare to paralyze the British frontier. After defeating the French and claiming her North American empire the British certainly did not expect to be thwarted by what they regarded as a ragtag group of savages. But their hard-won empire was quickly swept away. In a desperate attempt to hold on to their North American possessions, the British military struck back. Commanders ordered the use of whatever measures were necessary to "extirpate" the Indians. At Fort Pitt this took the form of distributing smallpox infected blankets in a rudimentary practice of germ warfare. No prisoners were to be taken and orders went forth to put "to death every one of that nation [Seneca] that may fall into your hands."[2] The bloody conflict raged on, terrorizing settlers and emptying the frontier. The natives did quite well in the beginning but eventually their efforts were weakened by the effects of disease, shortage of supplies, and conflicting individual agendas. Different groups made peace separately until the whole affair was over by 1765. Native resistance to the British Empire did not yield permanent possession of their lands. But it did force the British to back off their harsh attitude toward the Indians and to resume the accepted course of diplomacy.

AMERICAN REVOLUTION

Whatever breathing room the northeastern tribes gained from exerting their power during Pontiac's War vanished a decade later when the "great Father across the ocean" got into a squabble with his North American "children." The British attempts to downplay the impending conflict by putting it in terms of a family did little to mask the reality of a country again torn by war. The outbreak of what U.S. history records as the American Revolution brought new challenges to the first Americans. American Indians had a great deal more to do with the struggle to win independence from Britain than most Americans realize. It was the debts incurred from fighting the Indians and French that led Britain to tax her North American colonies. Likewise, the British attempt to avoid another costly war by enacting a dividing line between colonists and the Indian Country, known as the Proclamation of 1763, greatly enraged the colonists and fostered their spirit of rebellion.

Political Considerations

Despite their indirect influence on the outbreak of war, few native groups wanted anything to do with it. Natives wanted to focus on their own concerns and issues. In native experience, squabbles among whites had a nasty tendency to turn out badly for everyone. However, it is exceptionally difficult to stay out of a conflict taking place in your homeland, especially when you have ties to one or the other of the combatants. When the Iroquois sent a delegation to Philadelphia to declare their neutrality in May 1776, Washington said ". . . it will be impossible to keep the [Indians] in a state of neutrality."[3] The reality was that by 1776 most tribes had been influenced by white contact for generations. Many viewed the conflict as an opportunity for them to gain something by assisting one side or the other.

While pressure mounted on both sides several influential voices spoke for peace. Seneca chief Cornplanter had lived through the French and Indian War and knew the cost of violence. A chief as well as a warrior, Cornplanter had to think of the women and children, the future of the tribe. He saw only death and destruction in a white man's war. "War is war. Death is death. A fight is a hard business."[4] Although he counseled peace, Cornplanter was outvoted by whiskey-fueled young warriors among the Seneca and Mohawk. However, as a leader in a true democracy Cornplanter prepared his followers for a war he did not seek.

Those who would avoid war had a hard road ahead of them, but men like Shawnee chief Cornstalk continued to advocate peace. Western Indian communities had been drained by war, most recently Virginia Governor Lord Dunmore's attempt to assert control over the backcountry. The Shawnee's defeat at his hands in 1774 left them with little appetite for further conflict. Chief Cornstalk carried a message of peace from a clan mother to the Americans in 1775. The message reflected the concerns of women who had seen too much disruption and sought only a return to peace. ". . . if the white people entertain designs to strike us I beg you will tell me—I depend on you that I may move out of danger with my children."[5] Fighting for sovereignty was important, but so was raising and protecting the next generation.

The largest native power in the Northeast, the Iroquois League, had decisions to make. William Johnson—the Englishman who swayed Iroquois loyalties in the French and Indian War—had died, his influenced replaced, but not equaled, by his nephew

Guy Johnson. Still, most Iroquois had allied with the British in the past and saw little reason to go against them now. Natives continued to value and indeed require European trade goods, which were primarily supplied by the British. Indians found that Americans were less likely to have desirable trade goods and more likely to encroach on native lands. As the two easternmost members of the Iroquois League, the Mohawk and Oneida nations had been the most impacted by white contact and thus would be the most likely to take sides in the upcoming war.

The British actively courted the powerful Iroquois League, having seen their effectiveness in the French and Indian War. Powerful, charismatic Mohawk leader Joseph Brant, who had close ties to the British, used his standing to push his people toward an alliance. His efforts were aided by the behavior of Americans who had inspired the deep hatred of many natives. Brant traveled to London in 1776 where he met the monarch and the royal court. Brant made it clear that the Mohawk expected British support in the coming conflict, in order to "see these bad children chastised."[6] The Mohawk would fight, but for their own interests in containing the Americans' seemingly insatiable land hunger.

Religion

Other forces were also at play. For nearly a century the northeastern tribes had experienced change through contact with Euro-Americans. One of the forces driving wedges in native culture had always been Christianity and it came into play with the Oneida and their Tuscarora allies. One village provides an informative example of the situation of the Oneida people. Oneida had established Oquaga in the 1730s along the important Susquehanna River. It became a magnet for people seeking safety or fleeing encroaching white settlers. This created a diverse population beyond the Oneida cultural core. In many ways, this village reflected the cultural continuum between traditional native practices and new European innovations. Residents adopted the practice of keeping domesticated animals which required only slight modification of their age-old practice of penning up wild animals for fattening. Some of the new ideas came from Christian missionaries who had been invited to the village to "assist us in setting up husbandry."[7]

Of course the missionaries brought more than just agricultural knowledge, so that many residents of Oquaga practiced Christianity. An energetic Presbyterian missionary named Samuel Kirkland arrived in 1767 and made even greater inroads among the Oneida. He won the Indians' trust by learning their language, setting up schools, and sharing his meager resources with the people. Kirkland became a man the Oneida villagers could trust and turn to for counsel. However, his presence in the Oneida villages created a rift both between traditionalists and Christians, and between Presbyterian converts and Anglican converts. As the American Revolution arrived, various Oneida factions were at odds with each other and with their Iroquois brethren. The division between arrival and patriot intruded into the Oneida world. Samuel Kirkland was a patriot.

The Oneida leaders knew they needed to create a consensus to protect Oneida interests. Therefore they declared their neutrality to Governor John Trumbull of Connecticut in 1775. "We have heard of the unhappy differences and great contention between you and Old England. We wonder greatly, and are troubled in our minds. . . . we cannot intermeddle in this dispute between two brothers. The quarrel seems to be unnatural. . . . we are unwilling to join on either side in such a contest. . . . Let us Indians be all of one mind, and live with one another; and you white people settle your own disputes between yourselves."[8] The concept was clear; Indians needed to remain united and look after their own future. Unfortunately, the forces of change in the Oneida community prevented that unity.

The Oneida leaders did struggle for a long time to maintain Iroquois neutrality. Familiarity with whites pushed the Mohawk toward the British side and the Oneida toward the American. Their close relations with their neighbors led the Oneida to scout for the rebel cause. Younger warriors followed the lead of their elders, such as 80–year-old Chief Shenandoah who was very attached to both Christianity and the rebel cause. As the conflict heated up, Iroquois League members found themselves on opposite sides of the war. The inevitable civil war came on August 6, 1777, near Fort Stanwix, New York. The British planned an attack on the fort the Americans named Fort Schuyler. The British force included Mohawk Joseph Brant leading Mohawk and Seneca warriors against an American command assisted by nearly 100 Oneidas. The clash was intense and bloody. When the smoke cleared, the field was littered with Iroquois dead killed by Iroquois hands. The American Revolution had done what hundreds of years of native warfare could not—it broke the Iroquois League apart. The results devastated the homeland of the Iroquois. Everyone suffered in the ensuing cycle of retaliation.

The Americans reacted strongly to defeat by Mohawk and Seneca warriors. George Washington ordered General John Sullivan to lead an expedition into the heart of the Iroquois homeland. His orders were to "lay waste to the lands of the Iroquois."[9] Sullivan followed orders, burning over 40 Indian villages and scorching their crops, orchards, and stored food. With the men away fighting, the women and children could only watch helplessly as fields, homes, and food supplies vanished before the fires of the enemy. The loss was devastating. The Indians knew they could not replace what the army had destroyed. Sullivan's officers and men were amazed by the prosperity of the Iroquois lands they were destroying. "The Indians live much better than most of the Mohawk River farmers their Houses very well furnished with all necessary Household utensils, great plenty of Grain, several Horses, cows and wagons. . . . The town, which consisted of 128 houses, mostly very large and elegant. . . . encircled with a clear flat which extended for a number of miles, where the most expensive fields of corn were and every kind of vegetable that can be conceived. . . . There are great number of apple and peach trees here, which we cut down [and] destroyed. . . ."[10] This comment reveals the success of the Iroquois economy and underscores the incredible losses brought by the war.

The destruction caused 5,000 Indians to flee to Fort Niagara for British protection. Native war parties continued to leave from Fort Niagara, 50 in 1780 and again in 1781, to strike the American frontier. If the British expected the warriors to fight for their cause they had to support the women and children who had been driven from their homeland by the enemy. Fort Niagara became a refuge for Britain's native allies. By 1779, the more than 3,000 Indians drawing rations there were members of the Mohawk, Seneca, Cayuga, Onodaga, Tuscarora, Delaware, Chugnut, Shawnee, Nanticoke, and Mahican tribes. Some families tried to farm abandoned land and in some way recover the self-sufficiency they had known before the conflict.

Despite their suffering, the Seneca and Mohawk had enough strength to exact revenge on American allies the Oneida and Tuscarora by ravaging their homeland. The raid revealed the complete breakdown of the concept of the Iroquois League of friendship. The idea of friendship or alliance with whites proved equally hollow. When the Europeans ended the war in 1783, the Iroquois discovered that the British had never mentioned their Indian allies in the treaty they signed with the Americans. There was nothing in return for their loyalty to the great father across the ocean. The Iroquois had paid a high price for their involvement in the white man's war. Only two villages remained untouched by the war. Thousands had been driven from their homes, lost family members to violence, and suffered from starvation and disease. The Iroquois League would never regain the power, unity, and influence it enjoyed before the American Revolution. And in their diminished state, the Indians had to face their aggressive neighbor the new United States.

Social Disintegration

Many natives in the "frontier" areas of rapidly expanding white settlement had not known peace for decades. The bloodshed of the European power struggle flowed right into the colonial dispute. For hundreds of people in dozens of villages this meant men were away on war parties almost ceaselessly. The whole fabric of society stretched as warfare dominated life. Men had less time to help with the heavy labor of agriculture or to supply critical protein through hunting. Mourning for lost loved ones was more frequent, and everyone felt the stress of the endless conflict.

The natives caught up in a seemingly endless cycle of violence usually saw the Americans as the aggressors. It was Americans who encroached on native lands, killed their game, and cut their trees for houses.

When we passed through the country between Pittsburgh and our nations, lately Shawnee and Lenape hunting grounds, where we could once see nothing but deer and buffalo, we found the country thickly inhabited and the people under arms. We were compelled to make a detour of 300 miles. . . . We saw large numbers of white men in forts; and fortifications around salt springs and buffalo grounds.[11]

Chief Cornstalk, 1776

As their native enemies increased, Americans did little to stem the tide of support for the British. While on a peace mission to the Americans, Shawnee chief Cornstalk and his young son were imprisoned and killed by soldiers. The Shawnee then joined the British in retaliatory violence against the Americans. The Shawnee had had nothing but trouble with land-hungry Americans. Virginia Governor Thomas Jefferson urged a war of extermination against the Shawnee in the Ohio country. Kentucky and Virginia militia frequently crossed the Ohio River to burn Shawnee villages again and again. George Rogers Clark's punishing campaign unleashed a vicious cycle of retaliation that rocked the backcountry. Armies and war parties constantly crossed through Indian country. There was little discipline and seemingly little strategy apart from shocking violence. At Gnadenhutten, Ohio, American militia murdered 96 Delaware Moravian converts. The Indians' pacifist beliefs, which prevented them from fighting the war, did nothing to stop the Americans.

It seemed as though conversion to Christianity or friendship with the Americans was little valued anyway. The Mahican of Stockbridge, Massachusetts, supported their white neighbors and fought for the patriot cause. While Mahican warriors were away, whites took their land so that at the end of the war Stockbridge was no longer an Indian town. The Declaration of Independence ignored the reality that the patriots had Indian allies when it said that the king brought on the frontier the "merciless Indian savages, whose known rule of warfare is an undistinguished destruction of all ages, sexes and conditions." The Gnadenhutten massacre, Sullivan expedition, and other American actions prove the reverse was true. The Americans had such a bad reputation that many Indians could not wait for the chance to get revenge.

Southeastern Nations

Independent of the Iroquois and northeastern tribes, southern natives had to make their own choices in the American Revolution. Cherokee life had changed drastically in the last several decades. They suffered serious population loss due to the nearly constant warfare, the ravages of imported diseases, and the overhunting of wildlife. Their lands were very fertile, making them almost irresistible to American farmers. In attempting to keep the peace, elder chiefs had signed away much of the Cherokee ancestral lands until it seemed the settlers would leave little for the Indians. The Cherokee anger at encroaching Americans was something the British hoped to tap and direct for their own purposes. The Cherokee had their own ideas and young warriors struck hard and fast at illegal squatters. Dragging Canoe led the defiant Cherokees in a bloody frontier war. They targeted American forts in North Carolina, and the violence spread to the frontier areas of present-day Tennessee and Alabama.

The Americans retaliated in a scorched earth policy that brought untold suffering to the Cherokee people. As had become their practice, the whites made war on civilians. American troops received orders to "cut up every Indian cornfield and burn every Indian town." During September 1776, the Americans destroyed more than 36 Cherokee towns. People fled to the mountains in fear for their lives. Cherokees now lived as refugees with nothing to eat when just a few months previously they had been wealthy. The destruction of their livelihoods continued. In 1779, American troops burned 11 towns, over 20,000 bushels of corn, and stole 20,000 pounds worth of goods. People became desperate, and chiefs responsible for the future of their people had to act. When older chiefs pled for peace to stop the destruction, the younger warriors saw them as weak and cowardly. This internal disagreement over the proper way to deal with white aggression further weakened the Cherokee people. While the defiant warriors fought for traditional Cherokee principles, the chiefs entrusted with the safety and well-being of the tribe could not tolerate the destruction. Tribal members divided over the issue of resistance to Americans. The American Revolution had split another native power group.

All participants pay a price for waging war. The American Indians of the Revolutionary period seem to have paid especially dearly. With the war officially over after the Treaty of Paris, Indian Country woke to a harsh new reality. After years of nearly constant warfare, the native nations were weakened. Entire villages had been lost. Even if a tribe had maintained its land base, dwellings had to be rebuilt, fields replanted, and some attempt at a normal life reconstructed. No one could awaken departed loved ones; no one could replace overhunted wildlife; no one could be sure of what would come next for the native peoples of the East.

FIGHT FOR OHIO COUNTRY

The British claimed that their former native allies had not been abandoned but "remitted to the care of neighbours."[12] The neighbors were quickly revealed as rapacious land seekers. The new reality that eastern natives awoke to was that the aggressive American settlers now had a new, organized government and an army to back it up. The one feature of power the Americans did not have was money, and they quickly sought to remedy that by turning "empty land" they had "won" from the British into cash. The young American government desperately needed more land to act as a safety valve for the pent up demands of their new citizens. In addition, the issue of debts owed to Revolutionary War veterans threatened to destroy the fledging political experiment of the United States. The "empty" land of Ohio promised to solve all of these problems. The only obstacles to that plan were the men, women, and children who lived on that land. So began the fight for Ohio.

Americans approached Indian relations with confidence in their right to control all the land yielded by Britain in the Treaty of Paris. James Dean, member of the Continental Congress, advised that "I would never suffer the word 'nation' . . . or any other form which would revive or seem to confirm their former ideas of independence. They should rather be taught that the public opinion of their importance has long since ceased."[13] Americans seemed to care little that the land they coveted for expansion was also the homeland of natives. In 1785 in the Treaty of Fort McIntosh the United States told assembled chiefs that two-thirds of Ohio was U.S. land. Of course that was easy to say when the rightful possessors, Miami and Shawnee chiefs, were not present.

The new government quickly moved to organize the newly won lands by means of the Northwest Ordinance of 1787. This document set out a plan based on values and morals that may have reflected the best intentions of the new nation but certainly were never carried out. Article III promised "The utmost good faith shall always be observed towards the Indians; their lands and property shall never be taken from them without their consent; and, in their property, rights, and liberty, they shall never be invaded or disturbed, unless in just and lawful wars authorized by Congress. . . ."[14] These lofty words would quickly ring hollow in the ears of Native Americans. Individual American citizens certainly did not intend to act with "good faith." Relations on the frontier were exceptionally violent. In Pine Creek, Pennsylvania, in 1790 a judge ordered a jury to find guilty a man accused of murdering an Indian because of the overwhelming evidence. The jury not only found the murderer innocent, but raised a subscription to pay his court costs. The relentless pressure of westward expansion meant an inevitable clash in Ohio. Indians regarded the Ohio River as the final acceptable boundary between white and native lands. By 1789 there were 20,000 white settlers coming down the Ohio.

Economic Adjustments

When faced with the continued intrusions of a white dominated market economy based on agriculture, native groups had two choices—participate or reject. Those who participated and grudgingly engaged in the yeoman farmer ideal of the new republic found it to offer little protection. Whites wanted Indian lands no matter what they were doing on them. Farming offered little protection against land hunger. Those who sought to avoid the expansion of the market into their ancestral homelands and avoid white contact really had to leave the area. Some groups crossed the Mississippi to escape the aggressions of Americans. Spanish territory provided refuge for a few decades.

Those who stayed in Ohio realized a conflict with the United States would be inevitable so preparation was the best defense. Once again the tribes of the region found themselves forced to deal with a bewildering array of power dynamics. The Iroquois League's political and military power exerted in the region had collapsed. Their British allies had abandoned the Indians in the peace settlement yet retained control of several interior forts. The British naturally harbored ill-will toward the Americans, and hoped to create problems for the new nation on the frontier. But could they be trusted? Natives once again had to evaluate the intentions and reliability of foreigners in their own quest for sovereignty. The British offered encouraging words, arms, food, and other supplies to tribes who opposed American expansion. The reality was that the natives had few options for obtaining these necessary items.

Social Adjustments

The nearly constant pressure of whites brought changes and adaptations to Indian culture. Many of those residing in Ohio country could be considered as refugees. They had come to this region fleeing white pressure elsewhere. An area like the Glaize, on the Maumee River near modern Defiance, Ohio, represented the new world for natives. The Ottowas lived here before the American Revolution and warriors of other tribes often moved through on their way to raid settlers. As natives relocated their villages in response to white incursions, they migrated toward the Glaize. By 1792, three Shawnee towns, two Delaware, two Miami, and a European trading town clustered around the Glaize. Although they were tribally distinct, the residents shared many aspects of post-contact culture. Subsistence came primarily from agriculture as women tended large vegetable gardens and several acres of corn. The importance of agriculture is revealed in the ongoing practice of the Green Corn Ceremony, a harvest celebration. Men spent their time away from home on the warpath, hunting for food, and supplying the fur trade. Participation in the market economy allowed access to desired items such as the silver jewelry both men and women liked to wear. Some Indian women married white traders and acted as a bridge between cultures, and many natives had close relations with the British, French, and American traders in their midst. Interconnectedness did not guarantee peace, however, and the settlements at the Glaize became the headquarters for the militant resistance of American expansion.

Political Organization

As President George Washington mulled over the best way to "induce them [the Indians] to relinquish *our* territories and remove to the illimitable regions of the West"[15] the Shawnee, Miami, and Chippewa leaders had to devise a plan to keep *their* lands. Clearly it would take a united effort to stand up to American aggression. No one Indian nation was powerful enough to take on the Americans by themselves. Much like Philip 100 years previously, 18th-century leaders recognized the need for native coalitions. Their close residency fostered cooperation and a shared sense of destiny. A sense of pan-Indian identity cut across tribal lines and helped to foster the unity that would be required to hold a native confederation together against the Americans.

There were many conscious attempts to promote that sense of unity. Many Indian leaders saw it as the only hope for a future for their people. From the Great Lakes to the Gulf of Mexico, Indian leaders sought to communicate with each other with the goal of resisting U.S. expansion. Tribes with similar self-interest, which we refer to as the Western Confederacy, first met in 1785 and continued to insist that the United States deal with the whole group rather than with individual tribes. In 1787, the Huron, Mohawk, Oneida, and Shawnee met in the Creek Nation to discuss plans for a "general defense." Leaders invoked the names of great warriors who had resisted whites so that their descendants could remain free. On a practical level, cooperative strikes targeted American river trade by attacking boats on the Tennessee, Cumberland, and Ohio Rivers. Some individuals rose to prominence in this vibrant, defiant atmosphere. One was Blue Jacket—a Shawnee leader who gathered his 300 followers near the Glaize. People resided in bark cabins, tended vegetable gardens, farmed corn, and pastured horses nearby.

Into this atmosphere of native unity, confidence, and resistance the U.S. Secretary of War Henry Knox sent General Josiah Harmar in command of 1,500 poorly disciplined militia in 1790. Harmar had orders "to extirpate, utterly, if possible, the said [Indian] banditti."[16] He was to destroy the Miami, Shawnee, and Delaware villages along the Maumee River in Indiana "by a sudden stroke, by which their towns and crops may be destroyed."[17] In the face of this aggression, the leaders of the seven Indian villages at Kekionga (present-day Fort Wayne, Indiana) moved their women and children to safety. Harmar burned 185 deserted log houses and about 20,000 bushels of corn in the fields. Proud of his destructive activities, Harmar failed to realize that the warriors fully intended to meet his army.

A native force representing the spirit and physical makeup of Indian unity met the invading Americans. Blue Jacket led the Shawnee, Little Turtle led his Miami warriors, and they drew support from Delawares, Pottawatomies, Chippewas, and Ottawas. As Blue Jacket later said, the native warriors were "acting in a cause of justice" to protect their homes.[18] In two engagements the motivated, unified native force proved to be more than a match for a demoralized, poorly supplied American army. Little Turtle lured Harmar into an ambush, even setting villages aflame to give the illusion of a panicked flight. Deep in the forest the Indian force attacked and the Americans lost 183 men. The rest survived only because Little Turtle had made his point and allowed them to leave. The Indians' stunning victory over Harmar's men gave confidence to the natives who now knew they could repel invasion. On the other hand, it frightened and enraged frontier settlers who realized that their new federal government could not protect them.

While Indians relished their victory, they also knew it was not the end of American attempts to force them from the land. Warriors had to continually be on the alert for the next threat, plan the next defense. Women lived in fear of the next invading army and had little hope for a peaceful future for their children. That was the problem with this system. Natives had to win every battle. One defeat meant a land-yielding treaty. They had to stay unified and prepared, which was very difficult. Readiness status thus overrode normal activities like hunting, and retarded social activities as well. Who had time or energy to court, celebrate, or even mourn traditionally when the Americans would come back any day?

The Americans did come back. The fledgling federal government could not give up so easily, or they would find that they had lost more than just Ohio. In order to maintain federal authority and maintain the loyalty of westerners, President Washington had to control Ohio. His new government committed to driving

Indians to the cession of lands by force rather than by diplomacy. In May 1791, Congress authorized the recruitment of 3,000 troops. Their leadership was given to the territorial governor, Arthur St. Clair, a revolutionary war veteran and former British army officer. He was ordered to make a permanent military post in the Miami country to intimidate the Indians. St. Clair promised to make "strong war" against the natives and to wreak "vengeance" and "utter destruction." It turned out to be the other way around. St. Clair may have had battlefield experience in the traditional wars, but he took the field with a very weak army against an unfamiliar enemy. The result was a disaster for the United States. Such a disaster that it remains the worst defeat of a U.S. Army by Native Americans.

St. Clair's army suffered from massive desertions, terrible morale, and poor supplies. As the American army proceeded slowly on their fort building expedition the Indians prepared to drive them out. A force of 1,000 Miami, Shawnee, Delaware, Wyandot, Six Nations, Ottawa, Ojibwa, and Pottawatomie warriors watched the Americans' every move. On November 4, 1791, Little Turtle led an attack that routed St. Clair's army. St. Clair thought his position so strong that he did not bother to build defenses. The Indians hit the Kentucky militia so hard that half the men went down and the rest abandoned their camp and artillery. The rout was complete as St. Clair lost nearly two-thirds of the army while the survivors fled back to one of their new forts. The Western Confederacy could rightfully celebrate a well-deserved victory.

Political Considerations

This impressive success gave the Indians great confidence in their ability to hold onto their lands. In 1792, a Grand Council was held at the Glaize. The council decided to demand recognition of the border at the Ohio River as stipulated by the 1768 Treaty of Fort Stanwix. After St. Clair's disastrous defeat, the United States sent commissioners to negotiate with native leaders since the military approach had not worked. The commissioners, however, would not agree to the Ohio River boundary. Indian leaders declared that "money, to us is of no value."[19] They offered the novel idea that the United States should take all the money it was offering the Indians in treaties and annuities and was spending on raising offensive armies and instead offer it to white settlers in lieu of the land they had purchased from the federal government. To the Indians' way of thinking everyone benefitted from this plan. They made their views clear; all they wanted was to be left alone.

You have talked to us about concessions. It appears strange that you should expect from us, who have only been defending our just Rights against your invasion; We want Peace: Restore to us our Country and we shall be Enemies no longer.[20]

Native leaders tried to explain why they had to resist American demands for more land.

Our only demand is peaceable possession of a small part of our once great Country. Look back and view the lands from whence we have been driven to this spot, we can retreat no further, because the country behind hardly affords food for its present inhabitants.[21]

President Washington and Secretary Knox had no intention of trying a new approach to Indian relations or of allowing the great native victory over St. Clair to go unanswered. The fight for control of the frontier would continue. Congress increased both the military budget and the size of the army to meet the perceived threat to American expansion. The newly raised army, the Legion of the United States, would be led by Anthony Wayne. As Wayne prepared his new command for Indian warfare, the Indian leaders also gathered their forces. It had been difficult to maintain the native confederacy over the three years that the United States prepared for battle. Little Turtle also knew that British support was critical for any native success, and worried about the reliability of his white allies.

Both sides realized the pivotal role the British played in the struggle for the region. Wayne tried a last attempt to avoid war by sending a message to the confederacy that the British would not help them and they should make peace. In 1794, the United States was negotiating with Britain for their withdrawal from the forts in the old Northwest. This difficult situation revealed weaknesses in the native coalition. They could not realistically defeat Americans on their own even with an impressive coalition, and therefore had to rely on the assistance of unreliable white allies for help. Leaders of the various tribes in the confederacy had conflicting opinions on the best response. Little Turtle of the Miamis counseled against continued fighting. He said "the trail has been long and bloody; it has no end"; he knew the whites would never stop coming for

Miami lands. Little Turtle's view did not reveal cowardice but rather the understanding that he was responsible for protecting women and children, for the future of the tribe. As much as they needed their lands they also needed peace in order to plant, to have husbands and sons at home, to continue their daily lives. However, the vocal Shawnee leader Blue Jacket denounced Little Turtle and spoke strongly for war. Blue Jacket emerged as the leader of the confederacy and Little Turtle, though reluctant, led his Miami warriors in support of the confederacy's decision.

The towns at the Glaize became the targets for Anthony Wayne. He established Fort Defiance at the site of St. Clair's disastrous defeat and moved out to engage the Indians. Wayne's 1,000 men met Blue Jacket's 500 warriors in an area near present-day Toledo, Ohio, where a tornado had knocked down large trees. The ensuing Battle of Fallen Timbers lasted only an hour as Wayne's force overwhelmed the outnumbered Indians. The United States drove the Indians from the field with bayonets, cannons, and cavalry. "We were driven by the sharp end of the guns of the Long Knives. Our moccasins trickled of blood in the sand, and the water was red in the river."[22]

When they saw the tide shifting the Indians retreated to the British fort Miami. To their disgust their supposed allies refused to open the gates. Wayne had not destroyed the natives' ability to fight, but their abandonment by the British did undermine much of their determination. It turned out that Little Turtle had been right. It would be nearly impossible to hold off the Americans without access to British supplies. Accordingly, 1,100 natives from eleven tribes met with Wayne at Greenville in the summer of 1795. The United States demanded and received two-thirds of Ohio and a small portion of eastern Indiana. U.S. officials promised a lasting boundary between Indians and settlers which they would prove unable or unwilling to enforce. Little Turtle spoke eloquently for the traditional land rights of the Miami, but in the end the military might of the United States had opened the region to white settlement.

The Treaty of Greenville and the loss of Ohio can only be regarded as a major blow to natives' struggle for land rights. The Western Confederacy fought well and hard but it was not enough. Still, the idea of uniting various tribes in opposition to land-hungry Americans did not die at Fallen Timbers. Others took up the cause and once again looked to the British for help in challenging American domination. The timing was right in 1811 for another attempt to unify competitors to the United States' expansion. The British and the Americans were approaching war at the same time a native coalition came into its greatest strength.

TECUMSEH

The fighting in Ohio in the 1790s was merely the opening salvo in the United States' campaign to settle the lands organized under the Northwest Ordinance. After Ohio at the end of the 18th century, Americans clamored for the opening of Indiana to settlement; this brought them into direct conflict with one of the greatest Indian confederacies in history. The coalition led by Tecumseh and his brother Tenskwatawa, known as the Prophet, represented the high point of post-contact spiritual and military fervor of eastern tribes.

The Shawnee were the architects of one of the strongest native coalitions to challenge the United States. A remarkable set of brothers rose to prominence in the early 19th century and together led a pan-tribal resistance movement. The coalition built by the Shawnee brothers Tecumseh and Tenskwatawa offered both a serious challenge to the future expansion of the United States as

Shawnee military leader Tecumseh led a pan-Indian resistance against U.S. expansion. (Ohio Historical Society)

well as a new concept of Indian identity. Together they gathered thousands of Indians from dozens of tribes eager to defy Americans' expectations of continued growth. Motivated by the spiritual teachings of Tenskwatawa and led by the military genius of Tecumseh, the native coalition offered the only real hope of regaining past prosperity.

The Shawnee of the 18th century had wandered widely in their attempts to find a peaceful home. During Tecumseh's childhood, Ohio was the battleground where the Shawnee sought to maintain their traditional life against the ever encroaching white settlers. Tecumseh's father died in battle against the settlers in 1774, and his older brother was killed fighting Americans in 1792. Tecumseh witnessed the Western Confederacy's struggle against Harmar, St. Clair, and Wayne. From all these experiences the young Shawnee warrior shaped his vision of a pan-Indian movement that would unite to resist American incursions. Tecumseh's grand plan extended farther than any previous native coalitions. His conception—that all indigenous peoples shared an identity that existed in direct contrast to white America—was far ahead of his time. He sought to unite all the tribes between the Appalachians and the Mississippi River, from the Gulf of Mexico to the Great Lakes. Most native people of his time would not accept this innovative idea, but they did recognize great leaders who would help them maintain their traditional homelands.

Shawnee Politics and Religion

The first appeal to northeastern tribes came not from the warrior Tecumseh but from his brother Tenskwatawa. At first glance, this younger brother had none of the leadership traits of his brother. He was neither a great hunter, nor a warrior, nor a chief. He was, however, a powerful spiritual leader who inspired thousands of demoralized, refugee people with his message of renewal and hope. Known as the Prophet, he preached a return to traditional ways and strong resistance of white practices. Those who flocked to Tenskwatawa's preaching formed the core of Tecumseh's resistance movement. He mobilized his brother's followers into a dedicated, militant group. Tecumseh traveled widely, seeking to energize the remaining strength in Indian country into an organized resistance movement. In addition to every Indian he could inspire, Tecumseh also needed the assistance of the British. In the opening decades of the 19th century the British and Americans inched closer to conflict, a situation that could only benefit the Indian coalition seeking help against the United States.

The brothers did not immediately seek conflict. Like most leaders, they longed for harmony, prosperity, and security for their people. It was unlikely that their resurgent indigenous society would be allowed to co-exist with the aggressive American frontier culture, but it could be attempted. They gathered their followers at a new location along the Wabash River in Indiana. The town—known to whites as Prophetstown—boasted 200 homes, 100 acres of cultivated fields, and rich hunting areas. While Tecumseh traveled to spread the message of pan-Indian unity and resistance, the Prophet invited believers to come to him on the Wabash. Here he preached the evils of alcohol and other white vices and promoted a return to empowering traditions. The Prophet's teaching offered hope, pride, and a sense of self-worth to demoralized people. The Shawnee and other Indians had struggled to maintain a sense of identity as natives amid all the pressures of the new century. The world had changed so rapidly that the traditional ways seemed irrelevant in a world dominated by white economic forces. Now this Shawnee religious leader extolled the virtues of traditions.

Shawnee religious leader Tenskwatawa, also called "The Prophet." (Ohio Historical Society)

Only by rejecting white ways and returning to the successful paths of their ancestors could 19th-century natives hope to be happy. Tenskwatawa had showed his power many times and now thousands flocked to hear his message of renewal in dark times.

The existence of a thriving native town where many tribal groups mixed in harmony frightened American officials. They could not let such a powerful display of Indiana sovereignty continue. Consequently, the governor of Indiana Territory, future President William Henry Harrison, decided to move against the Prophet and the growing coalition before it was too powerful. In November 1811, Harrison marched 1,000 soldiers toward Prophetstown. This put the Prophet in a difficult position. His brother was the military leader and he was away; in addition the Indians were low on ammunition that would be desperately needed to hunt game in the coming winter. They did not want an armed conflict, but that's what Harrison brought. As a religious leader, the Prophet did what he could to prepare, calling on the spirits for assistance and bolstering morale with grand claims of supernatural support that would turn the tide in their favor. Outnumbered probably two to one, the Indians made a creditable defense of their town but eventually had to withdraw. The real loss came then, when Harrison torched the town, stealing cooking utensils and desecrating Indian graves as well. The Shawnee had lost everything, including their stored grain, on the brink of winter. This was a serious blow to the fortunes of the new confederacy and made them more dependent than ever on British assistance.

In January 1812, Tecumseh returned from a remarkable six-month journey of 3,000 miles traveling through 11 present-day states to spread the message of Indian unity. He found the destruction of his village and the scattering of his followers. He saw "the great destruction and havoc, the fruits of our labor destroyed, the bodies of my friends laying in the dust, and our village burnt to the ground, and all our kettles carried off."[23] His anger at the Americans and at his brother would do little to restore their fortunes. So Tecumseh set about repairing his coalition, gathering needed supplies, and preparing to strike back at the Americans. Despite setbacks his timing could not have been better; in June 1812 the United States declared war upon Great Britain. Tecumseh believed that throwing in with the British was the only hope to save Indian lands, culture, and independence.

In the summer of 1812 the frontier echoed with the sound of shots as Indians, Americans, and the British struggled for advantage. One by one the American forts at Detroit, Chicago, and Michilimackinac fell until in six weeks every American post on the upper Great Lakes west of Cleveland had fallen. It seemed that the pan-Indian resistance was off to a great start. As the British observed, "They appear determined to continue the contest until they obtain the Ohio for a boundary."[24] This was the same goal that Little Turtle and the 1790s confederacy had sought, and the same level of success against Americans that that group had achieved against St. Clair. Unfortunately, this greater confederacy would meet a similar fate, again betrayed by the British, as Little Turtle had been at Fallen Timbers.

The end came at the Battle of the Thames on October 5, 1813. Tecumseh had put his life, his cause, and his loved ones in the care of the British and now they failed him. Tecumseh led 500 Shawnee, Delaware, Creek, Mesquakie, Sauk, Pottawatomie, Kickapoo, Winnebago, Wyandot, Ojibwa, and Ottawa warriors. They held the right of the line attacking the American forces while the British troops arrayed on the left. Only a few minutes into the battle the British broke, their commander fled, and the resistance collapsed. Left on their own the Indian forces could not hold off the 3,500 Americans under William Henry Harrison. The battle quickly turned to a rout as the British lost over 600 men and the Indians withdrew into the swamp. By far the greatest loss that day was the life of Tecumseh, felled by an American bullet. As the great leader's body crumpled, the hope of a resurgent Indian confederacy to resist American expansion died with him.

RED STICKS

Tecumseh's endeavors ended in 1812 but his influence lived on. His name has entered the history books as an example of a powerful, intelligent Indian leader. Non-Indians keep his memory alive as a martyr to the cause of Indian resistance, respected for his fighting, but his message misunderstood. Yet, his message did spread far beyond the Wabash River of Indiana. In his remarkable journey in 1811 Tecumseh spoke with hundreds of Indian groups. His speeches brought huge audiences and he lived up to his reputation as a great orator. An observer described the experience:

His eyes burned with supernatural lustre, and his whole frame trembled with emotion. His voice resounded over the multitude—now sinking in low and musical whispers, now rising to the highest key, hurling out the words like a succession of thunderbolts . . . I have heard many great orators, but I never saw one with the vocal powers of Tecumseh.[25]

Many tribes were moved by the powerful pleas of Tecumseh but most could not overcome their tribal ties to embrace a pan-Indian vision. However, the message of resistance resonated strongly among southern Indians pushed incessantly by white farmers.

Creek Politics and Religion

The Creek Confederacy in Alabama had become a loose con-glomeration of people of many ethnic backgrounds, but most had held to traditional religious beliefs. As a group they had suffered loss of population, land, and security at the hands of Americans. They listened to Tecumseh's preaching combining religious renewal with action against whites. A strongly anti-American group goaded into action by the message moved quickly to implement the plan of resistance. They became known as the Red Sticks for the red color that signified war in Creek culture. Their activism against Americans coincided with the War of 1812 so they allied with the British. The rest of the Creek confederacy remained loyal to the Americans which made the Red Sticks' uprising a civil war among the Creeks. White settlers used the opportunity of official war to strike at a group of Red Sticks who had sought Spanish assistance in Pensacola, Florida. Hundreds of whites, including the attackers, then sought safety at Fort Mims, Alabama. The Red Sticks retali-ated against the poorly defended fort killing nearly 400 people there. This was a great victory for the Red Sticks, and is considered the only time in history when Indians successfully stormed a large fortification. The United States quickly declared Fort Mims to be a massacre, and organized a force to punish the Red Sticks.

The Red Stick faction was now committed to a war in which it was terribly outnumbered, having to fight Americans, traditional tribal enemies allied with the United States, and fellow Creeks. From the fall of 1813 through the spring of 1814 the Red Sticks fought valiantly at Calabee Creek, Tallushatchee, and Talledega. The end of the resistance came at Horseshoe Bend on the Tallapoosa River, Alabama. The Red Stick warriors hid their women and children in a safe spot and then prepared to defend the bend. Andrew Jackson with Tennessee, Creek, Choctaw, and Cherokee forces nearly destroyed the Red Stick warriors. More than 1,000 Red Stick warriors died. Most survivors and their families fled south to the questionable safety of Spanish Florida. One officer described their pitiful state—"such objects I never saw the like of, absolute skin and bone."[26] Jackson would eventually pursue them there, invading Florida in 1818. But first he forced an enormous land cession on the Creeks. The Treaty of Fort Jackson gave the United States 23 million acres, half of all the Creek land, ironically most of it from those who fought *with* Jackson against the Red Sticks.

SEMINOLE

The Red Sticks found refuge in Spanish Florida among the Seminole. The Seminole were a post-contact group composed primarily of Creek Confederacy members who had fled white settlement in the 18th century. The newcomers came into a region convulsed by tension. The conflicting interests of natives, white settlers, runaway slaves, and Spanish and American officials threatened to engulf Florida. The Seminole practiced a unique social strategy. They welcomed runaway slaves into their midst, treating them with various degrees of autonomy, all of which were an improvement over slave life. Some Africans married into the tribe, creating a group of mixed-race people that defied the accepted categories in 19th century society. Flush with victory over the British, the Americans—particularly war hero Andrew Jackson—set their sights on controlling the Florida peninsula and ending Seminole sovereignty. In 1816, Andrew Jackson oversaw an attack on Negro Fort, a former British installation held by renegade blacks, most of whom died when it blew up. This was just the opening salvo in the United States' attempt to control Florida. From 1817 through 1818, in what is often called the First Seminole War, Jackson's troops skirmished with various Indian forces, disrupting native life throughout North Florida. Finally, in 1821, Spain ceded Florida to the United States. Rather than ending the clashes with Native Americans, U.S. possession of the region simply set the stage for greater conflict.

After the United States took control of Florida, it moved to contain Indians onto less desirable land, attempting to place the Seminole on a reservation in the center of the state. Conflicts continued between the Seminole, the military, and white settlers throughout the 1820s. Then, in 1830, the Indian Removal Act legislated the removal of southeastern Indians from lands east of the Mississippi. The Treaty of Payne's landing, signed in May 1832, committed the Seminole to removal and incorporation into the Creek Nation upon their arrival in the West. Probably fraudulent, certainly not reflective of the will of the people, the treaty heralded a struggle between the United States and the Seminole. That armed conflict became known as the Second Seminole War, the longest, costliest, and least successful America Indian War in history.

The Second Seminole War lasted over seven years and cost the United States about $40 to $60 million and 1,500 soldiers' lives. It cost the Seminole people their homeland. From 1835 to 1842 the United States poured more and more resources into the attempt to drive the native people out of Florida. Famous military leaders like Zachary Taylor and Winfield Scott chased down illusive bands of Indians with both regular army and militia troops. Scott's orders were not to negotiate with the Indians until he had reduced them to unconditional surrender. The Seminole operated under loosely organized band leadership, so each chief and his band of a hundred or less followers resisted the incursion of their homeland. They struck at farms, plantations, and army forts. Sometimes they acted in consort, resulting in pitched battles like that of Dade and Okeechobee. Despite their incredibly superior numbers, the American forces could not gain the upper hand and so resorted to treachery to find victory. General Thomas Jesup had supplied the Indians with white cloth so that they could come in safely; however, he chose not to honor the flags of truce. Under his orders, several resistance leaders like Osceola and Micanopy were captured under flags of truce and imprisoned. Additionally, bribes were liberally distributed to chiefs to coerce them to surrender their followers. Each deception, each capture, each death reduced the Seminole's ability to resist the Americans. Food was always scarce since everyone was on the run, and women and children fled to isolated, marginal areas to escape the soldiers. Starvation was as much a threat as military engagements.

The continued conflict cost both sides dearly. The United States continued to spend millions of dollars to remove the Seminole from Florida. Many Seminoles were captured and deported, while others surrendered and agreed to go west to their fate. By 1843 the government had deployed 40,000 men and managed to ship some 3,800 Seminoles to Indian Territory where they settled in uneasy proximity to the Creek Nation. About 300 Indians remained in Florida. Despite incredible odds they had managed to survive. They had completely altered their lifestyle by withdrawing to the protection of the Everglades and creating a new subsistence style appropriate to the swamps. That was not quite the end of the hostilities with the Seminole, as newly arrived white settlers continued to push for total removal of all Indians. From 1855 to 1858 the American government waged the Third Seminole War to remove 163 Seminoles from Florida. The rest were left to their fate, considered too inconsequential to bother a mighty nation. The southeastern Indians had lost their homeland for good.

BLACK HAWK WAR

In the north, the fertile lands of Indiana continued to lure settlers. They wanted Indians removed. In January 1829, the Indiana Legislature petitioned Congress to remove Indians from within its boundaries because their existence tended to "materially impede a system of internal improvements . . . jeopardizes the peace and tranquility of our frontier."[27] Native people in Indiana would have found this claim to be laughable. If anyone jeopardized peace it was the Americans who squatted on Indian land. A Pottawatomie leader grumbled that the "plowshare is driven through our tents before you have time to carry out our goods and seek other habitation."[28] The behavior of whites "driving their plowshares" continued to divide natives. Some favored the easier avenue of cooperation, while others gathered strength for resistance. American officials sought to exploit divisions and use whatever tools, such as alcohol, that would weaken opposition to their demands. Indian Commissioner Lewis Cass offered to give the Pottawatomie enough whiskey "to make every man, woman, and child drunk" if they would sign away their lands.[29] White officials would gather signatures from any Indian, chief or not, to put a veneer of legality on treaties granting land cessions. Tribes could not be expected to abide by agreements made by individuals not recognized as leaders. This is just how the bloody Black Hawk War came about.

The Sauk and Mesquakie (Fox) were Algonquian speakers living in the region east of the Mississippi River. They had been in contact with whites for a century and allied with each other after the French decimated the Mesquakie in the 1730s. Their traditional lifestyle included hunting, gathering, and agriculture as well as frequent raids against enemies like the Osage and Cherokee. Once Europeans showed up, the Sauk and Mesquakie traveled to St. Louis to trade with the Spanish and also maintained trading ties with the British. Lewis and Clark traveled the region in the early 19th century and estimated a population of 2,000 Sauk and 1,200 Mesquakie.

Political Considerations

In 1804, an American treaty pledged the Sauk and Mesquakie people to vacate 50 million acres of northwest Illinois, northeast Missouri, and southern Wisconsin. The signers were not the preeminent leaders of the tribe, and they did not meet with the Americans prepared to cede land, but rather to secure the release of an imprisoned Sauk. In addition, the treaty signers were "drunk the greater part of the time they were in St. Louis."[30] Naturally, many tribal members did not regard this treaty as valid. Natives had a very different view of such documents than whites. They valued the rights or agency of the individual. For example, Black Hawk did not feel bound by the latest treaty defining tribal boundaries because he neither attended the council nor signed the paper. No one could tell a Sauk warrior what to do or where he could go. In fact many resistant Sauk refused to sign any papers lest they be tricked by whites. Although government officials did not immediately force the Sauk and Mesquakie off the land, they did attempt to curtail their traditional raiding against the Sioux. In 1808, the United States built Fort Madison in present-day Iowa which immediately brought them into conflict with the Sauk. The presence of the American military was not welcomed by the tribe. Black Hawk made his feelings about Americans clear: "Why did the Great Spirit ever send whites to this island, to drive us from our homes, and introduce among us *poisonous liquors, disease and death*? They should have remained on the island where the Great Spirit first placed them."[31]

When the War of 1812 broke out the natives had an opportunity to act on their dislike of Americans. The British held the loyalty of Sauk, Mesquakie, Pottawatomie, Kickapoo, Winnebago, and Ottawa warriors through liberal distribution of trade goods, especially coveted arms and ammunition. This was not a traditional war against traditional enemies. The whites had their own agendas and their own style of fighting. "Instead of stealing upon each other, and taking every advantage to kill the enemy and save their own people, as we do . . . they march out in open daylight and fight regardless of the number of warriors they might lose."[32] The Indian warriors had to defend and supply their families and the British became the best option, but Americans then regarded them all as enemies. Black Hawk especially became a noted enemy to Americans.

The United States tried to exploit tribal divisions by befriending the Sauk leader Keokuk—who represented peaceful elements of the tribe, in opposition to his rival, Black Hawk. While Black Hawk and other warriors were away fighting with the British, the rest of the tribe left behind needed leadership and protection. Keokuk stepped into the vacuum of power and gained status. This change of leadership reveals the pressures operating on native tribes. Warriors were away from home for long periods of time. White conflict stretched on for years, much longer than traditional raids had taken. The resulting stress and strain on the community gave rise to improvised and non-traditional solutions. Men like Keokuk, who otherwise did not have claims to power, rose to leadership. U.S. officials sought every advantage in pressing their claims against the Indians so they actively courted Keokuk and his views.

Economic Pressures

As white settlers poured into Sauk and Mesquakie country to exploit iron ore deposits, the situation worsened. As the wild game disappeared, Indian hunters roamed farther and farther from home in order to feed their families. Hunting trips took them into Sioux territory in search of meat and also brought inevitable native versus native clashes which terrified whites. White traders contributed to the feeling of chaos as they traded whiskey for pelts and skins, thus driving an unsustainable economy fueled by alcohol. The tension took a huge toll on Indian families, and everyone looked for relief. Keokuk saw removal west of the Mississippi River out of proximity with whites as the only hope for the Sauk people. Black Hawk believed they must stay and fight for the lands that were rightfully theirs. Indian Commissioner William Clark prevailed upon Keokuk's beliefs and convinced some Sauk chiefs to cede a forty-mile-wide strip of land as a buffer intended to keep peace. Black Hawk did not sign the treaty, and was later told that Sauk lands would be opened for sale and settlement to whites.

Black Hawk did not intend to give up the lands east of the Mississippi—for which the Sauk held a "sacred reverence"—without a fight. He knew the United States would be a formidable opponent, however. He had learned from the past, and worked to create a tribal confederacy to resist American encroachment on Indian land; he also expected help from the Sauk's old allies, the British, in Canada. When the seasonal cycle of resource utilization brought Black Hawk's people east of the Mississippi River in the spring of 1831, the stage was set for a clash. General Edmund

Sauk leader Black Hawk tried
to remain in his birthplace
east of the Mississippi River.
(Library of Congress)

P. Gaines, commander of U.S. troops, told Black Hawk he must
move west of the Mississippi—to which the chief responded that
his people intended to stay and "lay their bones with those of
their ancestors." He was "satisfied with the lands the Great Spirit
has given him. Why then should he leave them?"[33]

Black Hawk could not realistically expect the Sauk warriors to
hold off the American forces alone. He had, however, allies among
the Kickapoo and Winnebago, and he held out hope that his
old friends the British would come to his aid. He listened to the
counsel of a half-Sauk, half-Winnebago man named Wabokieshiek
who was regarded as a prophet. The Prophet urged Black Hawk
to stand firm for the village, that he could expect assistance and
success. The counsel of a man in contact with the powerful spirit
world was not taken lightly. Black Hawk prepared to remain where
the bones of his forefathers lay. His people planted their corn crop
in their village fields, but white settlers plowed it up. As the situation grew desperate and rival Keokuk siphoned off his followers,
Black Hawk offered a compromise that would save his people—he
would leave his village after the corn crop came in so his band
would have food. The white commander insisted that they had to
leave immediately.

Gaines had 1,400 militia which Governor Reynolds of Illinois described as entertaining "rather an excess of *Indian ill-will*, so that it required much gentle persuasion to restrain them from killing, indiscriminately, all the Indians they met."[34] Bloodshed was avoided that year when the Sauk returned west for the winter, but the likelihood of violence resurfaced in 1832 when Black Hawk crossed to the east side of the Mississippi River with 1,000 people, including 500 mounted fighting men. The new American commander, General Henry Atkinson, had no doubts as to the proper reception for the Sauk, Mesquakie, Kickapoo, and Winnebago with Black Hawk. He would "treat them like dogs." Atkinson—who the Indians called White Beaver—promised that "if Black Hawk's band strikes one white man in a short time they will cease to exist." And he had just the men to do it—2,600 undisciplined militia men who yearned for a chance to kill Indians.[35]

The militia had trouble finding Black Hawk's band. They kept moving, seeking any refuge. The constant flight and aggression of white settlers meant the Indians could not successfully hunt or gather, so starvation became the enemy. Subsisting on roots and bark was an unrealistic strategy, but their supposed allies did not supply the corn the Sauk so desperately needed. The group traveled to the Prophet's village where they learned the bitter news that not only would the Winnebago not aid them but neither would their old allies the British give them any assistance. The British flag they flew over their camp now seemed a pitiful act of defiance. When his last hope of aid from the Pottawatomie vanished, Black Hawk had little choice but to seek peace with the Americans.

Black Hawk sent three warriors with a flag of truce to his closest pursuers, several hundred mounted soldiers. This is when the federal government's reliance on untrained, Indian-hating militia changed the course of history for the Sauk people. The Illinois militia men under Major Stillman seized Black Hawk's messengers and killed some scouts in a weak skirmish that shed little blood but nonetheless destroyed any hope for peace. General Atkinson realized that the incident "closed the door against settling the difficulty without bloodshed."[36] Black Hawk felt the same way.

What was now to be done? It was worse than folly to turn back and meet an enemy where the odds was so much against us—and thereby sacrifice ourselves, our wives, and children, to the fury of an enemy who had murdered some of our brave and unarmed warriors, when they were on a mission to sue for peace.[37]

The region now descended into chaos as armed groups of whites and Indians took the opportunity to settle scores and gain advantages. A group of Pottawatomies attacked and killed settlers, and then were killed and scalped by the men of Colonel Dodge's command.

The U.S. Army ramped up efforts to regain control of the area. While Black Hawk had to lead warriors as well as care for the safety and well-being of women and children, the army poured in more military might. President Andrew Jackson ordered General Winfield Scott to travel to Illinois to take command of the operation with 800 regular army troops. Although the command was hit by cholera—which reduced their ranks by three-fourths—the order showed the intent of the United States to crush the Sauk's bid for freedom. In July 1832, the combined militias of Illinois and Wisconsin caught up to Black Hawk's band and engaged the warriors in the Battle of Wisconsin Heights. The Indians had discarded many of their possessions in their desperate flight, and many elderly and children suffered starvation and could not keep up. The militia killed them and moved on to engage the warriors. Again, the militia spurned a peace offering from one of the chiefs. Colonel Henry Dodge knew he had the advantage: "Be assured that every possible exertion will Be made to destroy the Enemy crippled as they must be with their wounded and families as well as their want [lack] of provision supplies."[38]

As Black Hawk's band dwindled due to deaths and desertions of his allies, the United States pursuing force grew stronger. Black Hawk moved his 500 remaining followers westward to cross the Mississippi River and tried once again to surrender with a white flag to a steamboat full of soldiers. The response was gunfire that killed two dozen warriors. Black Hawk, the Prophet, and 30 or 40 followers headed north to the Chippewa territory, leaving the main band huddled on the eastern bank of the Mississippi River in Wisconsin, unwillingly to flee farther. In the early morning hours of August 2, 1832, the U.S. Army opened fire on this camp. The battle of the Bad Axe was really a massacre as the army pounded the Sauk for eight hours. Soldiers shot any Indian they saw, including women attempting to swim the river with children on their backs. The riverbanks were stained red with Indian blood. Those who miraculously escaped to the west bank were killed by a Sioux acting in consort with the government. The death toll numbered in the hundreds. "It is impossible to say how many Indians have been killed, as most of them were shot in the water or drowned in attempting to cross the Mississippi."[39]

The government cleaned up the end of what came to be known as the Black Hawk War by scouring the countryside for any Indians that could be held responsible for the conflict. For their participation, real or imagined, the Winnebago, Sauk, and Mesquakie would be forced to yield yet more land. On behalf of the Sauk, Keokuk signed the Treaty of Fort Armstrong, or Black Hawk's Purchase, which stripped another six million acres from the tribe and placed them on a small reservation along the Iowa River. Black Hawk surrendered in August, and along with several other men was imprisoned in St. Louis. Along his journey Black Hawk traveled for the last time through his beloved country.

I surveyed the country that had cost us so much trouble, anxiety, and blood, and that now caused me to be a prisoner of war. I reflected upon the ingratitude of the whites, when I saw their fine houses, rich harvest, and every thing desirable around them; and recollected that all this land had been ours, for which me and my people had never received a dollar, and that the whites were not satisfied until they took our village and our grave-yards from us, and removed us across the Mississippi.[40]

After a winter in chains, Black Hawk and five others were sent to Fortress Monroe, Virginia, via Washington, D.C., where they met with President Jackson. In the East, people clamored to see real Indian warriors when they traveled, and several artists sketched and painted them while in prison. Frontier settlers had no such fascination with live Indians, and hanged and burned their effigies. Eventually Black Hawk was returned to his family in Iowa. His bid to keep his people in their ancestral lands had failed. It cost all the Sauk and Mesquakie people land and loved ones. Black Hawk was no hero to his tribe for the bloodshed he had cost them. His rival Keokuk had been appointed as the highest chief of the Sauk by the United States and Black Hawk retained little influence until his death in 1838.

Another chapter of the Indian Wars had closed. So many men and women from hundreds of tribes had fought to keep their traditional lifestyles and land east of the Mississippi. The focus now went westward across the great Mississippi River. The march of white settlers toward the West seemed unending to native people. Looking back, we can see the pattern of pressure and military domination spooling out across the centuries. For native peoples, the pressure was more isolated. Within a person's lifetime the whites could arrive and then dominate, and native life was forever changed. Although many tribes had heard of others' experiences with whites, ultimately each group had to deal with the current challenges on their own.

NOTES

1. Colin Calloway, *The Scratch of a Pen: 1763 and the Transformation of North America.* New York: Oxford University Press, 2006, 66.

2. Calloway, *Scratch of a Pen*, 73.

3. George Washington, The writings of George Washington from the original manuscript sources: Volume 4, http://etext.virginia.edu/ etcbin/ot2www-washington?specfile=/texts/english/washington/ fitzpatrick/search/gw.o2w&act=surround&offset=5224256&tag= Writings+of+Washington,+Vol.+4:+To+MAJOR+GENERAL+PHILIP+ SCHUYLER+New+York,+April+19,+1776.+&query=it+will+be+impos sible+to+keep&id=gw040406.

4. Alvin Josephy, Jr., *500 Nations: An Illustrated History of North American Indians.* New York: Alfred Knopf, 1994, 269.

5. Josephy, *500 Nations*, 262.

6. Brant to Lord Germain, 1776, quoted in Colin G. Calloway, ed., *The World Turned Upside Down: Indian Voices from Early America.* New York: Bedford/St. Martins, 1994, 150.

7. Joseph T. Glatthaar, and James Kirby Martin, eds, *Forgotten Allies: The Oneida Indians and the American Revolution.* New York: Hill & Wang, 2006, 51.

8. Calloway, *The World Turned Upside Down*, 149.

9. http://sullivanclinton.com/, accessed November 11, 2009.

10. Josephy, *500 Nations*, 269.

11. Josephy, *500 Nations*, 275.

12. Robert Utley and Wilcomb Washburn, *Indian Wars.* Boston: Houghton Mifflin, 1977, 112.

13. Utley and Washburn, *Indian Wars*, 112.

14. http://avalon.law.yale.edu/18th_century/nworder.asp.

15. Josephy, *500 Nations*, 286.

16. Wiley Sword, *President Washington's Indian War: The Struggle for the Old Northwest, 1790–1795.* Norman: University of Oklahoma Press, 1985, 87.

17. Harvey Lewis Carter, *The Life and Times of Little Turtle: First Sagamore of the Wabash.* Urbana: University of Illinois Press, 1987, 90.

18. Douglas R. Hurt, *The Indian Frontier: 1763–1846.* Albuquerque: University of New Mexico Press, 2002, 109.

19. Colin Calloway, *A World Turned Upside Down*, 182.

20. Calloway, *A World Turned Upside Down*, 182.

21. Hurt, 113.

22. Calloway, *A World Turned Upside Down*, 205.

23. John Sugden, *Tecumseh: A Life*. New York: Henry Holt and Company, 1998, 257.

24. Sugden, 311.

25. Josephy, *500 Nations*, 312.

26. Sugden, 385.

27. Francis Paul Prucha, *The Great Father: The United States Government and the American Indians*. Lincoln, NE: University of Nebraska Press, 1995, 245.

28. Hurt, 168.

29. Hurt, 168.

30. Donald Jackson, ed., *Black Hawk: An Autobiography*. Urbana: University of Illinois Press, 1955, 61. Black Hawk told the story of his life to Antoine LeClair, a mixed blood interpreter, and J. P. Paterson, a newspaper editor. They published the story as the autobiography of Black Hawk. This is a modern edition of that story.

31. Jackson, 69.

32. Jackson, 80.

33. Hurt, 178.

34. Hurt, 178.

35. Hurt, 180.

36. http://lincoln.lib.niu.edu/blackhawk/page2a.html, accessed November 11, 2009.

37. Jackson, 146.

38. http://lincoln.lib.niu.edu/blackhawk/page2c.html, accessed November 11, 2009.

39. Agent Joseph M. Street, quoted in Jackson, n. 115.

40. Jackson, 165.

3

THE FAR WEST

By the mid-19th century the United States looked beyond the Mississippi for its future. The lands of the Louisiana Purchase, which once looked so expansive, now beckoned eastern Americans and new immigrants. The prosperity and success of the United States was built on the availability of cheap land. By the 1840s the only place to go for that was west of the Mississippi. This political and economic reality came in stark contrast to previous U.S. policy. In just the past decade or so the government had forced native peoples out of their lands between the Atlantic and the Mississippi River and promised them new homes and peace in the West. Those promises were quickly going to prove to be hollow, and the continued U.S. expansion ushered in a new era of Indian Wars.

ECONOMIC PATTERNS

American expansion would also bring the country into direct contact with many indigenous nations who were at the peak of their power. The native nations west of the Mississippi were much more diverse due to the geographic regions of the West. Prairies, deserts, mountains, and high elevation forests dictated a wide variety of survival strategies. Most western groups did not practice agriculture, although there were some exceptions. This meant that many western natives lived a nomadic or semi-nomadic lifestyle.

Continued movement of entire communities in pursuit of resources created different lifestyles and different priorities. Mobile people experienced war differently than settled people. War was not less disruptive, less terrifying, but it did create unique problems for the people who roamed the West.

Until the mid-1800s the expansion of the Americans and thus their conflict with Indian peoples had followed a roughly continuous east to west course. Then suddenly, directly in mid-century, the pattern changed. The occasion was the discovery of gold in 1848 at Sutter's Mill on the American River in California. This set off a rush which brought 80,000 emigrants to California in 1849. The array of new arrivals was simply staggering. White and black Americans, Mexicans, Australians, Argentineans, Hawaiians, Chinese, French, English, and Irish flocked to the rumored sources of great wealth. One sentiment these diverse people had in common was a total disregard for the rights of native inhabitants. Within two decades the non-Indian population of California was 380,000 people. The United States had recently claimed jurisdiction over the Far West by virtue of the Treaty of Guadalupe Hidalgo, which cemented their victory in the Mexican-American War. With a stroke of the pen Mexico had passed off its "control" over the indigenous peoples of California and the Southwest. Mexico, as well as Spain before her, and the United States after, had an abysmal record of Indian relations in California.

California Diversity

The indigenous people of California were a very diverse group. The variations in culture were responses to the wide variety of resource areas. From seacoast to desert, mountains to grasslands, each region required unique cultural adaptations. The sheer variety of native life is reflected by the nearly 100 languages spoken at the time of European contact. This diversity in California's indigenous people made them independent; it also made them very vulnerable. There would be no confederacies, no pan-Indian movements in the area. There would be little unified resistance to the onslaught of outsiders. Most California people lived in fairly small units of no more than 500 persons. In a pure democracy it was difficult to organize for or wage war. Warfare was not a central part of the culture. It usually only occurred over the defense of territory, game, or members' safety and was waged formally, on a small scale, and quickly. It might be as simple as lining up, discharging arrows at the enemy, and returning home.

Much of the disruption of California native lifestyles occurred before the United States took possession. The Spanish arrived with a desire for wealth and a strong commitment to the spread of Christianity. The missions they built from San Diego to San Francisco took a terrible toll on the native population. Forced labor, physical abuse, destruction of culture, starvation, and disease combined to decimate the local populations. Some notable resistance occurred such as rebellions at San Diego, San Gabriel, and Santa Ynez. By the time the Mexicans ended the missionary system in 1834 the world of California Indians had been destroyed. Mexicans had taken their village land and missions became huge rancheros where surviving Indians worked as peons or serfs.

When the United States took possession in 1848, there were few native peoples left to resist them. Those who remained faced a new wave of abuse at the hands of miners. Areas of refuge such as remote valleys and torturous mountains which had allowed remnant populations to hang on, now became areas targeted by gold seekers. It seemed not a single square foot of California was left undisturbed in the relentless pursuit of gold. Loss of their land was the least of the abuses heaped on the California Indians. Miners overran their land, killed the remaining game, and captured women and children. Captive females were sexually abused while

Pomo women gathered seeds, a traditional resource use often interrupted by conflict. (Library of Congress)

children were sold into slavery. Shooting Indians became a sick form of sport for whites. A "sporting" party might wipe out an entire camp of indigenous people in an afternoon. "It was as close to genocide as any tribal people had faced, or would face, on the North American continent."[1]

Pomo Culture

The people we refer to as Pomo Indians were actually a diverse group of over 70 distinct tribes, speaking seven languages. They lived along the coast of north central California in shoreline, valley, and lake regions. This gave them access to a wide range of food types with little travel. Inland the land provided nuts from oaks, chestnuts, buckeyes, and conifer trees as well as wild grass seeds, fruit, and berries. They hunted mammals and many bird species like quail, pigeons, doves, woodpeckers, and blue jays. The lake shores and coast offered bounties of fish and waterfowl like ducks, geese, swans, cormorants, and herons. The resource areas were used communally and community leaders held elaborate ceremonies to set boundaries. However, individuals could control specific trees for harvesting.

The Pomo people traded extensively for items not available in their area. Men and women wove baskets that are still renowned for their quality. The technique of basket-making bound the Pomo in a common culture and was a recognizable trade item. Two forms of money created from shells and magnesite emerged to facilitate trade. The Pomo developed an arithmetic system to keep track of the value of their currency. None of this successful economic strategy helped protect the Pomo people from violence. They lived in relative peace in native California and only became threatened by the arrival of whites—first Russians, then Mexicans, then Americans. The Americans arrived in the mid-19th century and threatened to annihilate a people already weakened by disease and Russian attacks.

Any form of resistance to the Americans was generally futile. Two Americans had captured hundreds of Pomo Indians and forced them to work on their cattle ranch at Clear Lake, California. The chief described conditions of his people in captivity.

About 20 old people died during the winter from starvation. From severe whipping, four died. A nephew of an Indian lady . . . was shoot [sic] to death. . . . if this order was not obeyed, he or she would be whipped or hung by the hands . . . many of the old men and women died from fear and starvation.[2]

When these Pomos struck back and killed their white captors the U.S. Army arrived to dispense their version of justice. Unable to find the men responsible for the killings, the soldiers simply went after the Indians they could find. They massacred more than 130 men, women, and children they found fishing, and proceeded to butcher every other native person they came upon. The California newspapers of the time are full of similar accounts of atrocities. Native peoples lived in terror of the capricious violence of whites. On top of losses to random violence, diseases brought by new arrivals swept through remaining native groups. Not surprisingly, the Indian population of California dropped from 300,000 to just 30,000 in one century. The loss of 90 percent of their people meant few native California communities remained viable. Entire groups of people disappeared from the land while survivors suffered extreme dislocation and poverty.

Much of the devastation of indigenous lives went unanswered by violence. One historian described them as "gentle as the climate in which they lived."[3] While this is clearly a romanticized view, it is true that warfare was not as enshrined in the culture of California tribes as it was in other regions—such as the eastern Iroquois or the Plains Tribes. However, all people will fight to defend their homes and loved ones if they can. The problem in the Far West was that the few occasions when Indians tried to resist had terrible consequences. So the losses in California went largely unnoticed by the rest of the country until the 1870s. In 1872 the existence of a relatively unknown tribe in northern California captured headlines across the nation.

MODOC WAR

The Modoc people lived in northern California, along today's Oregon border. Their main settlements were situated around Tule Lake, although they migrated widely in search of resources. They hunted antelope, deer, mountain sheep, rabbits, and squirrels, fished, and supplemented this with gathered roots and seeds. There was little in this nomadic, somewhat materially impoverished lifestyle that garnered any respect or admiration from whites who arrived in the 19th century. When John C. Fremont led an expedition into Modoc country in 1846 he began a tradition of misunderstanding between whites and the Indians of the region. As whites entered the area seeking gold and other fortunes they clashed frequently with the Modocs. Within three decades the Modocs would fight for their lives and culture against the U.S. Army.

Modoc Social Organization

The Modoc are described as a naturally suspicious people. They distrusted their neighbors, some of their relatives, and all newcomers. They seem to have categorized other groups as enemies, present or potential. In hindsight this may seem a wise path in regard to whites. However, it exacerbated misunderstandings between the two cultures, and sparked reactions that hindered peaceful relations during negotiations. Seemingly quite in contrast to their innate suspicion was the Modocs' enthusiasm for aspects of white culture. They often adopted white dress, went by white bestowed nicknames like Scarface Charley or Curly Headed Doctor, and after mid-century traded with and had friends among white settlers.

Accommodation with intruding white culture may have been the Modoc's only choice. As soon as white settlers pushed their wagon trains through to northern California they wanted the Indians off the land. The indigenous people claimed far too much of prime ranching land in the opinion of the newcomers, and the U.S. government was constantly petitioned to fix the matter. In 1864, the U.S. government obliged by forcing a land cession of 14 million acres from the Klamath and Modoc. The natives received just three-quarter million acres for a reservation located entirely on Klamath territory. This left the Modoc with no access to their traditional hunting lands.

The stress of the loss and confusion about the proper path forward for their people divided the Modoc. A resistance leader rose to prominence—Kientpoos, whom the whites called Captain Jack. Fighting the loss of Modoc land, Jack left the newly assigned reservation and returned to his home. Much like Black Hawk in Illinois, Jack found that whites had already moved into his ancestral territory. Jack stubbornly stayed on, trading with, drinking with, and seeking advice from a few white friends. These white friends played an unusual role among the remaining Indians. Such men often issued passes, vouching for the character of the Indians. "Charlie, the Indian to whom I give this paper makes a living for himself and his family by farming, driving teams, etc. and wants me to give him this paper certifying to the fact that he is a civilian Indian and not a wild Indian . . ."[4] These passes reveal much about what had happened to Modoc society in the brief two decades since Fremont's expedition. They had become dependents of whites, conforming to white economic models and reliant on white assurance that they were good people fit to remain among settlers on their own homeland. At least a few Modocs did not accept this situation willingly.

To his credit Captain Jack tried reservation life in order to keep peace. Like Geronimo he found the situation intolerable and left. He left with eight times as many people as he brought in, a testament to the difficulties of reservation life and his leadership skills. His group returned to their homeland at Lost River and demanded that whites either leave or pay rent on the land they had seized. To further make their point about their traditional rights to the area, Jack's followers used white hayfields for their livestock, demanded to be fed in white houses, and took household utensils. These somewhat harmless attempts by Modocs to assert their rights caused white settlers to demand complete removal of the Indians, and it then became a U.S. Army operation.

Life for Jack's Modocs was tolerable if not perfect. It certainly was better than conditions on the reservation where so many were starving. The renegades successfully pursued traditional subsistence techniques. These Modocs followed Jack because he remained committed to the old ways. Had he accepted the whites' plans he would have lost his adherents. The band did not want war. They really just wanted to live as closely as they could to traditional ways on their homeland. But whites simply would not allow it. When in accordance with custom Jack killed a medicine man who failed to heal his niece it should have been an Indian affair. However, whites insisted that he be arrested. Some observers realized the dangerous potential of disparate cultural traditions. "The white people should not meddle with them in their laws among themselves . . . Let them settle all these matters among themselves and then our people will be in no danger from them."[5] Jack easily eluded those trying to serve the arrest warrant but it meant he could never go into the reservation. He continued to deal with government officials, always demanding that his people needed a place on their ancestral homeland. As so often happened in the saga of the Indian Wars, the final conflict was instigated by an unqualified official who ordered a force to arrest Captain Jack, Black Jim, and Scarface Charley.

In November 1872, the Modoc villages of men, women, and children were attacked by soldiers and settlers. The firefight lasted only a few minutes but the results were tremendous. The Modocs fled, the women heading for safety in the Lava Beds on the south shore of Tule Lake and the men taking vengeance on whatever white men they could find in the area. The Modoc War had begun.

During the attacks by the U.S. Army many Modoc fled to the harsh land-scape of the lava beds. (Library of Congress)

The United States poured men, money, and materials into the project to defeat the Modoc once and for all. As the army prepared to attack the Modoc Stronghold in the Lava Beds, the Modoc turned to the spiritual powers of their medicine man—Curly Headed Doctor—who promised to deflect white man's bullets from believers. The Doctor ringed the Modoc Stronghold with a red-painted, braided fiber rope. No white man could cross this line alive, and the carefully performed ceremony made Modoc warriors impervious to bullets. On its first test the medicine seemed to work. The Americans' first attack had been soundly rebuffed. The Modocs even finished the fight better armed than they began as they collected the weapons discarded by panic-stricken soldiers.

Political Considerations

The native victory was impressive but it created problems among the Modoc. Captain Jack was pleased and grateful for the victory though he knew that the United States would not give up, but would come at them again, perhaps with greater losses next time. The band was remarkably small and could not afford an all-out conflict. Accordingly, Jack sent word that he was tired of war and wanted it to end. However, it was not solely his decision to make. As a Modoc subchief, Jack did not have the power to coerce his followers. They followed him because they respected his leadership, but that could change. Many warriors were thrilled with the effectiveness of Curly Headed Doctor's medicine and had no intention of surrendering their advantage. The dispute raged in the Modoc camp as Jack sought negotiations with whites, and Curley Headed Doctor and Hooker Jim planned to defend the Stronghold. It is ironic that Jack, the Modoc leader most vilified by settlers and whose name became synonymous with the Modoc War, was the one negotiating for peace.

The ensuing tragedy shows the misunderstanding of cultures and the tensions brought to bear on natives by the challenges of white invasion. Captain Jack pursued a difficult course between the demands of his people to act bravely in defense of their tribe and the overbearing power of the U.S. military, which continued to close a net around the Modoc Stronghold. The pro-war Modocs following Curly Headed Doctor felt they had to force Jack to fight. They decided that if they murdered the members of the commission coming to negotiate with Jack, the whites would quit. The Indians would have withdrawn from the fighting if their leaders went down, and they expected the same of the whites. Shaming Jack by dressing him in women's clothing, the rebels provoked Jack into agreeing to the murders. Jack knew they would probably all die for the act, but if that is what they wanted from their leader, he would do it. Accordingly, the Modocs killed General Edward Canby and another commissioner when they came to negotiate. The die had been cast by the rebel Modocs. The United States would now expend whatever it took to retaliate for the death of a U.S. Army general. The Commander of the Army, General William Tecumseh Sherman, ordered the Modocs to be exterminated.

It took several days for the army to get into the Modoc Stronghold. The small band of warriors bound themselves with rawhide bandages for protection against the sharp lava terrain and used their knowledge of every crevice to gain the best firing positions. Women and children sought shelter in the caves which they protected from bullets by building stone barriers. Only the relentless pounding of artillery drove the Modocs out and then they were not destroyed but displaced. They engaged the military again in the rough lava formations that they knew so well and again won that day, but lost a subsequent skirmish at Dry Lake. The constant fighting took a toll on Modoc morale, and led to more and more internal disputes. Hooker Jim broke from Jack's leadership and took his followers away. They had goaded Jack into fighting the whites and now they deserted him.

Jack had only 33 fighting men left. His band was destitute. They had almost no water, little food, worn out clothing, and poor weapons. Jack probably would have surrendered for the sake of his people, but he knew the whites would hang him for the murder of General Canby; he had no choice but to fight. As the spring wore on the army pressed the Modocs and one by one the leaders began to surrender—Bogus Charley, Steamboat Frank, Hooker Jim— until only Jack and his few remaining fighters were left. With the intelligence of Jack's probable hiding places provided by the surrendered Modocs it was only a matter of time until the army found him. Captain Jack had been sold out by his own people. The very men who had put women's clothes on him and goaded him to fight now came to Jack riding white men's horses and advising him to surrender. Americans had always been able to capitalize on the divisions within tribes and it worked this time too. The original pro-war Modocs now acted as allies of the United States.

The United States and the Modocs chased Jack's little band for days and were rewarded with the incremental surrender of exhausted men. Scarface Charley, then John Schonchin—who helped murder the commissioners and knew he would be hung— reluctantly gave up their weapons and freedom. When at last Captain Jack surrendered, his reported words encapsulated the nature of the long struggle "Jack's legs gave out."[6] With that Captain Jack resigned his fate to the will of the U.S. government. The Modoc War was over. The cleanup campaign brought more bloodshed as settlers shot a wagonload of prisoners en route to an army camp. Jack and John Schonchin were shackled together for the few remaining days of their lives—one more insult to Indian dignity. Jack and several other Modocs, who spoke little English, were tried in a military court without counsel. The court quickly ruled that all six men should die by hanging. At the last minute President Grant

Modocs Captain Jack and Schonchin were blamed for the Modoc resistance and hung. (Library of Congress)

commuted two sentences to life in Alcatraz prison. On October 3, 1873, Captain Jack, Black Jim, Boston Charley, and John Schonchin died on the gallows. The Modoc had been defeated in war and the survivors forced onto a reservation. Although the U.S. Army had been the tool, much of the pressure for the Indians' removal had come from the citizens of Oregon. The same intolerant settlers would soon turn their attention to another quiet but proud leader and his people, and seek to drive them out of their homeland.

NEZ PERCE

As the fertile land of the Pacific Northwest continued to fill with white settlers, indigenous people came under greater and greater pressures. Violent skirmishes, indignities, and fraud became daily occurrences as newcomers disregarded traditional land-use rights. Traditions, harmony, and lives slipped away, often with little fanfare. Occasionally, however, the violence escalated into what the United States commonly called a war no matter who its opponents were, and captured national headlines. Such an event occurred in 1877 in the Nez Perce War, or more accurately, the Nez Perce Tragedy.

The Nez Perce tribe should have been the success story of the western Indians' relations with the United States. These were the people who had been so helpful to Lewis and Clark when their expedition came through Nez Perce country. The Corps of Discovery forged close ties with the group, and rumors persisted that William Clark fathered a child there. Subsequent white contact continued to yield good relations. Americans who dealt with them praised the Nez Perce highly. They regarded them as honorable, sincere, and trustworthy. Which is why it came as such a shock that settlers of the 1860s could harbor so much hatred for these people.

Nez Perce Culture

They called themselves the Nimiipuu, which translates roughly as "the people." The French label "pierced noses" may have been a mistaken characterization of their cultural practices, but the name has stuck for centuries. Occupying the mountainous region between the plains and the Pacific coast, the Nez Perce shared culture traits of both regions. After the arrival of European horses the people became excellent horsemen, and are often credited with breeding the American Appaloosa horse. Breeding skills allowed the Nez Perce to sell excess stock, so their renown as horse breeders spread through the West. They focused on improving endurance and speed, which would sadly turn out to be life-saving skills as they were drawn into war with the U.S. Cavalry. Horses became a form of portable wealth with some individuals owning more than 1,500 animals. Horses gave the people mobility and extended their range so that they interacted with groups along the Columbia River in the west and nomadic Plains Tribes to the east.

A journey to the plains required crossing challenging mountain terrain, but the entire tribe—men, women, and children—often made the trip, honing another set of skills they would unfortunately need to survive U.S. attacks. The vast herds of bison lured the Nez Perce eastward as they sought valuable hides. Hunters might stay on the plains for extended periods, and while there they developed trading relations with the Crow people, and later with white settlers. The Nez Perce originally hunted with a bow made of wild sheep horn that other groups admired. The men would and could fight, but the Nez Perce culture did not focus as much on warfare as many of their neighbors. Most accounts describe them as dignified, honorable people, slow to anger but quick to punish indiscretions. Theft and rape brought swift penalties and lying was considered a terrible breach of morality. Although the language contained no profanity, being called a liar was a strong insult.

The society was quite democratic and egalitarian. Families lived in related bands of 30 to 200 people. The bands each had a home-land territory but ranged widely in their exploitation of natural resources. Because they were not engaged in agriculture, hunt-ing, fishing, and gathering wild plants provided the basis of the economy. Band leaders or chiefs might direct the daily activities of several villages, but each village followed its own men in times of crisis. With a concept of limited leadership, chiefs gave advice and counsel but not orders. Since oratory and independence were both highly valued, men had to be convinced, not forced, to take action. Any collective action required lengthy debate and resulted only in a consensus that left individuals free to act as they wished. There was considerable friction among bands so it is misleading to refer to Nez Perce policy or Nez Perce decisions as though they all agreed. Despite our common terminology, the United States could not deal with a "tribe" or a tribal leader of Nez Perce. However, by the mid-19th century the federal government tried to do just that.

In 1853, Congress created the new territory of Washington in the Northwest. The new governor equated future success with ending Indian land rights. He quickly convened a meeting at which he convinced 54 Nez Perce headmen to yield over a third of their ancestral territory. The governor had insisted, as whites always did, on dealing with just one leader so that a Nez Perce called Lawyer rose to untraditional prominence. The Nez Perce were badly divided and now faced an onslaught of white demands which escalated with the discovery of gold on tribal lands. Miners illegally surged onto Indian lands, bringing disease, alcohol, and other destructive elements. The Nez Perce struggled to cope with their rapidly changing world, particularly the devastating effects of liquor.

Within a decade the influx of settlers emigrating along the Oregon Trail meant the United States wanted to reduce Nez Perce territory. An 1863 treaty, referred to by the Nez Perce as the "Thief Treaty," gave seven million acres of Nez Perce tribal land to the U.S. government. This instrument took some of the most spectac-ular areas of the Nimiipuu homeland like the Wallowa Valley, the Salmon River region, and the Snake River Valley and the important gathering spot of the Camas Valley. These were the bountiful natu-ral areas that had allowed the tribe to build considerable wealth based on impressive horse herds. The new reservation contained only land claimed by Christianized bands of Nez Perce and, not coincidentally, they were the only leaders who signed the treaty, under the watchful eye of the U.S. military. Lawyer had given away the lands of other bands while his people retained theirs. Many leaders did not sign the treaty and declared to Lawyer that they were no longer affiliated with his followers. Those band leaders who did not sign certainly did not consider themselves bound by the terms. Only the U.S. government believed that the bands who had no representative present at the negotiations had given up their homelands.

One of the bands that did not sign lived in the Wallowa Valley and was led by Tuekakas. The old chief whites called Joseph died in 1871 after extracting a promise from his son Heinmot Tooyalakekt that he would never relinquish the lands of the people. The son, known to whites as Chief Joseph, struggled to honor that deep desire of the traditional Nez Perce he led, but in the end lost his people's fight for freedom.

The Wallowa Valley, like so many areas of the Nez Perce territory was wonderful grazing land. White settlers moving into the area with dreams of cattle baronies soon overgrazed the neighboring Grande Ronde Valley and during a drought in 1871 cast covetous

Nez Perce leader Chief Joseph tried to hold his people together during their long flight from the army. (Library of Congress)

eyes toward the lush, well-managed Wallowa Valley grasses. When stockmen laid claim to Nez Perce land in 1872, Joseph carefully explained that his band had not signed away their land and that it was not open for settlement. The logical argument had little effect on dampening white land hunger. In one year the number of white-owned cattle grazing in the Wallowa Valley increased 300 percent. Undeterred by the Nez Perce's traditional rights, the settlers endlessly petitioned the government to remove the Indians. The government acquiesced to their demands and opened the valley to settlement in 1876. Reckless exploitation wiped out the game and the ubiquitous sockeye salmon in 30 years. As settlers took the valley as their own they continually clashed with the native residents. Lewis and Clark had described the Nimiipuu men as affable and gentle, rarely moved to passion, but not lacking courage when attacked. They would not give up their homeland without a fight.

Nez Perce dealings with white intruders and eventually the U.S. Army were drastically altered by forces outside of their control. In 1876 the command of George Armstrong Custer was wiped out by Plains Indians. Humiliated, terrified, and vengeful whites everywhere regarded "the Indian problem" with a new attitude. Immediate and overwhelming force became the only way to deal with natives. Generals assigned to western regions knew they had to act decisively in order to keep their jobs. General O. O. Howard ("the Christian general") showed little brotherly love for the Nez Perce. Even after his own study concluded that the Indians owned the Wallowa Valley, Howard decided that non-treaty bands had to move. The army would then occupy the valley to ensure that the Indians did not return. To make these demands even more outrageous, the general insisted that band leaders had only 30 days to move their people from their homelands. It seemed impossible for the Indians to meet these conditions or to successfully resist them. The Nez Perce situation was desperate.

I have carried a heavy load on my back ever since I was a boy. I learned then that we were but few, but the white man were many, and that we could not hold our own against them. We were like deer. They were like grizzly bears. We had a small country. Their country was large. We were content to let things remain as the Great Spirit Chief made them. They were not; and would change the rivers and mountains if it did not suit them.

Chief Joseph[7]

The band chiefs had to attempt the impossible. They had to move all the people, all their possessions, and huge horse and cattle herds numbering in the thousands to the small territory the whites "gave" them. Much had to be left behind, including valuable livestock which would surely fall into the hands of white settlers. This just added insult to injury. Bands led by Joseph, White Bird, and Toohoolhoolzote faced a journey that would crush most groups. The terrain was arduous, as they had to drop down into the aptly named Hells Canyon and then cross the Snake River at flood stage. Since the river was swollen by spring rains the Nez Perce asked to delay their journey, but a group of settlers petitioned for their immediate removal. This created incredible hardship for the elderly, children, and newborn livestock. Almost all the calves and many of the older horses and cattle were lost to the river but the people made it. Exhausted and frightened the Nez Perce clambered out of Hells Canyon into Idaho Territory. One of the wealthiest bands in the interior Northwest was now homeless and impoverished.

The Nez Perce came out of the canyon shaken by their experience but grateful for their success. All the bands met for one last taste of freedom before their exile to the reservation. Although the people were comforted to be together, it was hard not to be bitter about the future. They had tried hard to live peacefully with whites who came into their land and now seemed to be punished for it. Young men coming of age as warriors struggled to swallow the memories of past abuse. The elders were demanding that they walk away without a fight. It was too much to bear. Tensions simmered under the surface and headmen were alert for any signs of trouble. Trouble came in the form of three teenage boys. Wahlitits' father Eagle Robe had been shot by a white settler squatting on his land. The murder went unpunished. In his last night of freedom Wahlitits took some friends and rode out to settle the score. By the time the three boys returned to the Nez Perce camp they had shot five white men and started the Nez Perce War.

Nez Perce Attacked

The leading Nez Perce men knew the die had been cast. Whites would never allow these deaths to go unpunished and they rarely distinguished between individual Indians when seeking revenge. Chiefs had hoped to avoid war because of the cost to the women and children. They had always to balance their honor and courage against their responsibility to the people. Joseph's wife had given birth to a daughter a few days before. The proud father would have much preferred to spend time with his family, but duty called him to support the people. Joseph helped the 600 Nez Perce men, women, and children gather their possessions again and head for White Bird Canyon where they might have a chance at defense. This was not an offensive army; it was a settlement of people bracing for an attack. The U.S. Army was coming, goaded on by settlers demanding revenge against the "red devils" and "incarnate fiends."

As the army approached the Nez Perce camp at White Bird Canyon the Indians tried one more time to avoid bloodshed. They sent out a white flag and asked for a parlay, but a white settler charged and fired on the flag, intentionally shattering any chance for peace. The Nez Perce did not want battle but had prepared for the one they knew would come. With less than 70 sober fighting men and an obligation to protect women and children, they divided the force. One group protected the camp from a direct charge while the other two rode up the valley to strike the flanks of the attackers. The boys who started this mess, Wahlitits and friends, wore red blankets to show their bravery by attracting enemy gunfire.

In the ensuing battle of White Bird Canyon the Nez Perce fought admirably. One of the first shots took out the bugler so the army couldn't control troops, as this was the main means of communication. The warriors rode expertly trained horses. They could drop off, shoot, and remount, or shoot from beneath the horse's neck for protection. They fought equally well in unison or separately. The Nez Perce women also participated by stripping guns and ammunition from dead soldiers and getting them to the warriors. The volunteer soldiers fled in the face of this skill and aggression. Of the 85 U.S. Army privates, fewer than 10 had ever fought Indians and none of them were well-trained at firing from horseback. Those who had forgotten to tighten their girths simply slid right off their mounts. The mismatch left 133 U.S. dead and no Indian casualties. The Indians also collected 63 rifles from the battlefield so they would be better armed next time. The battle of White Bird Canyon was a great military victory for the Indians but clearly there would be retribution.

The American press made the U.S. defeat into a fiction. They inflated the 70 Nez Perce warriors into a force of 300 or 400. They played up the tactical genius of Joseph who was hardly on the battlefield and was not the military leader. Nez Perce had camp chiefs, like Joseph, who were responsible for the village when it moved or was under attack and war chiefs who led in battle. For some reason Chief Joseph was doomed to become the symbol of Nez Perce resistance. There was a full-blown panic in the Northwest of a full-scale Indian War. Claims abounded that all the tribes would now rise up to join the rebellious Nez Perce. This revealed whites' total lack of understanding of native culture. Joseph was no Philip or Tecumseh, planning a pan-Indian uprising, organizing and fighting for a concept. He was just a man trying to honor his father's wishes, to protect his people's future and to find a place to live in peace.

As with so many Indian tribes after the coming of the whites, the Nez Perce were a divided people. Christian Nez Perce whose homeland became the reservation scouted for the U.S. Army against their brethren. Both sides taunted each other across the Salmon River as the army chased the non-reservation Indians. "You call us cowards when we fight for our home, our women, our children. You are the coward! You sit on the side of the government, strong with soldiers. Come over. We will scalp you!"[8] However, the Christian Nez Perce were under pressure, too. The media accused them of aiding the renegades, thus stirring up demand for removal of *all* Indians. Whites made little distinction between the Indians so the resistance of non-reservation Nez Perce had consequences for all Nez Perce and created hard feelings.

Nez Perce Flight

While the newspapers escalated the fear of an Indian War, the U.S. Army consolidated forces against the Nez Perce. Despite the hardships, the Indians had no choice but to leave the area. They had to travel over extremely rugged terrain. They marched for two days, the old and the young, including Joseph's newborn baby. To lighten the load many left behind valuable possessions. Really tough decisions had to be made. How can you choose between ceremonial items passed down through generations, or food, or a light enough pack to carry without failing? Heart wrenching choices were decided in a few minutes and then the arduous journey began. The chiefs had decided to cross the Salmon River putting distance between themselves and the army. It was not easy to cross the swollen river with all their people and 3,000 horses, but they took the time to construct bullboats—bison hides stretched over a willow frame—which transported people and goods. Although it was hard, the Nez Perce made the crossing look easy compared to the army which struggled to get across. "We didn't seem to have engineering skill enough to devise ways and means across, said one soldier."[9] And they were not dealing with women, elderly, and babies.

As the Indians moved forward they had to protect the non-combatants. The warriors were not at liberty to launch an offensive attack on their pursuers. Joseph and other village chiefs stayed with the camp as it moved while warriors rode on the flanks and occasionally intercepted soldiers or foolhardy civilians bent on getting a lick in on the Indians. It was hard to be constantly on guard against the various detachments of infantry, cavalry, and volunteers that were chasing them. But to let their guard down was very dangerous. The group trudged over open prairie where they had often gathered the desirable camas plants in peaceful times but now could only hurry on hoping to avoid harm. The Indians' ranks had been swelled by the arrival of the respected chief Looking Glass and his people. When 60 troopers had approached his village Looking Glass sent out a white flag. The civilians with the army immediately fired upon it which set off a charge on the undefended camp. As the Indians fled, the whites drove off horses and cattle, and plundered tipis.

General Howard finally caught up to the fleeing Nez Perce along the Clearwater River. The Indians had taken to calling him "General day-after-tomorrow" for his constant tardiness during this epic campaign. But this slowness sometimes masked greater advantages. Howard's 500-man force now included howitzers and Gatling guns which he fired down the steep walls of the Clearwater canyon onto the Indian village in the valley below. Chaos and panic struck the camp along with the army's bullets and cannonballs. Joseph tried to ready the camp for another flight as warriors held off the attackers to buy them time. In the confusion Joseph's own wife and infant were left behind before being rescued. The only thing that saved the Nez Perce was the soldiers' incompetence and greed. The infantry faltered at the stream crossing and then the soldiers fell to looting the abandoned Nez Perce camp and gave up all pretense of a chase. Howard contented himself with telling the media and the president that he had just won a conclusive victory at the "Battle" of the Clearwater.

The army had scored a victory over the Nez Perce, costly not for the loss of life but the loss of belongings left in the panicked scramble to break camp. In a familiar pattern the Nez Perce regrouped and prepared for the next attack, but it did not come that day, or the next, or the next. General Howard had other matters to attend to and was confident that he could choose the time and place for the final blow to the Indians. He even interrupted his plans to meet with a supposed peace emissary from Joseph. However, the young warrior on horseback merely mooned Howard and rode away. The Nez Perce thus gained valuable travel time while Howard delayed.

Nez Perce Political Divisions

This was a challenging time for the Nez Perce. They had lost critical supplies and lacked a clear plan for the future. Quarrels raged as chiefs debated the best strategy to protect the people. Joseph probably proposed returning to the Wallowa Valley area to make a final stand in his homeland. War chiefs would not accept the risk of traveling back through that country and instead urged an eastward movement. Travel east, over the Bitterroot Mountains, would take the Nez Perce to Montana where they expected friendly relations and trade from white settlers and Flathead Indians. Chief Looking Glass in particular had great confidence in the idea that once in Montana the Nez Perce would be safe; after all it was the Idaho settlers who hated them. This naïve view of natives' problems with whites seems ludicrous viewed in the context of the 19th-century Indian Wars. However, leaders could only govern from their own experiences and understanding of issues. Nez Perce had traded peacefully with whites in the Bitterroot Valley in years past and saw no reason for relationships to have changed. The concept of racial hatred and a federal army with an assigned goal of their capture would have been inconceivable to Nez Perce leaders.

The Lolo Pursuit

In order to get to theoretical safety in Montana the people had to cross the Bitterroot Mountains on the Lolo Trail. It was reputed to be the worst trail in North America—narrow, precipitous, and clogged with mazes of fallen timber. It had nearly been the undoing of the Lewis and Clark expedition. Nez Perce bison hunters crossed it regularly but now women, children, elderly, and a horse herd had to negotiate the rugged trail while being pursued by the U.S. Army. The physical demands were almost unimaginable and added to that was the tension in camp every night. Leaders still did not agree on their ultimate goal as they herded their people forward. White Bird urged a journey to Canada, out of reach of the aggressive U.S. Army. Looking Glass wanted to travel some 600 miles to eastern

Montana into the territory of the Crow Indians whom he regarded as allies. This would take the Nez Perce far from their homeland, never to return. Joseph saw no point in this. "What are we fighting for? Is it our lives? No. It is this fair land where our fathers are buried. I do not want to die in a strange land."[10] This English rendering of Joseph's thoughts probably captures his general feelings on the need to stay connected to their homeland. Joseph was outvoted; the majority of chiefs agreed with Looking Glass. Joseph was not compelled to continue against his will but knew his people would have little chance striking out on their own. With a heavy heart Joseph continued to travel with the main group in his role of camp chief, responsible for the well-being of the non-combatants.

The terrain of the Bitterroots made this a daunting task. Everyone had to force their way through thick, tangled brush and trees which cut arms and legs. If horses fell off the side of the trail they had to be left for dead and their load was lost. Food was scarce so people gathered berries and snacked on the inner bark of pine trees for sustenance. Amazingly, under these terrible travel conditions the Nez Perce kept high spirits. They were together, traveling known territory, and anticipating a welcome in the Bitterroot Valley. The U.S. Army was in a considerably lower mood. Exhausted from an arduous campaign in the wilderness they were in no shape to cross the Lolo Trail. Howard's jurisdiction ended at the Idaho boundary anyway so he hesitated to push forward with troops already undone by less harsh terrain. Howard devised a plan to take an easier, more circuitous route to the Bitterroot Valley. The only troops left to contest the Nez Perce mountain crossing were under command of Captain Charles Rawn and they did little to slow the Indians. At the end of July 1877 the Nez Perce entered the Bitterroot Valley of Montana and the jurisdiction of General Alfred Terry. It seemed to the Nez Perce people like a victory. Whites had not seriously challenged them in their crossing. The only opposition they had faced was a weakly manned fortification which offered no fire and was thereafter referred to as "Fort Fizzle." Now they peacefully entered an area where they had friends among Indians and settlers. Maybe Looking Glass had been right.

Nez Perce in Montana

In the relative peace of Montana the Nez Perce chiefs again debated strategy. White Bird and Toohoolhoolzote spoke for a movement through the Flathead reservation on to Canada where they had heard Lakota leader Sitting Bull enjoyed refuge from the U.S. Army's endless pursuits. Looking Glass insisted on his plan to cross the Continental Divide into Crow Country where the Nez Perce would be welcomed as friends. Joseph did not rise to speak to the council. He merely remarked "When we were fighting for our own country, there was reason to fight . . . but since we have left our country, it matters little where we go. I have nothing to say."[11] So the man the whites chose as the symbol of the Nez Perce War was not the instigator or the mastermind of the violence; he had lost his home and now all that remained was protecting his people wherever they were. Looking Glass prevailed again and the group was joined by a few more lodges led by the mixed blood Lean Elk who knew the country they now traveled.

The journey up the Bitterroot Valley was easy, and they traveled and camped with no sentinels, no rear scouts. The valley is broad and flat with plentiful resources and people began to enjoy themselves. Everyone wanted to think that the worst uncertainty, the unexpected violence, was behind them now. Some warned that the group should be more careful but Looking Glass dismissed the fear. One young man, Wahlytits, considered to have medicine power, dreamed of violent death and warned the camp that they would all be killed. As Yellow Wolf later remarked, "Looking Glass was against anything not thought of first by himself."[12] The 700 men, women, and children went into camp in a meadow on the Big Hole River. The spot had long been used by parties traveling to and from the buffalo hunting country. They called it *Iskumtselalik Pah*, the Place of the Buffalo Calf. The chiefs laid out a V-shaped camp of 89 tipis along the winding, willow choked banks of the Big Hole. The location had all the resources necessary to replace items lost in the recent battles. Women could cut new tipi poles from the slender pine saplings, men could hunt deer and elk on the forest edge, camas grew in the meadow, and the horse herd grazed on the hillside. Almost everyone settled in to rebuild, relax, and rejoice. The evening of August 8th the warriors paraded, the women danced, and everyone enjoyed a glimpse of their old life.

Big Hole Battle

The next morning the dream was shattered by the roar of guns and yells of soldiers. The sleeping camp awoke to horror. The 149 men of the Seventh Infantry under the command of John Gibbon plus 34 civilians had snuck into a position 200 yards from the camp

Nez Perce families erected these ghost tipis to honor the memory of their ancestors killed in 1877 by the U.S. cavalry along the Big Hole River. (Courtesy of Clarissa W. Confer)

in the pre-dawn darkness. Counting on the element of surprise, the army expected to wipe out the village quickly. Their plans went awry when civilians prematurely shot and killed an elderly Nez Perce named Natalekin who had risen early to check on the horses. The element of surprise had lost its edge so now the soldiers crossed the stream and launched a furious attack on the village. Naked warriors rushed from tipis, grabbed weapons, and dashed for the cover of the stream. The army charged through the camp attacking anyone they encountered. They poured particular fury on the tipis which now sheltered only non-combatants. Gibbon had ordered three volleys aimed low because the Nez Perce would be lying down sleeping; the brutal strategy worked well. Many women and children were shot while still under their sleeping robes. Joseph's nephew scrambled out of his grandmother's tipi as she was shot and huddled on the slope with other horrified children to watch the carnage. The camp was in chaos and quickly devolved to hand-to-hand fighting as women, young boys, and elderly grabbed up any weapon to defend themselves. Warriors had to both fight and try to protect their families. As Wounded Head watched, his two-year-old toddled toward soldiers who shot him and then the mother who ran to grab the child. Women and children sought protection in the willow thickets at the stream bank but the soldiers soon began firing into the bushes there.

The army later claimed that the soldiers had not targeted women and children but they were the majority of the victims of the attack. Some soldiers made a choice not to fire on the unarmed but many did not. "This tepee here was standing and silent. Inside we found the two women lying in their blankets dead. Both had been shot. The mother had her newborn baby in her arms. Its head was smashed, as by a gun breech or boot heel," Yellow Wolf remembered.[13] Survivors bore the emotional scars of the trauma for the rest of their lives. It seemed impossible to describe. Unable to express his rage and grief Yellow Wolf declared that "some soldiers acted with crazy minds."[14]

Within 20 minutes the soldiers had occupied the camp. Gibbon thought he had whipped the Nez Perce and ordered his men to stop pursuit in order to burn the camp. Further carnage ensued as hidden children burned to death in tipis. "We found the bodies all burned and naked lying where they had slept or fallen before reaching the doorway."[15] The lull in the firing allowed chiefs to organize a resistance at the far end of the camp. White Bird could be heard exhorting his warriors.

Why are we retreating? Since the world was made, brave men fight for their women and children. Are we going to run to the mountains and let the whites kill our women and children before our eyes? It is better we should be killed fighting. Now is our time. Fight! Shoot them down. We can shoot as well as any of these soldiers.[16]

White Bird's rally wounded Gibbon and drove the soldiers from the camp into a siege situation on the hillside. Just as the men desperately used knives to dig shallow pits for protection the 12-pound cannon finally made it to the battlefield and set up on the hillside above the siege area. It fired only two rounds before it fell silent. Nez Perce warriors triumphantly captured the howitzer and a pack mule with 2,000 rounds of much needed small arms ammunition. From the hillside the soldiers witnessed the anguish of returning warriors who found the camp destroyed. The wails of grief filled the valley. Even Gibbon recorded that "few will soon forget the wail of mingled grief, rage, and horror which came from the camp . . . when the Indians returned to it and recognized their slaughtered warriors, women, and children."[17]

However shocking the scene there was no time to mourn or to bury the dead—the survivors had to get out of there. While his brother Ollokot kept the soldiers pinned down, Joseph oversaw the move. They buried the few bodies they could under a collapsed stream bank, loaded the immobile on travois, and slowly started the survivors on a 12-mile journey to the rendezvous point. It was a sad, slow trip.

All along on that trail was crying. Mourning for many left where we thought no war would come. Old people, half-grown boys and girls, mothers, and little babies. I can never forget that day.

Black Eagle[18]

The Nez Perce would be more grief stricken when they learned the fate of those relatives left on the battlefield.

At the same time, the Bannock scouts began to disinter the Nez Perce dead, scalping and mutilating the bodies. They scalped one dead warrior, then kicked him in the face, and jumped on his body and stomped him. In fact they did everything mean to him that they could.

Tom Sherrill[19]

Modern Nez Perce remain grieved over the treatment of their dead; the lack of proper mourning rituals was a serious cultural affront. The camp area is today a sacred place that holds the bones of ancestors.

The Battle of Big Hole was over but the odyssey of the Nez Perce continued. Every day was struggling. Fighting and hurrying on. Faint for food; tired with the hard travelling. Many difficulties I cannot explain. Little children, some of them wounded. Women dying of wounds on the trail. Men left to die or be killed by the soldiers and scouts because they were too old to travel further, or shot too badly to ride.

Raven Spy, Nez Perce Warrior[20]

The battle just a year after Little Big Horn had attracted national attention and more and more army resources were committed to stopping their flight. General Sheridan amassed over 1,000 of the army's most experienced Indian fighters to stop the Nez Perce. The Nez Perce still needed a war leader, but Looking Glass had been discredited by his failure to prepare before Big Hole. White Bird and Toohoolhoolzote were too old, Ollokot too young, Joseph was needed as a camp chief, so the task fell to Lean Elk. He would lead the 700 people and 2,000 horses over the Continental Divide on a route that would take them through the newly created Yellowstone National Park.

The open spaces and resources of Yellowstone provided a welcome respite for the exhausted, stressed Nez Perce. They split into family groups and traveled slowly. It was a deceiving peace because there are few exits from the Yellowstone region and the army moved to block each of them. Looking Glass rode ahead to contact the Crows and seek their help. He returned with devastating news. The Crow warriors not only would not be fighting with the Nez Perce, many had signed up with the U.S. Army to fight against the tribe! Looking Glass had not understood the larger picture from the beginning. He had not grasped the national effort that the United States could launch against one Indian tribe after another. None of the old alliances were relevant—the rules had changed. Now the Nez Perce had no plan. Another debate broke out and this time split the tribe. Looking Glass led his followers north; Joseph turned his band south. However, Joseph's fate was not his to control. Yellow Wolf's warriors had been out raiding, and as the cavalry pursued them it blocked Joseph's planned route. He had no choice but to turn around and follow Looking Glass. Once again the Nez Perce were traveling in a large group pursued by various units of the U.S. Army.

As the Nez Perce wound around seeking an unobstructed path to the north they never knew when they would have to fight. Outside of present-day Laurel, Montana, the army bore down on the travelers yet again. At Canyon Creek the mounted warriors once again threw up a protective line around the non-combatants hurrying to reach camp. The high rocky ridges gave the Nez Perce an excellent line of fire on the army which had so many losses it had to set up a field hospital on the valley floor. Although the soldiers considered this engagement a battle, the Nez Perce suffered only three wounded and some lost horses. Far worse was the constant harassment of the traveling group by Bannock and Crow scouts who managed to drive off several hundred horses. Yet the group continued northward, crossing the Musselshell and then the Missouri Rivers. They were a long way from home with little hope of ever returning to their beloved lands. They had been traveling under great stress for months and nearly everyone wanted a break. The designated leader Lean Elk knew that would be a foolish chance to take when they were so close to Canada. For reasons that are unclear Looking Glass disagreed vehemently and out-argued the council. When Lean Elk realized he had lost he said "alright, you can take command, but I think we will all be killed."[21] The fact that a discredited chief changed the course of Nez Perce history speaks strongly to the power of oratory and persuasion in Indian culture.

At the end of September 1877, the Nez Perce entered a broad valley near the Bear Paw Mountains. They were just 42 miles from the Canadian border but the people were exhausted. Looking Glass took command again and allowed the ragged group to rest. From south to north the chiefs—Joseph, Ollokot, Looking Glass, White Bird, and Toohoolhoolzote—set up their bands' camps. They had lost their tipis at the Clearwater and Big Hole battles and had to pitch canvas and blanket shelters. They had only half the horse herd that had begun the journey. The valley offered fresh buffalo meat and fires of buffalo chips and a chance to relax. The Nez Perce knew that General Howard was far behind as usual so they felt little concern. As at Big Hole, Looking Glass appeared unconcerned about reports of activity near the camp. Everyone dismissed a vision Wottolen had revealing an impending battle. Once again they misunderstood the depth of the U.S. Army's commitment to their capture. General Nelson Miles, who had recently hounded Sitting Bull and Crazy Horse, now turned his attention to the Nez Perce. He led his battle hardened Fifth Infantry into the valley right behind the travelers.

Newly popular photography allowed settlers to see images of the Nez Perce leaders. The man in the middle may be Chief Joseph, or his younger brother Ollocot. (Library of Congress)

On the morning of September 30 individual families slowly prepared for the day's march. Suddenly, a scout on a nearby hill furiously waved his red blanket and yelled a warning. Moments later the U.S. Army rushed into the camps. Participants later reported that the ground shook and rumbled like thunder from the charge. Crow and Cheyenne warriors led the attack and made immediately for the Nez Perce horses that were to be their prizes. Joseph yelled for people to save the herd and a few hundred plunged across the stream, mounted, and fled the camp. As Joseph turned back to the defense he said "It seemed to me there were guns on every side, before and behind me. My clothes were cut to pieces and my horse was wounded, but I was not hurt. As I reached the door of my lodge my wife handed me my rifle saying: 'Here's your gun. Fight.'"[22] There would be no distinction between camp or war leaders now; everyone fought desperately to save their lives.

Only about 75 warriors were left but they fought hard and held off General Miles' forces, including 200 men from the Seventh Cavalry who sustained 53 casualties. Miles was in the embarrassing position of being unable to crush a smaller Indian force in a surprise attack. He hastily reported that the Nez Perce "fight with more desperation than any Indians I have ever met."[23] But as the survivors huddled in hastily dug pits without food in a light snow, it was clear the Nez Perce were near the end. Many of those who fled early tried to continue on to Canada, walking the four to six days it took, but many of them perished from hunger or Indian violence.

At Bear Paw those who remained took stock. Ollokot, Lean Elk, and Toohoolhoolzote were dead. Looking Glass would soon be shot. Joseph, the protector of the camp, was left to deal with the consequences. While talking to General Miles under a flag of truce Joseph was seized as a prisoner. Miles had built up the chief as a mastermind and instigator and he was not going to abandon the fabrication. In the end Joseph considered the hungry, cold children, and those like his family, wandering in the hills scared to come near the army, and chose to surrender. He was later asked why more people did not flee. Joseph replied, "We could have escaped from Bear Paw Mountain if we had left our wounded, old women, and children behind. We were unwilling to do this. We had never heard of a wounded Indian recovering while in the hands of white men."[24] General Howard noted that at the time of surrender the people, although "covered in dirt, their clothing was torn, and their ponies, such as they were, were thin and lame" still possessed a "dignified bearing."[25] Old Chief White Bird did not want to end like this and consequently did not come in to the surrender meeting. When General Miles accepted the gun from Joseph as the sole representative of the free Nez Perce it cemented Joseph's inaccurate reputation as the commanding Nez Perce military leader. Joseph pledged his future peace with the now famous words, "From where the sun now stands I will fight no more forever."

The anticlimactic end to the long arduous Nez Perce War was reservation life. This was the fate the Nez Perce had begun the journey in order to avoid. White Bird and his followers slipped off to Canada while the rest of the Nez Perce awaited their fate at the whim of the government who chose to regard them as renegades. Miles had promised Joseph that he would be returned to the Nez Perce reservation in Idaho in the spring. Instead, the survivors were shipped from their beloved mountains to Fort Leavenworth, Kansas. Camped on the Missouri River bottomlands the Nez Perce suffered from debilitating malaria. When the time came to be sent to their permanent homes on the Quapaw reservation, many like Joseph could not rise and dozens were dead.

Joseph spent the remainder of his life trying to get his people home. Finally, in 1885 the government relented and about 260 Nez Perce boarded trains bound for the Northwest. They left behind the graves of nearly 40 percent of their population who had died in the seven years of exile. And they never truly got home. Half went to the Lapwai reservation in Idaho and half with Joseph to the Colville reservation in Washington. Joseph continued to try to fulfill his promise to his father by regaining his ancestral lands. He traveled to Washington, D.C., met Buffalo Bill Cody and President William McKinley, and told anyone who would listen that his people needed to go home. They even offered to buy back their homeland from the white settlers in the Wallowa Valley. It was all to no avail. Joseph died in 1904 in Washington State, not the Oregon valley he cherished.

The 1870s saw the destruction of numerous impendent native groups west of the Rocky Mountains. The Modoc and Nez Perce had fought for their freedom and lost, while many other tribes and bands just lost without a military engagement. Each group was different with distinct cultural practices, but often shared the same experience. The intrusion of white culture, whether by missionaries, miners, or settlers, threw native lives into chaos. Alcohol, disease, and loss of land destroyed traditional lifestyles. The people could no longer rely on traditional food supplies and often faced hunger and starvation. Society unraveled as swift changes obliterated century-old practices. Random violence tore apart families and kin groups. The native cultures of the Far West were forever changed by the United States' 19th-century expansion.

NOTES

1. Josephy, *500 Nations*, 347.

2. Josephy, *500 Nations*, 347.

3. Dee Brown, *Bury My Heart at Wounded Knee*. New York: Henry Holt & Company, 1991, 220.

4. Keith Murray, *The Modocs and Their War*. Norman: University of Oklahoma Press, 1958, 42.

5. Murray, 62.

6. *New York Times*, June 17, 1873.

7. Brian Schofield, *Selling Your Father's Bones: America's 140 Year War against the Nez Perce Tribe*. New York: Simon and Shuster, 2009, 75.

8. Schofield, 104.

9. Schofield, 106.

10. David Lavender, *Let Me Be Free: The Nez Perce Tragedy*. New York: Harper Collins, 1992, 272.

11. Lavender, 279.

12. Lucullus Virgil McWhorter, *Yellow Wolf: His Own Story*. Caldwell, ID: The Caxton Printers, 1948, 108–110.

13. Yellow Wolf, quoted in *Guide to the Trails at Big Hole National Battlefield*. West Glacier, MT: Glacier Natural History Association, 1997, 6.

14. McWhorter, 136.

15. McWhorter, 137.

16. http://www.fs.fed.us/npnht/people/bigholequotes.shtml, accessed November 11, 2009.

17. John Gibbon, quoted in *Guide to the Trails at Big Hole National Battlefield*, 8.

18. http://www.fs.fed.us/npnht/people/bigholequotes.shtml, accessed November 11, 2009.

19. http://www.fs.fed.us/npnht/people/bigholequotes.shtml, accessed November 11, 2009.

20. http://www.fs.fed.us/npnht/people/bigholequotes.shtml, accessed November 11, 2009.

21. Lavender, 309.

22. Lavender, 314.

23. Bruce Hampton, *Children of Grace: The Nez Perce War of 1877*. New York: Avon Books, 1994, 297.

24. Chief Joseph, "An Indian's View of Indian Affairs," *North American Review*, April (1879): 431.

25. Hampton, 309.

4

THE NORTHERN PLAINS

From the 1840s through the 1880s the pressure on lands west of the Mississippi River increased dramatically. This brief, intense period brought tens of thousands of native peoples into direct and often violent contact with expanding white America. In one generation some tribes met their first white men and lost their lands and culture. It was a cataclysmic upheaval of an entire way of life. The best known conflicts of this traumatic time are often referred to as the Plains Wars because they engaged the iconic American Indian Plains culture. However, other people also fought the U.S. government's relentless surge of "civilization" which stripped them of their lands and independence. Over five decades every tribe west of the Mississippi River had to deal with U.S. expansion, and the ensuing conflicts can be roughly divided into northern and southern regions with Kansas as the approximate border.

DAKOTA WAR

It was the largest mass execution in U.S. history and it came at the end of a war no one expected. The hanging of 38 men closed out the bloody conflict known as the Great Sioux War, or Dakota War. The condemned men were not the Sioux that everyone in the 19th century regarded as synonymous with warfare—the "savage, wild" Indians of the plains that whites had been taught to fear from reports about the death of Lieutenant Colonel Custer. Instead, this was an uprising of Eastern or Dakota Sioux who had been living on a reservation in Minnesota for ten years.

Social Organization

The name Sioux is a relatively inaccurate term for a wide ranging group of people. These woodland peoples were pushed by native conflict and drawn by resources and slowly worked their way west of the Mississippi River. They called themselves the *Oceti sakowin*, or Seven Council Fires, and had three divisions based on dialect and location—the Dakota, Nakota, and Lakota. The Dakota division, or Eastern Sioux, had four groups—Mdewakanton, Wahpekute, Sisseton, and Wahpeton. They occupied most of Minnesota in the 17th century while their brethren migrated farther west onto the Plains. The Eastern Dakota maintained contact with their bison hunting cousins, often trading goods of the forest like walnut-wood bows and quarried pipestone for the meat and skin products of the plains. The northernmost of the Dakota villages harvested wild rice from marshy lakes and made maple syrup in the early spring. They hunted deer, fished, and supplemented their diet with gardens. The rich habitat which allowed for this native bounty also attracted white settlement. By the mid-19th century Minnesota Territory had become a magnet for immigrants from northern Europe who were familiar with the cold, wet climate and regarded it as the place for their American dreams of opportunity. The white population increased from 6,000 in 1850 to 150,000 in 1858.

The Dakota lands bore great pressure from increased U.S. immigration before the Civil War. The demand for newly open lands spurred the government to insist that the Dakota yield some of their territory. The 1851 Treaties of Traverse de Sioux and Mendota moved the Dakota from the woodlands of the Mississippi River in the eastern portion of Minnesota to a reservation along the Minnesota River. Here the people settled into two agencies— the Upper or Yellow Medicine Agency and the Lower or Redwood Agency. Yellow Medicine contained wooded land more like their old homes, so these residents had fewer adjustments to make than those at Redwood, but everyone was in a state of fluctuation. With white settlement came land cessions as well as intense pressure to acculturate. In 1858, U.S. officials demanded more Dakota lands to meet the growing needs of the new state of Minnesota. The chiefs were told that the state would take the land anyway and that the

Dakota lived there "by courtesy" of the Great Father. So they signed yet again. Dakota lands had been reduced from the Minnesota region down to a 10-mile-wide strip along 150 miles of the Minnesota River. This odd-shaped reservation was not even actually theirs because Congress left its authorization up to the executive branch which never acted on it.

Political Organization

Stuck on their narrow stretch of river lands the Dakota attempted to negotiate the rapidly changing world they faced. The government focused energy on Indian "regeneration" which meant that natives had to become Christian farmers. Most Dakota men had no interest in adopting what in their culture was the women's economic function. But the government denied them the opportunity to engage in their cultural role of hunter and warrior. So government policy essentially emasculated men and thus was not a success. Those men who did give up their traditional economic roles also yielded much of their traditional culture. They cut off their long scalp locks, becoming "Cut Hairs," gave up breechcloths for pants, tipis for houses, and traditional spirits for the Christian God.

Not surprisingly, tension grew between traditionalist, or "blanket" Indians, and the Cut Hairs. Those observing old ways regarded the acculturated as traitors to their culture, an insult to the ancestors. The government encouraged this split in Dakota society. They used the tribal monies to reward those who listened and conformed to white ways. Farmer Indians received more food and clothing, cows, oxen, and household items. Overall, the farmers received ten times more supplies than the other Dakotas. They had to attend church, send their children to mission school, and elect a government. In short, they had to stop living like Dakota. The division between lifestyles helped to destroy Dakota sense of community as about 10 percent of the people shunned tribal identity. This was exactly what the United States hoped to encourage.

Economic Life

Tensions ran high in the spring of 1862. The previous winter had been extremely hard and everyone suffered. The corn crop failed leaving the Dakotas with nothing to eat through a long, bleak spring. By June malnutrition stalked the villages, some of which turned to eating their horses and dogs in desperation. The only hope to stave off a complete disaster was the government annuity or annual payment and provisions that came in June. The resources came because the government owed them to the Dakota people as long-term payment for the land they had relinquished to the whites for settlement. The insatiable white appetite for land had pushed the Dakotas out of their territory and onto a small swath of their former domain, so the government had to relieve the Indians' appetite now.

The idea that the guaranteed payment might not come was really terrifying to the people. It had literally become an issue of life or death. Weak, thin children did not care that the United States fought a Confederate challenge or that Congress had made the appropriation late or that the Treasury could not decide whether to pay in gold or paper money. People had to eat. Since they could not rely on their own failed crops, the Indians' only other choice was to purchase goods from the white merchants. However, the traders suddenly cut off the credit they normally extended to the Indians. The profitable business of Indian trade relied heavily on the payment of government annuities. The general practice was to mark up prices outrageously so that the customer owed far more than he could provide in furs or other trade items and the balance came directly out of the government annuity. Without the federal money the traders had little incentive to provide for native customers.

The system was infuriating and clearly abusive. The traders took about $80,000 from the Indians every year. The government Indian agents favored the traders' claims prior to those of their charges. Each year as the Dakota males lined up to receive their annuity payment the traders pushed to the front of the line with their books. The white traders told the white agents how much money they were owed and it was handed over. No one checked the accounts, queried the Indians as to the accuracy, or questioned the appropriateness of the system. One historian described the Indians as "economic prisoners."

The economic captivity did not stop at the annuities. On the frontier, settlers lost no opportunity to fleece the Indians. It seemed as though they could smell the opportunity for profit. In 1851, when the Dakotas signed the treaty giving up their land the traders schemed to find more immediate profit. The chiefs who signed the treaty paper were then given a second paper to sign, supposedly just a copy. In fact, the second document asserted that the Dakota people owed undisclosed debts to the traders and that the full amount would be taken out of the treaty payment. This unprecedented action took most of the $495,000 paid to the Indians in exchange for the 24 million acres of land they gave up to the United States. Less than a half-million dollars for that vast territory was already a very low figure and then the traders ended up with most of it. To add insult to injury, the governor of Minnesota and his secretary took a 15 percent fee for handling the transaction by which the Indians lost their land. The scheming continued. In 1857, the Dakota sold one million acres to the government and again saw little of the money after fraudulent traders' claims were paid. The future Dakota adversary, trader Henry Sibley, claimed $145,000. The injustice was not lost on the Dakota people. As they struggled to conform to white conceptions of civilization they could not help noticing that whites had the best land, the most money, and it seemed to be at Indian expense.

My Great Father was to give me money and goods. . . . I was to receive a great quantity of money every year. The money left the hands of the Great Father but in passing from hand to hand, each one taking his part, nothing reached my hand more than a dollar. My heart was sad in seeing that.

Standing Buffalo[1]

Dakota Economic Crisis

The Dakota clearly had reasons for resentment and distrust of whites. Nothing in the spring of 1862 would improve that feeling. The Dakota's main contact with whites was the government appointed Indian agent. These appointments were political and often went to spectacularly unqualified, ignorant men. Thomas J. Galbraith lived up to that characterization. He was described by contemporaries as arrogant, stubborn, emotionally unstable, and a hard drinker. In a time of heightened apprehension these were not helpful qualities. His irrational stubbornness caused untold suffering. Observing the impending starvation of their people, on June 20th the Dakota chiefs asked Galbraith when the rations would be delivered. They hoped he would refute the rumors they had heard that there would be no annuity that year. The agent did deny the rumors but took no steps to alleviate suffering. Unbelievably, the ration portion of the annuity was already in Minnesota; only the cash payment had been delayed. Flour, pork, lard, sugar, blankets, hatchets, pots, and cloth all sat behind locked warehouse doors. The chiefs naturally requested that the Dakota's rations be distributed to the starving people. Galbraith refused. Procedure said that goods and money were to be distributed at the same time;

besides it was easier to do it just once. The agent sent the Indians away to fend for themselves and to come back in one month. He then requested troops to guard the storehouse of Indian goods from the Indians. One month later 5,000 starving Dakotas waited for Agent Galbraith at Upper Agency. When he tried to send them away again they refused. If they had to starve they would do it in front of him. Finally, Galbraith allowed the distribution of small amounts of rations, continuing his practice of giving far more to the farmer Indians, thus fanning the flames of resentment.

Militant young men revived the Soldiers' Lodge society of warriors which could act in place of the chiefs during a crisis. They determined that when the payment did come, it would all go to the people—none to the traders this time. Some wanted to go farther and urged military action against a weakened United States stretched thin by the demands of the Civil War. The people were not ready for war yet, but another month of starvation might change their minds. Still Galbraith insisted on preserving stockpiles of foods and goods in his warehouse. By August the warriors had to act. On the 4th, 800 warriors stormed the warehouse and seized food but were stopped by a contingent of soldiers under command of Lieutenant Timothy Sheehan. Sheehan restored order and then advised Galbraith to distribute food as the only means to avoid bloodshed. A meager allocation of pork and flour defused the situation until the chiefs from both agencies came to talk the next day. So far the activity had been from the Upper Agency but Chief Little Crow of the Lower Agency knew his warriors would join any full-scale action that broke out.

The talks of August 5th yielded one of the most thoughtless white reactions of the period. Chiefs met with Galbraith and several traders, including the influential Andrew Myrick. Little Crow represented the Dakota's situation. "We have waited a long time. The money is ours, but we cannot get it. We have no food, but there are these stores filled with food. We ask that you, the agent, make some arrangement by which we can get food from the stores, or else we may take our own way to keep our selves from starving. When men are hungry they help themselves." The other traders deferred to the dominant Myrick in deciding whether they would open their stores to the Indians. Myrick walked out with the callous reply, "So far as I am concerned, if they are hungry let them eat grass or their own dung."[2]

The traders and agent may have been reckless in their dealings with the Indians but the U.S. Army was not as foolhardy. The commander of nearby Fort Ridgely, Captain John Marsh, ordered Galbraith to distribute all the food he held and threatened the traders with arrest for any more interference. Everyone believed that fed Indians were happy Indians. Marsh took his troops back to the fort, Galbraith left on a trip, and Little Crow attended Christian church services. However, mere flour and pork could not undo decades of injustice or soothe the tensions of a racially and culturally divided area. Resentment of whites and their treatment of Dakotas lay just below the surface and could break forth at anytime.

The first rupture came on August 17, 1862. Four young Dakota men had been on an unsuccessful hunting trip. It was harder and harder to find game in a country overrun by whites and they were still hungry. When they found a nest of chicken eggs on the edge of white property the realities of their lives seemed stark. Here was food to be foraged on the homelands of their fathers yet they dare not touch it for fear of white retribution. What was the point of being a Dakota warrior if they had to live like this? Their own frustration led to boasting and challenges and accusations of cowardice. One young man claimed he would prove his bravery by shooting a white man and dared the others to accompany him. A dare like that is hard for young, agitated men to resist. The challenges to honor resulted in the haphazard killing of five whites,

Dakota leader Little Crow reluctantly agreed to lead his people against white settlers in Minnesota. (Library of Congress)

including two women. Once done such a deed cannot be reversed so all that remained was to inform the elders of the act. The chiefs' reactions were mixed. On one hand they were proud of the young men for their courage, for acting like warriors. However, the impulsive violence ensured retribution that would fall on all the people. The whites would execute the men for their actions and penalize the bands. The Soldiers' Lodge members decided that it was better to declare war on the whites than suffer more indignities against the people. Brave, but not imprudent, chiefs Red Middle Voice and Shakopee knew they needed to recruit all the Dakota warriors to the cause and for that they would need Little Crow.

Little Crow, or *Taoyateduta*, faced an agonizing decision. He had tried to live in both worlds and now he had to choose between them. Recently, after his people had rejected him as the band's Speaker in favor of a farmer Indian, he had begun wearing pants, moved into a brick house, and occasionally attended church, but wore his hair shoulder length and had four wives. As chief, he had long chosen conciliation over confrontation with whites. His belief that no good came from challenging whites lost him the allegiance of many younger members of the tribe who thought he gave up too easily. Now they asked for his leadership in a war against whites. He knew it would be folly, that many would die, yet he said yes.

Taoyateduta is not a coward, and he is no fool! . . . Braves, you are like little children; you do not know what you are doing. . . . We are only little herds of buffaloes left scattered; the great herds that once covered the prairies are no more. . . . the white men are like locusts when they fly so thick that the whole sky is a snowstorm. . . . if you strike at them they will all turn on you and devour you and your women and little children. . . . You will die like the rabbits when hungry wolves hunt them in the Hard Moon. Taoyateduta is not a coward: he will die with you.[3]

We cannot know why Little Crow agreed to lead in a war he believed was hopeless. Like Chief Joseph of the Nez Perce this chief was faced with the result of acts of violence carried out by hotheaded young men. Both chiefs knew fighting whites would bring suffering and loss. The alternative was to submit meekly to whatever retribution that whites demanded to settle their particular sense of justice. Perhaps it was better to die as a Dakota warrior, fighting for the peoples' lives, than rotting in a white prison. The years of lost land, stolen money, and recent hunger and insults boiled up and many men would go to war. If war was inevitable the Dakota nation should go into it with all of its resources. Little Crow would lead them.

On August 18, 1862, Little Crow ordered an attack on the Lower Agency. The first white man to die was a clerk at Myrick's store who ironically had three mixed-blood children and spoke Dakota fluently; the second was Andrew Myrick himself. His death spoke to the emotions that sparked the war. The man who declared that the Dakotas could eat grass had many arrows and a hay scythe buried in his chest and his mouth was stuffed with grass. "Myrick is eating grass himself," came the taunt.[4] The warriors killed twenty whites, burned buildings, and emptied the warehouses of provisions. The Dakota War had begun.

Native Warfare

Panic rolled across Minnesota as farming communities fled from their worst nightmare. Years of disregarding the natives among them had finally come to haunt them. Retribution was swift and violent. The Upper Agency bands decided to join those already at war. Groups of 20 or so warriors roamed the countryside killing whatever whites they encountered. Those Dakota not engaged in the war often tried to protect whites and the 15 percent of the reservation that was mixed-blood had a particularly difficult time. The violence against civilians troubled Little Crow as well. He wanted the warriors to attack the U.S. point of strength, the "soldiers' house" at Fort Ridgely. The young men preferred the easier target of towns where they could plunder poorly defended supplies. When Little Crow did organize an attack on the fort, the Dakota's traditional fighting style proved poorly suited to the task. War leaders asserted their authority but all Dakota warriors could act independently, a good strategy for fast raids on native enemies but ineffective against a strongly held position. As Lightning Blanket described it, "we did not fight like white men, with one officer; we all shot as we pleased."[5] A second assault two days later with 800 warriors resulted in a stronger rebuff in which the Indians retreated after six hours of fighting.

If the Dakota could not take the soldiers' house then they would go after the rich prize of New Ulm, a prosperous German-American town downstream from the reservation. On August 23rd the Dakota created a diversion by burning grass on the far side of the river which succeeded in luring out some of the town's defenders. The 2,000 townspeople barricaded themselves inside a three-block area and waited for the attack. The main body of 650 warriors advanced under the cover of smoke from buildings they set ablaze. As the defenders retreated toward the core of town the hand-to-hand combat moved from building to building. The Dakota warriors gained ground but lost daylight. As the day wore on Little Crow saw that they needed to take the town by nightfall and launched a renewed offensive which ran headlong into a desperate assault by the townspeople. Gaining no new ground, Little Crow called off the attack at sunset. The Dakota had not taken New Ulm but they certainly had bloodied it—32 dead, 60 wounded, and only 25 of the original 215 buildings left standing.

The tide of the war was about to change. The frontier settlers of Minnesota may have brought this war upon themselves with their behavior, but the United States would not leave them to their fate. Governor Ramsey had made his intentions clear, "The Sioux Indians must be exterminated or driven forever beyond the borders of the state."[6] The 1,400 soldiers of the of the Sixth Minnesota had finally arrived, led by Colonel Henry Sibley. The Dakota knew Sibley; he was the trader who took $145,000 out of

The warriors' attack on the town of New Ulm did great damage but spurred the government to greater effort to eradicate the Dakota. (Library of Congress)

their treaty payment. Now he was here to fight them. In the face of the increased troop strength at Fort Ridgely, the Dakotas began withdrawing northwest up the Minnesota River Valley toward the Upper Agency. More than 3,000 residents of the Lower Agency were on the move with 200 white captives, who experience had taught them could be exchanged for ransom. They also carried everything they owned—tipis, clothing, food, horses, and cattle. Everyone wore their finery and decorated horses with greenery and U.S. flags, giving the procession the air of a victory parade.

Political Considerations

Debates continued among the warriors as to the proper targets— the soldiers or the settlements. They also argued over the fate of the captives. Two distinct camps formed, the "hostiles"—mostly from the Lower Agency who wished to hold the captives and continue the war, and the "friendlies"—primarily Upper Agency Dakota who tried to free the captives and appease Sibley. Little Crow remained committed to the warriors he had agreed to lead in this conflict. The division of the Dakota was a fatal weakness. At a time when they needed all the strength they could muster, infighting threatened the existence of the whole tribe. Whites surely would make no distinction between hostiles and friendlies if they won this war.

Little Crow led his 100 warriors out on September 1st to Big Woods where they defeated a local militia and burned and looted two towns. War chiefs Big Eagle and Mankato surrounded a detachment of Sibley's forces at Birch Coulee near Lower Agency. The subsequent attack went so well for the Dakota that their women cooked meals for the engaged warriors. The defeat of his forces shocked Sibley into asking Little Crow for any discussion he might want. Little Crow responded with the Dakota's reasons for war—they had to beg for rations, their children were dying of hunger, and the traders had started it all—and the fact that he had white prisoners. Sibley blustered back with a demand for the return of the prisoners. Sibley felt emboldened by the reality Little Crow feared; the rifts in the Dakota nation threatened to be their undoing. Friendly Dakotas contacted Sibley and blamed the hostilities on Little Crow. They promised to return the captives to the whites.

Little Crow prepared to attack Sibley's forces camped at Wood Lake. He was hindered by the presence of friendlies in his councils who argued against the most effective night attack. The ensuing daylight attack was triggered prematurely and went poorly for the warriors. Chief Mankato fell in battle and his body was carried off the field, but 14 other Dakota dead who were left behind were scalped by Sibley's men. A further disappointment met them at camp when they learned the friendlies had taken the white captives and dug defensive positions to defend against Little Crow's men. Bitterly defeated by both whites and his own people in a war he did not seek, Little Crow told his followers to pack their belongings and flee westward.

I am ashamed today to call myself a Dakota. Seven hundred of our best warriors were whipped yesterday by the whites. Now we had better all run away and scatter out over the plains like buffalo and wolves. . . . I cannot account for the disgraceful defeat. It must be the work of traitors in our midst.[7]

The Dakota War was over and all that remained was the ugly retribution demanded by whites over their defeated enemy. It was going to be bad. "They must be exterminated and now is a good time to commence doing it" said one newspaper while another writer insisted the government should treat the Indians as "out-laws, who have forfeited all right to property and life." General John Pope, lately in charge of the U.S. effort in Minnesota, called for "punishment beyond human power to inflict." He planned to treat the Dakotas as "maniacs or wild beasts."[8] The Dakota who surrendered waited for the wheels of white justice to turn. It did not take long. Sibley created a five-man military tribunal to judge the Dakota warriors. He also sent out parties to gather up all the Indians they could find. Under the pretense of registering the Indians for their long delayed annuity payments he separated the men from the women and children and disarmed, shackled, and incarcerated the males, all of whom he blamed for the war.

The tribunal proceeded to "try" 392 Dakota men. The defendants were allowed no counsel, no witnesses, and few understood the proceedings. Nonetheless, 307 received a sentence of death by hanging. Both Sibley and Pope hesitated to carry out such an unprecedented execution without higher approval. When they informed President Lincoln of their plans he also realized the enormity of what they proposed. Lincoln insisted that all the trial records be sent to his office for review. General Pope bristled but eventually complied. After combing though the transcripts Lincoln's staff recommended the death sentence for just 39 men.

While all this took place 1,658 Dakota women, children, and elderly remained under Sibley's control. He finally decided to move them to Fort Snelling. The trip was a horrifying experience as whites rushed the wagon train bent on violence against the Dakota civilians. The elderly and children were pulled from the wagons by their hair and beaten. A white woman grabbed a nursing Indian baby and dashed it to the ground; it died a few hours later. While incarcerated at the dismal camp the Dakota suffered from hunger and died of measles. Many of the prisoners belonged to the friendly camp. As Little Crow expected, in the end the whites had made no differentiation between Indians.

As the Dakota suffered the cries for their destruction increased. Sibley and Pope warned that if the condemned men were not executed immediately the citizens would act without the government. The newly minted citizens of St. Paul wrote to President Lincoln demanding not just the execution but the banishment of every Sioux from the state. "The Indians' nature can no more be trusted than the wolf's."[9] The executions could be delayed no longer. On December 26, 1862, 39 Dakota men were set for execution. Due to confusion over similar names no one was sure if these individuals were the correct ones, but the gallows had been constructed and the hanging would proceed. The men sent messages to their families imprisoned at Fort Snelling and prepared for the end. At the last minute one man convicted on the testimony of children received a reprieve, so 38 went to the gallows. The warriors expressed confidence that they were headed to the Great Spirit but many received baptism in case the whites were right about Christianity. As they sang their death songs the platform dropped and the largest execution in U.S. history was done. Their shallow grave was raided that night by white doctors seeking specimens.

The convicted warriors suffered no more but the rest of the Dakota did. Little Crow had escaped to the west before Sibley captured him. After a fruitless effort to gain help from western Indians he returned to Minnesota. While picking raspberries near Big Woods Little Crow was spotted by whites now farming this formerly Dakota land. The state offered a $25 bounty for Dakota scalps so the whites immediately opened fire. Once the scalp was found to be that of Little Crow the killers received a $500 bonus. Little Crow's skull went on exhibition in St. Paul so everyone could savor the triumph over the Dakota.

Warriors with reduced sentences like Big Eagle went to prison in Iowa where half died of diseases like tuberculosis. The residents of Minnesota got their wish as the Dakota reservation was seized by the government. The land was of course immediately available for public sale. The U.S. Congress abrogated all previous treaties with the Dakota and appropriated their annuity money for a reimbursement fund for white victims. Determined to rid Minnesota of its Indian problem once and for all, the government sent the Winnebago with the banished Dakota. Banishment meant a cramped journey by steamboat down the Mississippi, a train ride across Missouri, and then another steamer up the Missouri River. All this to get to the Crow Creek Reservation. An observer described it as "a horrible region. . . . the soil is miserable; rain hardly ever visits it. The game is scarce, and the alkaline waters of the streams and springs are almost certain death."[10] Since nothing would grow the Dakota and Winnebago quickly starved, unable to survive on the issue of thin soup provided by the government. Those who could leave counted themselves lucky to find an abandoned army camp where they could glean undigested corn from the horse dung. The suffering scarred the Dakota people forever.

One of the most recognized native leaders, Hunkpapa holy man Sitting Bull. (Library of Congress)

One young Lakota who visited his cousins at Crow Creek vowed that his people would never allow the whites to take all they had. His name was Sitting Bull.

LAKOTA

The name and image of Sitting Bull are familiar to many Americans. In fact, he is one of the most recognized Native Americans in history. The life of this individual, from the 1830s to the 1890s, spanned the period of greatest conflict between his Lakota people and the U.S. government. All of the northern Plains Tribes faced the challenge of American expansion and most engaged in military conflict with the government, but the Lakota with their Cheyenne and Arapaho allies waged a decade-long fight for their land and their freedom. This struggle has come to represent the Indian Wars for many people.

Social Organization

The Lakota, the westernmost of the three major divisions of the *Oceti sakowin*, are also referred to as Tetons. Like the overall division of the Seven Council Fires, the Lakota further divided into seven groups. The Oglala, Brulè, Miniconjou, Two Kettle, Sans Arc, Hunkpapa, and Blackfeet (or Sihasapa) comprised the Lakota bands. Each followed its own leaders and the people of the bands interacted only occasionally during travel, hunts, and social or religious gatherings. They could not be considered a united political entity by modern standards but rather a large group loosely affiliated by kinship and culture.

By the time whites encountered them in the 19th century the Lakota lived a nomadic life perfectly adapted to the plains region. They had perfected a lifestyle centered around the greatest resource of the plains—the bison. Horses descended from European stock enabled the Lakota to be extremely mobile hunter gatherers. Once on the plains the Lakota gave up the gardening traditions of their eastern ancestors. The bison provided nearly everything the people needed. From meat, housing, and clothing, to rope, tools, containers, and utensils, the bison served as a walking commissary for Plains Indians. Therefore, human life centered on the bison, moving in accord with the animals' movements and thanking the Great Spirit for providing the bounty that sustained them. Other animals like wolves, coyote, and bear were also important, so the Lakota strove to live in harmony with their world by maintaining a balance that

Plains women spent hours preparing hides used in shelter and clothing, an activity interrupted by the constant movement required by warfare. (Library of Congress)

ensured the continuation of life for everyone. The arrival of whites promised to upset that balance.

The initial problem whites presented to the Lakota and neighboring tribes was not the same as that facing their Dakota cousins in the 1850s. In the regions close to the Mississippi and also much farther west in California and Oregon whites arrived to stay, drawn by land or resources. The new settlers wanted land, wanted it cheap and free of natives. However, the plains initially had none of the allure of the rich Mississippi bottomlands or the fertile western valleys. The only whites who had spent any time among the western tribes were explorers and trappers who often took Indian wives and generally shared much of the native lifestyle. Treeless, arid, and bleak to eastern eyes the plains existed only as a trail on the way to better places. Emmigrants in the mid-19th century just wanted to get through the area as quickly and painlessly as possible, preferably with no Indian contact.

That sentiment did not mean the emmigrants had no impact on the natives. As soon as whites breeched the supposedly permanent

Indian frontier along the Mississippi River they brought problems. The mere style in which whites traveled created impact. After 1846, when the Whitman/Spaulding party drove a wagon through South Pass, Wyoming, proving wagon travel across the Rockies was feasible, a flood of prairie schooners headed west. The extensive wagon trains decimated vegetation, fouled water sources, and killed or scared off game animals. Almost 200,000 people crossed the country in the decade from 1849–1859 and 350,000 by 1869. This was an unimaginable number of humans when viewed from the Plains Indians' perspective. Their entire tribes were smaller than just this partial white migration. In the long term the sheer volume of whites would challenge natives' understanding of the world and their place in it. The immediate problem now, however, was the U.S. Army.

The U.S. government did not sponsor these private attempts at emigration; however, the government's policy was one of expansion to the Pacific. Implicit in that manifest destiny was a promise to eliminate the Indian menace to white settlement. In many ways the emigrants acted as an extension of national policy, taking with them the tools of 19th century progress—democracy, Christianity, and agriculture—and a fierce pride in their national identity. The government would protect and promote this expansion of its sovereignty. In 1848, the army began construction of Fort Kearny along the Platte River in Nebraska. It was the first in a long line of army installations that would bring the blue coats into Plains Indian lives forever. By 1854, the army had 52 forts in the West and every one was meant to protect whites from Indians.

Each western tribe now had to decide how to deal with the newcomers and they did not have a universal reaction. Responses often corresponded to the level of interruptions in daily life. Those quickly ravaged by the diseases brought by the immigrants or starving because trails disrupted the bison migration patterns had to adjust swiftly. "Since the white man has made a road across our land and has killed off our game, we are hungry and there is nothing for us to eat. Our women and children cry for food and we have nothing to give them," said the Shoshone chief Washakie in 1855.[11] Washakie became well-known for his friendship with the intruders his people were not strong enough to defeat. The strong, confident Lakota who with Cheyenne and Arapaho allies dominated the region of Wyoming and the Dakotas were another matter.

At first the Lakota felt little concern over the changes they witnessed. The pale, thin people struggling with their wagons day after day seemed irrelevant to the Plains lifestyle. Curiosity drew Indians to the trains where they could trade for metal and cloth. Young men might test their newly minted warrior skills by harassing the travelers. Only when whites became too numerous or disruptive did the leaders plan strikes against them. This in turn alerted the army to the need for a show of force in Lakota territory.

In 1849, the government bought a trading post at the junction of the Platte and Laramie Rivers in southeastern Wyoming from the American Fur Company in order to better protect the Oregon Trail travelers. Fort Laramie was an important rest and resupply stop for white travelers located in the hunting grounds of the Lakota. Two hundred soldiers moved west to garrison the new installation, and fur trapper Thomas Fitzpatrick whom the Indians called "Broken Hand" became an Indian agent. By 1851, the government told Fitzpatrick to take action to ensure peace in the region. Although Fitzpatrick would have preferred a straightforward subjugation of the Indians, that was impossible with the meager western forces, so he planned treaty talks instead.

Political Considerations

The call went out across the northern plains from the Yellowstone to the Arkansas Rivers and between the Rockies and the Missouri River. The government planned a grand meeting and everyone should come. Each band chief evaluated the news and decided whether he and his people would participate. Some tribes like the Pawnee refused to take the risk of traveling into the country of their enemies, the Lakota. Other groups feared the recent outbreaks of cholera which whites had brought along the trails and had devastated native villages. Some leaders simply did not care, especially those who lived far from the emmigrant paths—what did whites have to do with them? The allure of the meeting was the promise of trade goods and good times. Indeed, no native conferences took place without extensive feasting and gift exchange, so in some respects it was an invitation to a celebration.

In all, about 10,000 people from the Lakota, Cheyenne, Arapaho, Shoshone, Crow, Assiniboine, Arikara, Mandan, and Hidatsa tribes showed up in September 1851. Many of these people, particularly the Crow and Lakota, were traditional enemies which added an air of tension to the gathering. So many tipis and so many horses could not fit at Fort Laramie, so the whole group moved out onto the flat meadows of Horse Creek below the fort. Even so, the grass would not sustain tens of thousands of Indian ponies for long, so as soon as the 27 wagonloads of presents were distributed, speeches made, feasts eaten, and dancing concluded, the government got to their point. Essentially, the United States wanted to manage the Plains Indians. They offered to pay annuities of $50,000 per year in goods for 50 years (which the Senate reduced to 15 years) in return for a commitment not to molest white travelers. This was fairly easy for the Indians to agree to as they all had become dependent on trade goods. Far more controversial were the demands that tribes adhere to designated hunting grounds and cease making war on each other. These provisions reveal how little the government knew about Plains culture. Hunting and warfare defined male life and could not be abandoned. The idea was preposterous. Furthermore, the United States had just given the Oglalas' Powder River hunting ground to their deadly enemies the Crow. Almost as ridiculous was the government's assertion that one man they chose, Conquering Bear, could sign the treaty and commit all the Lakota people to its terms. Conquering Bear could not even speak for all the Brulè Lakota, much less members of the other six bands. The Lakota fought among themselves frequently and the new pressures brought by the treaty made the divisions worse. As the great gathering broke up the government talked of peace on the plains; the Plains Wars would begin at Fort Laramie within a few years.

Lakota life changed in the decade of the 1850s. It did not affect all bands equally but it was coming. Whites had altered everything. Trade goods played a larger and larger role in daily life. Women sought glass beads for decoration, metal pots for cooking, mirrors for indulgence. Men needed iron for knives and arrow points, as well as guns and ammunition for hunting and warfare. Warfare had become more deadly when fought with white weapons. Bison herds shrunk from heavy hunting to meet market demands and dislocation due to white intrusions. White diseases swept away populations, sometimes catastrophically. In the midst of these stresses on Plains life the army became an ever stronger presence in their lives.

GRATTAN INCIDENT

After the Treaty of Fort Laramie, daily life seemed to return to normal. The distantly located bands left, and those near the Oregon Trail let the travelers alone. When the first bloody clash came no one expected it. It was hard for the Lakota near the Platte River to watch the endless wagon trains roll through their territory. In return for their compliance the government distributed food to replace the vanishing bison herds, but the people were often hungry. When a thin cow from the trail wandered through the Brulè camp it became dinner for a visiting warrior. The Mormon owner demanded retribution and the army overreacted. A young officer eager to make a name for himself led a detachment of 30 men into the Brulè camp. John Grattan's behavior sparked the Grattan Incident in which he and all his men died. Grattan demanded that Chief Conquering Bear surrender the cow killer. The chief explained that the man was a visitor and thus not under his authority but he offered payment or even his own surrender to appease the army. Grattan ignored the chief and ordered his men to fire artillery into the camp. Conquering Bear fell mortally wounded. When the warriors saw their chief fall they swarmed over the soldiers, killing every one of them. Grattan did make a name for himself by dying with 24 arrows in his mutilated corpse.

Both sides had to respond to the reality of what whites called a massacre. The young Lakota warriors urged an attack on Fort Laramie to avenge the death of Conquering Bear. The elders saw no reason for more war. They had honorably killed over 30 men and as it would have been with a raid on their enemies the Crow, the incident was over. Women packed up tipis and belongings and headed away from the place of conflict, thus settling the internal debate. The army on the other hand took to the warpath. The problem with the army system was that it did not matter how Grattan had behaved. It did not mater that he had acted foolishly and instigated the violence that killed his command. He, like Custer 22 years later, would be avenged.

BLUE WATER

The other problem was that the army did not much care which Indians it punished. General W. S. Harney marched 600 men from Kansas to punish the Lakota. He attacked the village of Little Thunder near Ash Hollow, Nebraska, even though he admitted in his report that the group was largely blameless for the Grattan Incident. Nevertheless, retribution was swift and furious. It was September 1855 and the Brulè village had just finished a bison hunt. The proper preparation of the bison was critical to the band's winter survival, so women worked hard to skin and tan hides and dry meat for storage. Once the work was completed the whole group could move on, hoping to avoid the soldiers reported to be in the area. Before they were ready soldiers appeared. Chiefs rode out with white flags to talk to General Harney. They could not know that Harney had declared, "By God, I'm for battle—no peace," or that he had ordered his men to surround the village. When Harney refused to yield, Chief Little Thunder rushed back to the village to tell his people to prepare for an attack. It was too late; less than half the people escaped. As the infantry fired down into the camp clustered in the valley of the Blue Water the cavalry charged down the hill. Women were shot down with their babies in their arms. One officer remarked that "there was much slaughter in the pursuit."[12] The Lakota dubbed Harney "the Butcher," or "Squaw Killer."

Native Warfare

In many ways the Blue Water Massacre marked a turning point in the Plains Indian Wars. The U.S. Army showed itself to be a new kind of enemy. They killed relentlessly, and targeted women and children. The Lakota's traditional enemies shared their values. There may have been hatred and intense competition for resources, but everyone used the same techniques and sought the same goals. Honor was valued above all and there was little valor in slaughtering defenseless children. Traditional warfare focused on hit-and-run style raids designed to maximize gains and minimize losses. The concept of *coup*—showing immense bravery by touching the enemy rather than killing him—had no place in warfare with whites. The Lakota would have to change their tactics if they were to survive this new threat to their people. Besides revealing the need for adaptation Blue Water also kindled the flames of hatred. As a young Lakota warrior, Crazy Horse came to this village of his relatives just after the fight and witnessed an entire Lakota village destroyed. Crazy Horse found women and girls raped, stabbed, and scalped. He would spend the rest of his life fighting the enemy that had done this.

The brutality practiced by the army may have earned it lifelong enemies but did achieve short-term results. Most of the Lakota bands moved away from the Oregon Trail, the "holy road" the whites were prepared to kill for. The Brulè associated the trail with senseless deaths. The Oglalas continued their internal feuding and moved away from each other, one group to the north to ally with Northern Cheyenne, while the other ranged south and partnered with Southern Cheyenne. The Lakota were mostly living a traditional life, moving seasonally through their territories, following bison herds, celebrating their greatest spiritual ceremony, the Sun Dance, each summer. If whites simply stuck to their one road and passed through Lakota territory, the Indians could adjust to the loss of that territory. But the whites wanted more.

POWDER RIVER, OR RED CLOUD'S WAR

The whites, first civilians and then increasingly the army, turned their attention to the Powder River country of present-day north-central Wyoming. While the United States thought it had deemed this to be Crow territory under the Treaty of Fort Laramie, the Oglala Lakota knew better. They had pushed the Crow out in the previous ten years and it was *their* hunting ground. When John Bozeman marked out a new trail with wooden stakes that stretched across the Powder River region to central Montana the Indians were not happy. They became less happy as gold seekers trickled through their land. Of course the army felt a need to protect these frontier travelers, so in the summer of 1865 General Patrick Connor led a punitive expedition through Powder River country. He built Fort Reno and ordered subordinates to kill every male Indian over twelve years of age.

Battle of Tongue River

In late August, Connor located Chief Black Bear's Arapaho camp set up on flat bottomland of the Tongue River near present-day Ranchester, Wyoming. The camp of 700 people awoke on August 29 to the sounds of gunfire as Connor's men charged into their midst. By using artillery the army overran the large camp, killing over 60 people including Black Bear's son. A soldier remembered that women and children, as well as warriors, fell among the dead and wounded. As a further blow, the Arapaho lost the contents of the village when soldiers turned their attention to destroying Indian property. Scores of buffalo robes, blankets, and furs were heaped upon lodgepoles, with tipi covers and dried buffalo meat piled on top and then burned. The army also ran off 1,100 of the Arapaho horse herd. This was a terrible blow as the people prepared for winter, and the army's cruelty drove more Arapaho warriors to fight alongside the Lakota.

The winter of 1865–1866 was especially hard as game got scarcer and scarcer. An invitation from the government to meet and talk promised food and trade goods. The Lakota chief Man-Afraid-of-His-Horse and the prominent war chief Red Cloud agreed to come to the meeting at Fort Laramie in June 1866. The government was rather vague about what it wanted, referring to a desire to "make and use" such roads "as may be necessary" through the Powder River country.[13] Only when a group of Lakotas ran into the army's fort-building expedition did the government's real intentions become clear. The deception infuriated Red Cloud who accused the white negotiators of treating the chiefs like children, "pretending to negotiate for a country which they had already taken by conquest."[14] The war chief would not tolerate permanent forts, symbols of conquest, in his land. The Oglala would do everything they could to halt movement on the Bozeman Trail. The Powder River War had just begun.

The Oglala had great confidence in their ability to defend their homes. Men trained their whole lives for warfare and welcomed the opportunity to prove themselves. Honor on the battlefield led to political power, social status, wealth, and spiritual blessings.

Oglala chief Red Cloud led the resistance to white incursions into the rich Powder River country. (Library of Congress)

Women always feared the inevitable losses of war. Conflict with the whites seemed to bring more wounds and deaths than ever before, but they were proud of their sons, husbands, and brothers, and looked forward to the victory dances celebrating the return of successful warriors. Meanwhile, women continued to run the daily life of the camps, preparing food, raising children, and making clothing and tools. The warriors focused their aggression on the hated symbols of white intrusion—the forts.

Woodcutter, Fetterman, and Wagon Box Fights

The expedition under Colonel Carrington sent to construct fortifications to protect the Bozeman Trail managed to build Forts C. F. Smith and Phil Kearny to supplement Fort Reno. The army now had a tentative presence in the heart of Oglala territory. Red Cloud regarded this as a huge insult to Oglala sovereignty, and continually harassed the forts, army detachments, and any gold miners foolish enough to attempt to use the Bozeman Trail. The Lakotas focused their attention on the largest fort, Phil Kearny. Warriors kept the fort under continual harassment, constantly picking off men and adding to the growth of the fort cemetery. The deaths lowered morale and made the army nervous but would not end their presence along the Powder River. The Indians had to plan something bigger.

Cultural Adjustments

This type of conflict required new strategies from the Lakota, Cheyenne, and Arapaho war leaders. Attacking large, fortified installations was not the same as hitting small, mobile camps of their traditional enemies. Colonel Carrington had concentrated most of his energy on his headquarters at Kearny, directing his men to construct a wooden stockade around the 17-acre fort. The stockade probably prevented a direct Indian assault but required enormous amounts of wood which had to be harvested from distant areas. The Lakota realized that when the whites went to the "pineries," as they called the woodlots, they were at their most vulnerable. Striking detached forces had a higher rate of success than assaults on fortifications. However, it still demanded a level of organization, coordination, and discipline uncommon in Plains warfare. Through the fall of 1866 the strength of the Indian camps on the Tongue River grew as Miniconjou Lakota under High-Back-Bone, Little Wolf's Cheyenne, and other bands arrived. With the proper planning the Indians had the strength to strike a major blow at the army.

High-Back-Bone seems to have planned the attack that resulted in the Fetterman Fight—but Red Cloud, Crazy Horse, and other notable warriors were involved as well. The Indians hoped to lure a substantial number of soldiers into an ambush situation. Confidence was high as a holy man had received a vision that foretold one hundred soldiers falling. They would need to maneuver the troops out of sight and thus the aid of the fort. A high ridge near the fort, Lodge Trail Ridge, a woodcutting detail, and an impetuous officer combined to create a near-perfect scenario for the Indians on December 21, 1866. Older warriors planned and oversaw the attack which required coordination and discipline. A handful of men would act as decoys luring the soldiers across the ridge to the valley of Peno Creek where 1,500 hidden Indians could attack. Warrior societies, whose role was to keep order at gatherings, admonished young men to stay quiet and concealed until the signal was given. Ten men, representing the assembled tribes, undertook the dangerous and daring role of decoys. Crazy Horse earned a reputation here for steely nerves as he remained within rifle shot of the soldiers to encourage them to follow him.

Captain William Fetterman played directly into the Indians' hands. A small party attacked a woodcutting detail and Fetterman rushed his command to their aid, saw the decoys, and ignored orders not to cross Lodge Ridge. As his men followed the decoys down the slope into the stream area, warriors sprang up from every direction. The overwhelming Indian force made short work of infantry and cavalry, pouring arrows into men and horses. They cut down the last soldiers, including Fetterman, who had huddled on a ridge along the Bozeman Trail. The trap had worked beautifully, the young warriors had acted well, and the triumph was complete. It was a great day to be a Lakota. However joyous the victory celebration, it could not last long. It was December, and participants had to return to their families and scatter across the countryside in order to find enough food to survive the long winter.

As the army shuffled blame for the Fetterman loss and called for the Indians to "be punished with vindictive earnestness, until at least ten Indians are killed for each white life lost," the Indians planned more attacks.[15] The composition of the Powder River camps created some challenges. The Cheyenne chiefs Two Moons and Dull Knife argued for an attack on Fort C. F. Smith, while Red Cloud insisted that Kearny remain the target. In the end there were enough warriors for both plans. On August 1, 1867, over 500 Cheyenne attacked a party of hay cutters and their military escort three miles from Fort Smith. The small group huddled inside a stock corral and waited out several hours of intense fighting until the frustrated warriors withdrew. The next day, Crazy Horse led a group of 1,000 mounted Lakota against woodcutters at a pinery near Fort Kearny. The Indians rode confidently into the attack with far superior numbers. The trapped soldiers and civilians hid behind wagon boxes that made a makeshift corral and prepared to die fighting. But after hours of attacks the Lakota had to withdraw as the Cheyenne had done at the Hayfield fight. With superior numbers and the element of surprise the Indians should have easily won these fights as they had with Fetterman. The difference was technology. The soldiers had been armed with Springfield breech-loading rifles which allowed for rapid fire. The warriors had planned their attack based on old weaponry. They rode in, drew fire from the soldiers, then charged in the lull moment when the soldiers had to reload—except at the Wagon Box and Hayfield there was no lull. Defenders could fire continuously against attackers

Soldiers and civilian employees armed with repeating rifles successfully used these types of wagon boxes as a makeshift defense against an attack led by Crazy Horse. (Courtesy of Clarissa W. Confer)

which greatly improved their chances. The Indians would have to adjust yet again to changing styles of warfare in order to defend their homes.

Treaty of Fort Laramie 1868

Despite the disappointing outcome of the August attacks, Red Cloud and his followers did not feel defeated. They had effectively closed the Bozeman Trail, kept the army in its forts, and stolen herds of livestock. When the government asked for a meeting, the Indians could negotiate from a position of strength. Red Cloud responded, "We are on the mountains looking down on the soldiers and the forts. When we see the soldiers moving away and the forts abandoned, then I will come down and talk."[16] After several fruitless months the government realized the chief was serious and ordered Forts Smith, Reno, and Kearny abandoned. Red Cloud and his men were indeed watching and immediately swept down and burned Smith and the hated Kearny to the ground. Eventually, Red Cloud—along with 125 chiefs and many seasoned warriors, arrived at Fort Laramie in November 1868 to sign a treaty guaranteeing the closure of the forts and trail through their hunting grounds. It seemed a victory gained from aggressive resistance to army incursions. In fact, it reflected the fact that whites had new railroads with which to access the Montana gold fields and the old trails simply were not worth defending. Many young warriors did not like the provisions reserving specific lands for the Lakotas and granting them hunting territories north of the Platte only "so long as the buffalo may range thereon in such numbers as to justify the chase."[17] However, most Indians neither understood nor worried about other treaty provisions outlining the government's plan for the civilization process. They were Lakota, Cheyenne, and Arapaho people living free on their own lands—it was a good time to be Indian.

Cultural Divisions

While traditional peoples continued to follow age-old patterns of life, the West changed around them, and it would not be long before their lifestyle would be untenable. It was hard to contemplate what that might mean. How to imagine what Lakota children born in 1870 would experience in their lives? It was a time of incredible change that would make a Plains bison hunting culture obsolete. So much of that culture focused on hunting, warfare, and constant movement that the government's vision of sedentary, Christian farmers threatened the very core of Plains life. Spirituality, leadership, social structure, and nearly every aspect of daily life had evolved to fit with the old life so a new lifestyle required major adjustments.

People who had no interest in change gravitated to the leadership of a few men dedicated to preserving the old ways. Most notable among those were the Hunkpapa Lakota holy man Sitting Bull and the Oglala war chief Crazy Horse. Their followers camped as far from whites as they could, avoiding treaty signings and ration distributions. In an unusual show of support that reflected the changing nature of the times, families of Oglala, Miniconjou, and Sans Arc Lakota and Northern Cheyenne joined Sitting Bull's Hunkpapa Lakota. This resistant group, labeled "hostiles" by the government, boasted extraordinary leadership which would be severely tested by the challenges of the 1870s and 1880s.

Approximately one-third of the Lakota and Northern Cheyenne people chose to remain free of government interference. The rest of the people managed some level of accommodation. Traditional life became harder as game grew scarcer and whites intruded farther and farther into Indian country. Winters especially could be really tough. The government offered a steady food supply if Indians would come to the reservation. Many decided it was worth it, including notable chiefs. In the coming decade Red Cloud passed from the center of Lakota resistance leadership, accepting an agency house from the government and abiding by his pledge not to go to war with whites anymore. There was no love lost between the reservation or agency Indians and non-agency Indians. Sitting Bull's perception of reservation Lakota was clear. "Look at me—see if I am poor, or my people either . . . You are fools to make yourselves slaves to a piece of fat bacon, some hard-tack, and a little sugar and coffee."[18]

Numerous Lakota and Cheyenne crafted a compromise existence—stay on the reservation eating government food in the winter, then slip away in the spring to resume a nomadic hunting lifestyle until the snow flew. This practice drove government agents crazy, but remained workable for years. The reservation Indians could often be counted on to supplement the war parties and social gatherings of the traditionals so that some summers seemed just like the old-time gatherings of people.

Although there were still many good times on the plains, the specter of white intrusion hung like a sword over the people.

What has been done in my country I did not want, did not ask for it; white people going through my country. . . . When we first had this land we were strong, now are melting like snow on the hillside, while you are grown like spring grass. . . . When the white man comes in my country he leaves a trail of blood behind him.

Red Cloud[19]

It seemed every month brought a report of some new invasion. Sitting Bull's people ranged in the region of the Yellowstone River in Montana. In 1871 and 1872, parties of surveyors for the Northern Pacific Railroad pushed into the Yellowstone country. The Lakota clashed with the railroad men but did not stop their progress. The Northern Pacific Railroad faltered due to the national financial collapse of 1873, not Indian aggression. That was fortunate; however the next threat loomed even larger.

The catastrophe that would strike the Lakota world was the same one that hit tribes all over the West—the discovery of gold. This time the whites targeted the sacred heart of Lakota life. Whites called them the Black Hills; Lakota knew them as *Paha Sapa*, the scared center of their world. The creator put the people in *Paha Sapa* and no matter where they roamed it was still the heartland, the place for vision quests and communication with the spirits, as well as abundant resources. From a legal point of view, the area had been guaranteed to the Lakota by the Treaty of Fort Laramie. None of this slowed white invasion.

In 1874, George Armstrong Custer led an expeditionary force into the Dakotas. He had long expressed an interest in seeing the area, and rumors of gold grew stronger in the 1870s. The army wanted to find a location for a new fort, so the scouting expedition served several purposes. The Indians knew Custer as the officer who slaughtered Black Kettle's Cheyenne village in 1868 so it added insult to injury when his expedition returned to trumpet the confirmation of gold in the Black Hills. Gold fever was about to be unleashed again. President Grant, whose son had accompanied Custer, realized the forces coming into play. He announced that the government would "prevent an invasion of this country by intruders so long as by law and by treaty it is secured to the Indians."[20] Strong words, but even the president could not long hold back the force of greed. As the *New York Tribune* noted, "if there is gold in the Black Hills, no army on earth can keep the adventurous men of the west out of them."[21] The army did not and perhaps could not stop the tide of whites streaming to western South Dakota. By the winter of 1875–1876, 15,000 settlers occupied the Black Hills.

Neither did leaders like Red Cloud react strongly to the invasion. His mild response pushed more young warriors off the reservation to live with Sitting Bull's band of resisters. Finally, Red Cloud protested—so the government sent yet another commission to negotiate yet another treaty to take yet more land from the Lakotas. However, the Black Hills were too important to sell. The Lakota people never agreed to this taking, and still in the 21st-century fight for their return to the people. This rejection of white plans for expansion showed Lakota solidarity. All the leaders agree the sacred *Paha Sapa* were not for sale. It also set the stage for the most infamous native battle in the West—Little Big Horn.

Sitting Bull and the free-living Lakota were furious about Custer's expedition, and referred to his trail as the "thieves' road." For their part the government had determined that Sitting Bull and the roamers must be forced onto reservations. On December 3, 1875 the commissioner of Indian Affairs issued an ultimatum that all Indians had to report to their agencies by January 31st or a "military force would be sent to compel them."[22] The whole plan was a farce. The "hostile" bands under Sitting Bull, Gall, and Crazy Horse were hunkered down in a harsh winter and would never have received the news of the deadline. Two months was a ridiculously short time frame to move people and all their belongings to the reservations, and no one traveled during a plains winter. Of course, these bands would not be coming in anyway; Sitting Bull and Crazy Horse had no intention of surrendering to the government.

The government cared little for the impossibilities of the plan—the next step was military. The report of Indian inspector Erwin Watson said "The true policy, in my judgment, is to send troops against them in the winter, the sooner the better, and *whip* them into subjection."[23] The army had been waiting for the support of the Indian department, and now proceeded to plan what they regarded as the final solution to the Indian problem. General Philip Sheridan had expected this assignment and was already planning a winter campaign against the non-reservation Indians.

The army's winter campaign was considered quite clever. They would strike the Indians hunkered down in isolated family camps low on food for people and ponies. Warriors from the reservation, "agency Indians," would not swell their numbers in a fight during the winter. Of course the harsh winter was no less grueling for troopers and cavalry horses unaccustomed to the cold and snow. Many easterners were beaten by the plains winter and the campaign fizzled. There was some grief in the Powder River country, however. Non-agency Cheyenne came out to hunt and camped on the Powder River. They had seen soldiers but were not expecting trouble. "We felt safe then. Many of our people thought they were not seeking us at all."[24] At dawn on March 17, 1876, U.S. Cavalry swept through the village of 450 people. The surprise attack scattered women and children, burned tipis, and ran off the horse herd. The now homeless people traveled through the bitter winter weather to take refuge with Crazy Horse's camp. The army had merely succeeded in angering the Indians and gaining the "hostiles" more support. As Two Moon told Crazy Horse, "My people have been killed, my horses stolen; I am satisfied to fight."[25]

LITTLE BIG HORN

In the spring of 1876 as the Lakota fattened horse herds on the greening grass, moved in search of game, and were joined by agency Indians from the reservations, the army planned a three-pronged assault intended to end their freedom forever. This year because of government's harsh treatment and army aggression at the Powder River in March, even more warriors left the reservation. All were welcomed by the non-treaty bands. Crazy Horse expected 1,000 warriors to swell his ranks.

As the Indian camps grew larger, reports came in of bluecoat movement. General Sheridan planned a three-prong movement sending General John Gibbon from the west, General George Crook from the south, and General Alfred Terry—with Custer under his command—from the east. The idea was to squash the Indians in a pincher movement, but it did not go according to plan. As warriors and their families flocked to Sitting Bull and Crazy Horse the mixed Lakota and Cheyenne camps reached unusual proportions. The people came together in their traditional patterns which included the annual Sun Dance. This multi-day ceremony propitiated the spirits and ensured harmony in the coming year. Sitting Bull participated in the Sun Dance held in the Rosebud Valley. He described for the people the vision he had seen while dancing. He saw, numerous as grasshoppers, soldiers and horses bearing down on an Indian village below. They came upside down, falling headfirst into the Indian camp. To all who heard it this portended a great victory over the bluecoats who would dare attack their villages of women and children. The army would take the field against large numbers of confident, angry warriors.

Native Warfare

Rosebud Battle

June 1876 found Sitting Bull camped along Reno Creek, between the Rosebud and Little Big Horn Rivers. The camp had about 460 tipis which sheltered 3,000 people—a mobile village that was large by Plains standards. The group had to be mobile because the tens of thousands of ponies associated with all those lodges ate up all the available grass in a few days. As General Crook followed his orders to move northward from Fort Fetterman toward the Yellowstone River, he headed straight for the huge Indian camp. Unwilling to let the army surprise the village as they had done in March at Powder River, Sitting Bull and Crazy Horse led their 1,000 warriors up the Rosebud valley to the enemy. The Lakota and Cheyenne warriors hit the army while it was resting, but were slowed by fierce fighting with Crook's Indian scouts. The battle between the two sides raged most of the day. As Wooden Leg remembered, "Sometimes we chased them, sometimes they chased us."[26] Two Moon remarked, "It was a great fight, much smoke and dust."[27] The warriors broke off the fight in the afternoon and rode back to their camp. This left Crook in control of the battlefield, usually considered a victory by the army, but he was much bloodied. The true victory belonged to the Lakota and Cheyenne. Crook had to retreat to Fort Fetterman to care for his wounded and resupply, so he was out of Sheridan's overall plan. The southern pincher was gone.

The Indians had lost men too and there would be mourning in some lodges, but overall they had scored an important victory. The victory called for a celebration which required a move to a place uncontaminated by death. Women packed tipis, loaded travois, and the whole group moved to a new location up the valley. Here they rested and celebrated their recent victory with dances and feasts. The arrival of friends and relatives from the agency added to the joyous atmosphere. The new arrivals swelled the village to nearly 1,000 lodges which could hold about 7,000 people. This was now the largest gathering ever known in the plains. George Armstrong Custer was about to ride right into it.

Little Big Horn (Greasy Grass)

I could whip all the Indians on the Continent with the Seventh Cavalry.

George A. Custer, June 25, 1876

Ho-ka hey! It is a good day to fight! It is a good day to die! Strong hearts, brave hearts, to the front! Weak hearts and cowards to the rear.

Crazy Horse, June 25, 1876 [28]

Amid all the hype surrounding the Battle of Little Big Horn it is important to remember that the Lakota and Cheyenne were a divided people. The army was not fighting an entire tribe; only a portion of the people engaged in war with the United States. In fact, the native population of the Plains Tribes continued traditional divisions. The United States has always been able to capitalize on indigenous rivalries and they used this to great advantage in the 1870s. Members of the Apsàalooke or Crow tribe frequently served as scouts for the army. Such service offered them the opportunity to strike a blow at their long-standing enemies the Lakota as well as providing food, clothing, and weapons. The scouts earned $13 per month just as regular troopers did and since they often made money hunting for the army, service could be quite a lucrative deal. It also offered an opportunity to fight with honor and courage against a worthy opponent. It was often the Indian scouts who clashed first with the army's target. The Seventh Cavalry under Custer rode with Crow and Arikara scouts in search of Sitting Bull's people.

As the large Indian camp fresh off a victory at the Rosebud moved up the valley to a new location, the other arms of the army's pincher movement moved forward, unaware that Crook was out of the game. Gibbon came from the west to meet with Terry and Custer on the steamer *Far West* on the Yellowstone River to plan the attack. The idea was that Custer would take troops south to cut off any Indian escape while Gibbon stayed north to block the Indians' retreat up the Little Big Horn. The generals believed this was their opportunity to annihilate the hostiles once and for all.

George Custer was very anxious to get to the Indian camp. The opportunities for advancement in the post–Civil War army came only by fighting Indians. Custer had several setbacks in the army that winter—Grant had forbid him to go with the Seventh Cavalry—so he was really looking for an opportunity for glory. From the start he seemed intent on doing whatever it took to chase down the village.

Although the command was ordered out for five days, Custer told officers to take rations for 15 days. He even stated that he would cut loose from Terry—his commander—so it should be no surprise that when he found a fresh Indian trail he followed it rather than his orders to proceed south.

The large native camp did head south, up the Greasy Grass or Little Big Horn River. However, when scouts came back with reports of large antelope herds, the entire group turned around and headed north. Thousands of people made camp on the Greasy Grass (named for the shining quality of the ridge). The wide valley made an appealing location. To the west were low grassy hills where the huge pony herd could graze. To the east the river hugged steep bluffs as it meandered through cottonwood trees. The wide, flat, bottom of the valley had room for the 1,000 tipis which stretched almost three miles. Each band set up in its own camp circle with the Hunkpapa at the southern end, Northern Cheyenne at the northern edge, and Miniconjou, Blackfeet, Brulè, Sans Arc, and Oglala in the middle. Sitting Bull climbed the high ridge opposite the village and left offerings to thank *Wahantanka*, the Great Spirit, for the people's protection. It was a wonderful spot and everyone settled in, aware of the constant possibility of white intrusion but not on high alert. If the army came the warriors had no doubt they could deal with them as they had at the recent Rosebud Battle. At the height of their power and confidence the Lakota and Cheyenne felt strong, but did not seek a fight. They did not know Custer desperately sought them.

In his search for Indians to fight, Custer was extremely fortunate to have Crow scouts with him. They essentially were going home; they knew the Bighorn River area well, knew the campsites, hunting areas, and stream crossings. They always had a much better idea of the movements of the enemy than anyone in the cavalry. The Indian scouts remained mostly separate from the white troopers. They camped apart and exercised a fair amount of independence. They usually rode ahead and reported back on what they had seen.

The Crow scouts were eager to fight the Lakota and Cheyenne whom they hated, but they were not suicidal. One of the most important features of traditional native warfare was the assessment of the odds and the capability to be able to fight another day. When they came to the site where Sitting Bull had held the Sun Dance earlier that month the scouts recognized powerful medicine. The signs of a large gathering grew stronger. On June 25, 1876, Crow scouts rode to a high point known as the Crow's Nest and

Crow scout Curly rode with Custer against long-time enemies like the Lakota. (National Archives & Records Administration / Double Delta)

there spotted far in the distance the evidence of a large native camp. Native warriors trained from childhood to sharpen their eyesight, to make out signs at long distances. They saw undulating dark spots which they described to whites as maggots and a churning dust cloud. They knew this was a huge horse herd that could only be associated with an enormous gathering of Indians. Although Custer could not see the described objects he apparently believed the Indian scouts. However, that trust did not extend to judgment. The scouts analyzed the enormity of the enemy and knew the smaller army force was no match. It would be foolish to attack a superior enemy force, wiser to confront them on another day as this size village could not be sustained for long. Custer had no patience for such talk. The scouts could do as they wished; the army under his command would move forward immediately.

Still fearful of losing the village he so desperately sought, Custer divided his force by sending Captain Frederick Benteen on a swing to the south to make sure the Indians were not below the army. Everyone else, despite the demands of hard riding the past few days, was to move forward at once. Custer left behind his mule train in the haste to get to the Indians. Captain Marcus Reno's command of 175, which included 15 Arikara scouts, was to cross the Little Big Horn and attack the Indian camp from the south. This would send him directly into Sitting Bull's Hunkpapa.

As Custer hastily made his plans on June 26, the Indian camp went about its daily business. It was a hot and lazy afternoon. The warriors had danced and feasted nearly till dawn so many slept during the heat of the day. A few, especially the camp police, had ponies tied by their tipis, but most of the animals were far across the valley with the rest of the herd.

I had no thought of any fighting to be done in the near future. We had driven away the soldiers, on the Rosebud, seven days ago. It seemed likely it would be a long time before they would trouble us again. My mind was occupied mostly by such thoughts as regularly are uppermost in the minds of young men. I was 18 years old, and I liked girls.

Wooden Leg[29]

Women completed domestic chores or dug wild turnips and picked berries along the river, watching the children splash in the water. It was hard to believe the cry "they are charging, the chargers are coming" when it spread through camp.[30] But it was true and the pandemonium began.

Reno's command had splashed across the Little Big Horn and charged into the southern end of the camp circles. Warriors rushed to their tipis urging their families to safety and grabbing their weapons. As bullets smashed through the tipis women grabbed children and fled to the western hills.

Like that the soldiers were upon us. Through the tepee holes their bullets rattled. . . . we women wailed over the children, for we believed that the Great Father had sent all his men for the destruction of the Sioux.

Mrs. Spotted Horn Bull[31]

Young boys tied sagebrush to ponies' tails and drug it back and forth to create a dust cloud to screen the men who sprinted to the herd to get horses. The initial defense of the village was chaotic, but effective. The Indians defending their homes and families fought hard to push Reno's men back across the river and up the steep bluffs. Unlike the soldiers, the warriors' loved ones were not 1,800 miles away, but just below the ridges where the men fought so hard to protect them.

Reno never received support from Custer and ended up in a siege situation on the ridge. Custer's favorite scout, Bloody Knife, lay dead and most of the other Arikara scouts left. They had warned the whites not to take on a village of this size. Now the Lakota and Cheyenne warriors had Reno's and Benteen's men pinned down. They would remain there for two days.

The quick push back of Reno's assault encouraged the warriors, although they lost some good men in the fight. Women walked among the enemy dead, stripping them of valuables and mutilating many bodies. They were especially violent toward the bodies of Indian enemies, making sure through the mutilation that they would not have an easy time in the spirit world. There was no time to relax, however, as word came of attacks on the other end of the camp. Custer had left Reno to his fate at the southern end of the village. He took the rest of the men under his command and moved north along the ridge seeking a way to get to the village.

We still do not know the exact movements of Custer, because all the men with him perished. Indian accounts indicate that some of the soldiers rode down a ravine called Medicine Tail Coulee and tried to cross into the northern end of the camp. There they would attack the Miniconjou, Sans Arc, and Cheyenne camps. Warriors swarmed to defend the village and easily overwhelmed the cavalry force. They rode confidently to the attack, some sporting scalps recently lifted from Reno's men. Warriors pushed the remaining cavalry onto the ridge where they surrounded them. Coming from behind, Indians shot the unmounted horse holders and moved closer to Custer's defensive spot on the hill where Sitting Bull had made his offerings the day before. Hundreds of warriors were there to punish the attack on their village.

We all yelled "*Hoka hey!*" and charged toward them, . . . I was mad, because I was thinking of the women and children down there, all scared and out of breath. These Wasichus [whites] wanted it, and they came to get it, and we gave it to them.

Iron Hawk[32]

Before the day ended Custer, along with all the officers and men in his immediate command, lay dead. The defeat of this northern group freed warriors to return to harassing Reno and Benteen at the southern end of the ridge. Soldiers there struggled with thirst and lack of ammunition. The wounded were placed in a bowl or depression for protection but during the hot, dry day dehydration became a serious threat. Soldiers lay in makeshift entrenchments listening to the victory cries of the warriors who had killed Custer. It seemed a hopeless situation, but the Indians had neither the inclination nor the time to continue the siege. Reports of soldiers coming south along the Little Big Horn prompted the entire camp to pack up and move away from further aggression.

The Indians did not realize the problems the victory in battle would bring. They had not sought the fight, they had responded to an attack. Rather than pursue the soldiers as the young wished to do, the chiefs chose to move the village away from the army. The general feeling was that the people could resume their lives.

In every way we were living yet according to our customary habits. We were not bothering any white people. We did not want to see any of them. We felt we were on our own land. We had killed only such people as had come for driving us away from it.

Wooden Leg[33]

However, white Americans were shocked and outraged at the news of Custer's defeat. One has only to look at the ongoing fascination with Custer more than 125 years later to get a glimpse of how this one defeat preoccupied non-Indians. Instead of settling the matter and gaining the non-agency Lakota and Cheyenne their freedom, the great victory set in motion the events that would force them all onto reservations. Just five years after the battle Sitting Bull announced that he was the last man of his tribe to surrender his rifle.

Americans demanded blood revenge. Immediately after Custer's loss a flood of soldiers spread around the region. Neither Crook nor Terry would venture out after the victorious Indians without major reinforcements. Of course, the Indians who defeated Custer no longer existed as a group. Many of the agency Indians had enjoyed the feasting, celebrations, and fighting they had come for and now headed back to the reservations. The large gathering could not be long maintained anyway and they split up to look for game. Sitting Bull and his Hunkpapa headed down the Little Missouri while Crazy Horse went up the Little Missouri toward the Black Hills with Oglala and Cheyenne.

Terry and Crook combined their forces so that with 4,000 soldiers they felt strong enough to venture out to look for Indians to fight. The quest was beset by rain, mud, and disillusionment. Crook had enough of Terry and the weather so he headed his force toward the Black Hills for resupply. As his situation got more desperate and the men had started eating horses, Crook sent Captain Anderson Mills ahead with some 150 men. Mills literally stumbled into the Indians Crook sought. Near Slim Buttes several groups camped, including Crazy Horse and Sitting Bull. Mills located Chief American Horse's Miniconjous in a camp with 37 lodges and attacked before daybreak on September 9th. Once again the army attacked a village of women and children, so the warriors had to ensure the safety of civilians before turning to the fight. Tipis had been tightly fastened against the rain so it was hard to get out quickly. The women and children fled to the bluffs where they watched the battle unfold. Their warriors pushed the soldiers back so that nearly everyone escaped. The fighting escalated as Crook's main column rode up and Crazy Horse, Sitting Bull, and other Indian leaders came from the nearby camps. The Indians lost about 40 people before the army continued on its way to the Black Hills. The Miniconjou lost everything when the army burned the village. Then Chief American Horse died from his devastating groin wound. This group had been intending to surrender at the agency, but the sight of their dead chief, women, and children caused them to rethink that choice.

Economic Struggles

After Little Big Horn the free Indians had trouble avoiding the army. General Sheridan decreed a "total war" which meant keeping troops in the field all winter to harass the roaming groups. These bands needed bison to survive so Sheridan planned to disrupt their supply. The strategy was effective enough to anger Sitting Bull. A message he dictated to the army said "I want to know what you are doing traveling on this road. You scare all the buffalo away. I want to hunt on the place. I want you to turn back from here. If you don't I will fight you again."[34] Meanwhile, the other part of the strategy, to establish military control over agency Indians, proceeded. The men on the reservations were stripped of guns, ammunition, and ponies. The non-agency Indians would get no help from their reservation brethren now. Red Cloud, who still spoke out for the rights of his people, was replaced as chief by the more compliant Spotted Tail. The government forced agency chiefs to sign away the Black Hills. Despite their obvious strength, in June the Lakota and Cheyenne who sought to live free now seemed caged on all sides.

The pressure convinced some leaders that they should talk about peace with white officials. Any peace conference meant nothing

without Sitting Bull's blessing so after much convincing the great
Hunkpapa leader met with General Nelson "Bear Coat" Miles. Bear
Coat, fresh off his success on the southern plains, demanded full
surrender. His aggressive style angered Sitting Bull, and they broke
off the talks before violence occurred. The two sides did then clash
at Cedar Creek with few casualties. The talks had shown Sitting
Bull the army's intentions to remain in his country, which created
serious problems for those seeking to pursue a hunting lifestyle.
It was also clear that not all the non-reservation Indians were
committed to the free life. Miles easily convinced the chiefs of 400
Miniconjou and Sans Arc lodges to surrender after Cedar Creek.
Sitting Bull and Crazy Horse would increasingly fight alone.

The two great leaders could not imagine living without guns or
horses, warfare or hunting, which whites demanded on the reservations. Many Lakota and Cheyenne felt the same way, but it was
getting harder and harder to live the life they wanted. There was
nowhere safe, nowhere to escape the U.S. Army. Life took on a
tense, anxious quality as camps moved continually to locate dwindling food resources and evade the army. Hunger and cold could
be as deadly as cavalry rifles. More and more groups went into
the agencies, drawn by the promise of food and clothing. Only a
few chiefs remained free—Sitting Bull, Crazy Horse, Dull Knife
(Morning Star), Little Wolf—and each day challenged them to
care for their people as the army poured men and resources into
the contest.

The Cheyenne were crippled in November 1876. General Crook
assembled yet another large expedition of cavalry, infantry, and
artillery against the Indians. Almost 2,000 men set out from Fort
Fetterman, including more than 400 Indian scouts, mostly Crow,
Shoshoni, and Pawnee. The Indian scouts riding with the cavalry
contingent under Colonel Ranald Mackenzie located a Cheyenne
village in a canyon on the Red Fork of the Powder River. Cheyenne
accounts reveal that the chiefs knew about the soldiers but
chose not to move the village, shamed into staying by the bravado
of war leader Last Bull. True to form, the army attacked the sleeping camp at sunrise on November 25, 1876. The previous night the
Cheyenne had celebrated a victory over the Shoshone with feasting
and dancing until near dawn. In the early morning light the Pawnee warriors raced into the village on fast Lakota ponies confiscated from the reservation. Bullets slammed into tipis killing
many before they had a chance to emerge. Warriors struggled out
naked into the confusion of the attack fighting to buy time for the

women and children to escape. It was snowing fiercely as Chief Little Wolf led the evacuation of the camp. The chief was wounded seven times that day, but continued his role as warrior and protector. The battle dragged on all day until the Cheyenne withdrew at dusk with about 40 dead. The real toll of the battle came when the army burned the camp and ran off the horse herd. In digging through the Indians' belongings soldiers found items from the Seventh Cavalry, taken at Little Big Horn. This may have added to their thirst for revenge. The Cheyenne lost everything—tipis, blankets, household goods, clothing, dried meat, and horses. They now faced the harsh Wyoming winter with no supplies. The temperature dropped far below zero that night and eleven babies froze to death. The desperate situation called for desperate measures as men killed and disemboweled ponies in order to put freezing children inside the shelter of their bodies. A march so harsh people left bloody footprints in the snow brought the survivors to Crazy Horse's camp. The Lakota shared what they had but resources were limited. The warriors did not have enough ammunition to hold off an army attack so the people had to keep running.

Battle of Wolf Mountains

The long winter of 1876–1877 continued this way. Just six months after the power and pride displayed at Little Big Horn, the victors struggled to survive. General Miles continued to prove his willingness to campaign in the winter which proved costly to the villages. Some chiefs even convinced Crazy Horse to ride in to talk to General Miles, but Miles' Crow scouts fired on the Lakota, thus ending the opportunity for discussion. Crazy Horse now raided for revenge and planned a decoy tactic to lure soldiers out of Fort Keogh. On January 8, 1877, Miles fought Crazy Horse's band in the Wolf Mountains for four hours in heavy snow. After fighting ended the soldiers could return to a sheltered fort with secure rations while the Indians moved camp yet again seeking elusive peace and sufficient game. Crazy Horse took his people to the familiar Powder River country.

Sitting Bull answered Crazy Horse's request for ammunition with a mule train he had gathered in trade. His Miniconjou had lost their camp along with its dried meat, robes, tipis, and many ponies, to the army in December. In fact, some soldiers at the Battle of Wolf Mountains wore coats made of the Hunkpapas' bison robes. With Sitting Bull's arrival most of the leaders of the non-reservation Indians were together. They divided sharply on the next course of action, some willing to surrender, others to fight on.

I am tired of being always on the watch for troops. My desire is to get my family where they can sleep without being continually in the expectation of an attack.

Red Horse[35]

In February the big camp had to split up to find game. The Oglala and Cheyenne headed for the Little Big Horn to ride out the winter. It was harder and harder to keep the band together as people departed for the reservations. Crazy Horse had to use the warrior police societies to keep people from leaving. Sensing the desperation of the people at this harsh time, the government began sending emissaries to the holdouts. Sometimes they sent kinsmen to extol the virtues of reservation life. Other delegations boasted prestigious leaders. Spotted Tail, now the chief of the Lakota according to the government, arrived as a peace emissary. Spotted Tail was a Brulè not an Oglala, and had long since forfeited any prestige he had among the non-agency Indians so his word would not sway Crazy Horse. But the condition of his people did. They could not keep running. The women and children were tired, hungry, and frightened. This was not a true Lakota life for them. Crazy Horse would not meet with Spotted Tail, but left a message that the Oglala would come in when the weather improved. The government emissary also received promises from Miniconjou chief Big Foot and other chiefs that they would bring their people to the reservation in the spring.

Surrender of Lakota

In April, General Crook sent Chief Red Cloud to find Crazy Horse with a promise of a reservation in the Powder River country. Red Cloud found 900 Oglala and their ponies starving, out of ammunition, and out of hope. Crazy Horse led his people on their last free journey to surrender at Fort Robinson, Nebraska. On May 6, 1877, one of the greatest Lakota leaders in history surrendered to the U.S. government. With him were 889 people who gave up 12,000 ponies and 117 guns. This was the culmination of a string of surrenders by various bands that put virtually all of the Lakota and Cheyenne under government control.

Meanwhile, the other major individual leading the non-reservation holdouts had chosen a different path. Both Sitting Bull and Crazy

Horse had become legendary in the eyes of white officials and thus bore the brunt of the military and political pressure to accept reservation life. Both men would rather die fighting in their homelands than accept such a life for themselves, but had to make concessions for their people. Crazy Horse chose to surrender with his band. Sitting Bull sought one last option—Canada.

Unfortunately, the end of fighting did not bring any measure of peace to the chiefs who had led their people in resistance for so long. Crazy Horse surrendered in May and was dead by September. Once on the reservation the army sought Oglala help in tracking the Nez Perce which disgusted Crazy Horse. He had clung to the old ways as much as he could and viewed with scorn those warriors who enlisted to fight with their former enemies. General Crook still feared the power of the legendary leader and ordered him arrested after hearing rumors that he meant to leave the reservation. In September 1877 Crazy Horse received a mortal stab wound while in government custody. Numerous contradictory accounts exist about how the killing took place, but in the final analysis the results are the same. Crazy Horse died in captivity, held by one of his own warriors turned policeman for the whites. The Oglala Lakota had lost their greatest leader, but he would be spared the heartbreaking toll of reservation life.

Cheyenne chiefs Dull Knife and Little Wolf led the Cheyenne people on a desperate trek to return to their homelands. (Legends of America)

Surrender of Northern Cheyenne

Others chiefs lived to see the suffering of their people. Cheyenne leaders Dull Knife and Little Wolf led 552 Cheyenne into Fort Robinson in April 1877. Forced to subsist on horse meat during the hard winter, many were skin and bones, wore only tattered clothing, and suffered from frostbite. The skinny ponies they surrendered were not in any better shape. As General Crook took satisfaction in having beaten another group of "hostile" Indians, they turned over a paltry 102 guns and 14 bows. It did not seem like enough to hold off the might of the U.S. Army, yet they had for years. The chiefs brought their people in because of the intense hardship, but also because of the promises the government made. The Cheyenne surrendered at the Red Cloud Agency at Fort Robinson and expected to remain there, among Oglala Lakota kin, in their homeland. But suddenly the government announced that the Cheyenne would be shipped south to Indian Territory. In the government's eyes it made sense to put all the people they labeled Cheyenne in one spot. They disregarded the cultural reality of the Plains. The Cheyenne had long before divided into southern and northern tribes. Dull Knife's people, the Northern Cheyenne, had shared their lives with the Oglala Lakota for decades. They had fought and hunted together, intermarried and raised Oglala/ Cheyenne children. Their home was in Wyoming, and they did not want to leave for an unknown place. Their protests fell on deaf ears and—with hollow promises of return if they did not like it—the Cheyenne began the long walk southward in May 1877.

Indian Territory (Oklahoma) was terrible. The two divisions of Cheyenne did not get along after three decades of separation. For people accustomed to the climate of the northern plains, the heat and humidity seemed unbearable. Ticks, mosquitoes, and flies plagued the camp on the river bottomlands and soon Cheyenne began to die from malaria and measles. Chief Dull Knife felt helpless as no complaints moved the corrupt Indian agent whose own store overcharged the Indians 300 percent. The government promises began to unravel as the annuities failed to show up. Corn, flour, rice, hominy, beans, and salt never came, and the beef supply was piteously short.

They gave us corn meal ground with cob such as a man feeds his mules, some salt, and one beef [cow] for 46 persons to last seven days. We ate it in three and starved in four days. . . . A great many starved to death. We had goods and provisions in our commissary, but our agent used them. The grass was so poor our horses died, and there was no wood.

Wild Hog[36]

The agent threatened to withhold even these meager rations if the Cheyenne did not enroll their children in the agency schools.

Sickness swept the Indian camps in the spring of 1878. Over a third of the people contracted measles and many would not recover since there was no medicine. Physical illness only exacerbated the suffering from heartbreak that so many Northern Cheyenne felt. They had lost everything they cared about. "I have been sick a great deal of the time since I have been down here—homesick and heartsick," said Little Chief.[37] Warriors remembered their free life hunting bison and glorying in their success in their beautiful homeland. This new life was a nightmare from which they could not awaken. Chiefs Dull Knife and Little Wolf had led these men in battle and led their families into this unbearable situation. They resolved to take action. On September 9, 1878, the Northern Cheyenne left the reservation in Indian Territory and headed for home.

Cheyenne Journey

The journey was truly a remarkable odyssey. Three hundred people braved incredible hardship to go home. The interpreter on the reservation knew the Cheyenne had been reduced to eating meat from dead horses and believed there would be a "large outbreak by the coming Spring, unless something is done to improve their condition at the agency."[38] Little Wolf had even told the Indian agent that the Northern Cheyenne were going home, but the agent apparently did not believe they would try such an impossible expedition. Once the government accepted the reality of the Cheyenne exodus they reacted strongly. General Sheridan gave orders to "spare no measures . . . to kill or capture the band of Cheyenne on the way north."[39] Generals Pope and Crook coordinated the pursuit of the band by nearly 2,000 soldiers. The Cheyenne thus had to make a running fight, holding off details of soldiers long enough to let the women and children move on.

As war chief, Little Wolf oversaw a series of skirmishes with the army that left the group battered but still moving so that by October the Cheyenne had crossed the Platte River into the familiar hunting grounds of Nebraska. They had traveled 500 miles in five weeks, lost most of their possessions and ponies, and arrived cold, hungry, and weak. The chiefs now disagreed on the best course of action. Dull Knife wanted to go to his friends the Oglalas at the Red Cloud Agency (it had been closed and the Oglala moved to Dakota Territory), while Little Wolf intended to push on to Montana to resume a free life. After the people made their choices Dull Knife ended up at Fort Robinson surrendering 148 people. The experienced chief did not trust the soldiers, so he had the warriors disassemble their working weapons, hiding barrels in the women's skirts and disguising small gun parts as ornaments. The Cheyenne prisoners crowded into an army barracks and enjoyed food, warmth, and medicine, while awaiting the government's reaction to their arrival. In December, Chief Red Cloud came down from Dakota to visit his old friends. "Our hearts are sore for you" he said, "but what can we do? The Great Father is all-powerful. His people fill the whole earth. We must do what he says. . . . You cannot resist, nor can we."[40] The fight had gone out of the old Oglala chief.

Dull Knife also did not wish to fight, but insisted that the Cheyenne must remain in their homeland. His message was clear—"tell the Great Father that Dull Knife and his people ask only to end their days where they were born."[41] The government had no intention of allowing this escape from an assigned reservation to succeed; it would set a terrible example for the thousands of other unhappy Indians. General Sheridan ordered the Cheyenne back to Indian Territory immediately, despite General Crook's assertion that it would be "inhumane to move them as ordered."[42] Dull Knife received the news in the building where Crazy Horse had bled to death less than two years ago. He responded ". . . I will never go back. You may kill me here, but you cannot make me go back."[43] As the army captain insisted day after day, the Cheyenne did not waiver. "You can starve us if you like but you cannot make us go south." The army took up the idea.

The first week of January 1879 the army cut off food, fuel, and water to the Cheyenne in the barracks. For five days the men, women, and children shivered and starved. Adults scooped snow from windowsills in an attempt to get water for children who were weakening. Still the people refused to surrender. The officers attempted to break their will by seizing and removing the leaders one by one. Dull Knife refused to be lured out of the barracks and instead prepared his people for one last fight. The soldiers had surrounded the barracks and nailed and chained the doors shut.

Better to die fighting on the prairie than die "shut up like dogs" they decided. Warriors reassembled five guns from the hidden parts, piled possessions against the windows, and put on their best clothes as befit proud Cheyenne warriors. At 9:45 PM the Cheyenne fired on the soldiers, then crawled out the windows. Arming themselves with weapons from the fallen bluecoats, the warriors made a skirmish line as women and children piled out windows and fled for the bluffs. Many warriors had their wish as more than half died in the first hour of fighting. No one had eaten for five days and most were weak and slow. Soldiers drew closer and shot or captured dozens of Cheyenne. The captives, many wounded, were pushed back to Fort Robinson.

Only 38 Cheyenne remained free and it took the cavalry days to capture them. They had to get the assistance of Lakota from the reservation to track these desperate people. The scouts located a group of Cheyenne hiding in a washout at Hat Creek Bluffs and the army opened fire into the pit. When the firing ceased, 24 lay dead and just eight survived. The bodies were robbed and scalped before burial. Dull Knife and his family had headed for the Red Cloud Agency in Dakota. Without provisions, they resorted to eating the soles of their moccasins, but they finally stumbled into the Lakota camps. Dull Knife was old, sick, and terribly worn from the journey, but still hoped to reunite with Little Wolf. Little Wolf's group had spent the winter in pits dug into the banks of a creek in Nebraska, and then in the spring finally reached their beloved Powder River country. But the soldiers were already there. Little Wolf surrendered his band in March 1879. The Northern Cheyenne survivors did get to go back to Montana, where Dull Knife died in 1883.

Surrender of Sitting Bull

Before most chiefs surrendered in 1877 some Hunkpapa leaders had headed for Canada, and by the spring Sitting Bull decided to join them. He vowed to watch the treatment of Crazy Horse and others who surrendered. If they were disarmed and dismounted, Sitting Bull would not return to the United States. In the first week of May 1877 Sitting Bull and his remaining 1,000 followers crossed into Canada. Canada was not home but home had been made unlivable by the U.S. Army. The Indians thought Canada promised freedom.

They told us this line was considered holy. They believe things are different when you cross from one side to another. You are altogether different. On one side you are perfectly free to do as you please. On the other you are in danger.

Robert Higheagle[44]

The Grandmother across the sea had to be kinder than the Great Father in Washington.

Canada beckoned to a people who had been thoroughly harassed by the U.S. Army. The refugees numbered over 4,000 from five of the Lakota tribal divisions. This large group created pressure in several ways. The resident natives resented their arrival, the U.S. Army regarded them as a irritating symbol of their inability to subdue ALL the Indians, and there were not enough resources for so many hunting people. All of this became the problem of the newly formed North-West Mounted Police. Small, but with no intention of being intimidated by natives, the force laid out the rules for the newcomers—the laws were inviolate. The Lakota could stay in Canada as long as they did not kill or steal, particularly across the international border. The Lakota granted the North-West Mounted Police, and its local commander Major Walsh, "Long Lance," both obedience and respect in return for the fair and consistent treatment they received.

Neither the United States nor Canadian governments wanted the Lakotas in Canada but could not figure out how to push them back. In the end, hunger did it for them. Swelled by the arrival of some of Crazy Horse's followers after his death, Sitting Bull's camp grew to 5,000. There just was not enough game for them all since the bison herds were staying almost exclusively south of the border. As early as 1879 some 200 lodges moved back across the border. Then even Sitting Bull's people had to cross into the United States to find bison. "All I am looking for is something for my children to eat," he explained. "But I will not remain south of the line one day longer than I can help."[45] The U.S. Army had watched the border carefully and the ambitious Nelson Miles seized his chance to strike at the infamous Sitting Bull. Miles clashed with stragglers at a hunting camp along the Milk River in July 1879, doing little damage but further cementing Sitting Bull's hated of Americans. "So long as there remains a gopher to eat I will not go back," he vowed.[46] However, hatred cannot sustain women and children, so by 1881 less than 200 Lakota remained in the hungry land of the Great Mother. On July 19, 1881, Sitting Bull led 45 men, 67 women, and 73 children into Fort Buford, Montana, to surrender. He was the last free leader of the mighty coalition that destroyed

Custer's command just five years earlier. Sitting Bull understood the significance of his act. "I wish it to be remembered that I was the last man of my tribe to surrender my rifle."[47]

By 1880, the U.S. Army had finally succeeded in clearing the western plains of native people. The major tribes of Lakota and Cheyenne allies had been forced onto reservations, as had their enemies the Crow. No nomadic hunters remained to roam the plains. Reservation life required a tremendous adjustment for a free-living people. Confined to the worst land in the West and required to abandon every vestige of their culture—from religious beliefs to economic pursuits—the Plains Tribes suffered terribly. Women often adjusted better than warriors as they could more easily adapt to different ways of pursuing traditional activities like meal preparation, child care, and artwork. Men however, whose entire identity focused on two roles—hunter and warrior— could not possibly adjust to a life which forbade either pursuit. The end of the wars on the northern plains opened a dark chapter in the lives of the indigenous residents.

NOTES

1. Gary Anderson, *Through Dakota Eyes: Narrative Accounts of the Minnesota Indian War of 1862*. St. Paul: Minnesota Historical Society Press, 1988, 293.

2. Duane Schultz, *Over the Earth I Come: The Great Sioux Uprising of 1862*. New York: St. Martin's Press, 1992, 28.

3. Anderson, 40–42.

4. Schultz, 49.

5. Anderson, 155.

6. Brown, 54.

7. Schultz, 237.

8. Schultz, 242.

9. Schultz, 258.

10. Schultz, 282.

11. Robert Utley, *The Indian Frontier of the American West, 1846–1890*. Albuquerque: University of New Mexico Press, 1984, 47.

12. Utley, *The Indian Frontier*, 117.

13. Robert W. Larson, *Red Cloud: Warrior-Statesman of the Lakota Sioux*. Norman: University of Oklahoma Press, 1997, 89.

14. Larson, 93.

15. William Tecumseh Sherman, in Larson, 102.

16. Utley, *Indian Frontier*, 119.

17. http://www.pbs.org/weta/thewest/resources/archives/four/ftlaram.htm.

18. Colin Taylor, *The Plains Indians*. London: Salamander Books, 1994, 235.

19. Colin Calloway, *Our Hearts Fell to the Ground: Plains Indian Views of How the West Was Lost*. New York: Bedford/St. Martin's, 1996, 154.

20. Brown, 276–77.

21. Robert Utley, *Bluecoats and Redskins: United States Army and the Indian, 1866–91*. London: Cassell, 1975, 244.

22. Brown, 285.

23. Robert Utley, *Cavalier in Buckskin: George Armstrong Custer and the Western Military Frontier*. Norman: University of Oklahoma Press, 1988, 143, 146.

24. Wooden Leg, in Jerome Greene, *Lakota and Cheyenne: Indian Views of the Great Sioux War, 1876–187*. Norman: University of Oklahoma Press, 1994, 4.

25. Brown, 287.

26. Thomas Marquis, interpreter, *Wooden Leg: A Warrior Who Fought Custer*. Lincoln: University of Nebraska Press, 1931, 200.

27. Robert Utley, *The Lance and the Shield: The Life and Times of Sitting Bull*. New York: Henry Holt and Co., 1993, 141.

28. Stephen Ambrose, *Crazy Horse and Custer: The Parallel Lives of Two American Warriors*. New York: Doubleday, 1975, 435

29. Marquis, 214.

30. Utley, *Lance and the Shield*, 148.

31. Calloway, *Hearts*, 146–147.

32. Calloway, *Hearts*, 145.

33. Marquis, 294.

34. Utley, *Lance and the Shield*, 169.

35. Utley, *Lance and the Shield*, 181.

36. Joe Starita, *The Dull Knifes of Pine Ridge: A Lakota Odyssey*. Lincoln: University of Nebraska Press, 1995, 40.

37. Starita, 40.

38. Starita, 42.

39. Starita, 43.

40. Brown, 344.

41. Brown, 345.

42. Starita, 57.

43. Starita, 57.

44. Utley, *Lance and the Shield*, 182.

45. Utley, *Lance and the Shield*, 206.

46. Utley, *Frontier Regulars*, 288.

47. Utley, *Frontier Regulars*, 288.

5

THE SOUTHERN PLAINS

Sitting Bull, Red Cloud, and Little Big Horn became fixtures in American history and served to define the struggle on the northern plains in the mid- and late 19th century. As the Lakota dealt with problems caused by the Oregon and Bozeman Trails, the tribes to their south—both allies and enemies—also had to cope with the arrival of strangers who coveted native land. The emigrant trails helped to split the bison into northern and southern herds so the people relying on those herds for sustenance also split. We can speak of the Southern Cheyenne who, while related to the Northern Cheyenne, pursued a distinct path in the late 19th century. South of Kansas were also diverse native peoples—Cherokee, Navajo, Apache, Comanche—who pursued their own strategies to survive a similar threat from white expansion.

INDIAN TERRITORY

In the early 19th century the U.S. government perceived the area west of the Mississippi, particularly directly south of Kansas, as a dumping ground for native peoples. Because it was thought that Indians could not co-exist with civilized whites, they had to be placed out of the path of natural U.S. expansion. From President Jefferson to President Jackson the solution to the Indian problem was to separate them from their valuable homelands that the whites desired and place the tribes on less desirable land. For over half a century that undesirable land was Indian Territory.

Under President Andrew Jackson's direction, Congress passed the Indian Removal Act in 1830. The terms required that the Five Nations—Cherokee, Creek, Choctaw, Chickasaw, and Seminole—relinquish all their land east of the Mississippi and relocate to Indian Territory. Tribal resistance led to favorable Supreme Court cases; however, by 1838 most of the members of these southeastern nations resided west of the Mississippi River. Once there, they had to rebuild their lives, including their governments, economies, and social systems. After the upheavals of the 1840s and 1850s, seemingly the last thing these nations wanted in the 1860s was warfare. But that is what came in 1861 with the outbreak of the Civil War.

When Americans went to war with each other in 1861 they repeatedly told native peoples that it was a white man's war. Much as they said in the American Revolution, officials declared that this conflict did not concern Indians. However, both the Union and the Confederacy soon realized the key geographic position of Indian Territory. At the very first escalation of tensions, citizens of the bordering states of Arkansas and Texas had pressured the residents of the Territory to ally with the Confederacy. Bound to the federal government by treaties, but to the south by strong economic and social ties, the Indian nations were in an unenviable and untenable position. When no practical promises of support came from the federal government, and unable to maintain the preferred neutrality, all five nations officially allied with the Confederacy (CSA) in 1861. Warfare had come to these newly arrived trans-Mississippi tribes and it would be bloody.

Political Considerations

The Five Nations charted an unusual path through the Civil War. Engaged in the white man's Civil War they fought both for and against organized American military forces, but not in the sense of Indian scouts. In Indian Territory the mostly acculturated Indian men were valued not for indigenous warrior tradition and unparalleled skills, but merely for more bodies in a conflict that would consume millions. As members of the Confederate military (and later the U.S. military when the Creek, Cherokee, and Seminole nations switched sides), native soldiers were expected to conform to white traditions encompassing drill, discipline, and military organization. Not surprisingly, they frequently ran afoul of a bureaucracy with which they had little experience on matters such as leave, enlistment terms, and behavior. Even more harmful for the tribes' future was the division that occurred among Indian peoples. By the end of the war members of the Creek, Cherokee, and Seminole nations wore both blue and gray uniforms on opposite sides of battlefields. This internal schism, an internal civil war, cost the tribes the one attribute they needed in the face of aggressive U.S. expansion—unity.

The native military experience in Indian Territory left a mixed record. Neither the United States nor the CSA respected their Indian allies. These troops typically received the worst supplies, from outdated weapons and condemned tents, to inadequate food and ammunition. The Union treated Indians as they would the U.S. Colored Troops. Indian men could not serve as commissioned officers, and instead were ruled by white officers who often had little understanding of Indian values or their motivation for engaging in the war. Colonel Charles DeMorse unapologetically stated his firmly held opinion that "the Indian is physiologically recognized as an inferior race." He added "no Indian is qualified by attainments for such duty as regulations of the army call for," due to the "well-known incapacity of that people to direct operations which require promptness and concentration of mind."[1] The Confederacy took a more enlightened approach, commissioning Indian officers and even promoting Cherokee Stand Watie to brigadier general. Watie was continually frustrated, despite his uniform stars, with the lack of support he received from the Confederate military establishment.

The general populations on both sides seemed mainly unaware that natives fought in their armies, much less appreciated their service. Most attention that Indian troops received was negative. After the battle of Pea Ridge, Arkansas, in 1862 the two sides engaged in an unflattering exchange of allegations of uncivilized behavior, pointing at non-American troops. The *New York Tribune* hurled accusations of scalping and other "barbarities" at native Confederate soldiers. The righteously indignant writers conveniently forgot that the government had a long tradition of paying bounties for Indian scalps. The CSA did little to defend their Indian allies, although Commander Earl Van Dorn counter-charged that Germans in the U.S. Army had murdered Confederate prisoners.

Despite the overt racism obvious in such charges and the lack of military support, Indian soldiers fought fairly well in the service of their respective allies. The fighting in the early years of the war focused mainly in the northeastern corner of Indian Territory, in the Cherokee and Creek nations. The first major set of engagements was particularly stressful. The Confederate Indian troops were asked to track down and fire upon fleeing civilians, primarily from the Creek nation. This naturally created a major challenge to concepts of identity and group affiliation as Cherokee and Creek soldiers questioned the consequence of shooting their kin. The whole affair, represented by the battles of Round Mountain, Chusto-talasah, and Chustenahlah in the fall of 1861, offered a challenging start to the war. Much as the U.S. Army routinely did, the Indians in Confederate service were expected to attack a primarily civilian native group. The issues raised by the demands of Confederate service were so difficult that an entire Cherokee Regiment gave up the cause. Before the battle of Chusto-talasah men "slipped away" from camp and from a Confederate military service that expected them to fight friends and relatives. Some went home, others to the federal Fort Gibson, and many joined the loyal Indians they had been supposed to fight. All the later condemnation of this act of "desertion" missed the complex pressures of kinship ties and tribal loyalty that complicated native military activity.

After the confusing start to the war, the conflict in Indian Territory deteriorated even more. Internal rivalries and conflicts, which simmered just below the surface in the 1850s, were spurred to the forefront by the larger war between blue and gray. Most of these tribal issues had their root in the long fight over Removal. The Creek continued to be divided between the pro-Removal McIntosh family which threw in with the CSA and the anti-Removal traditionalists who remained loyal to the United States. The Cherokee's longstanding rift over Removal had led to political assassinations in the 1850s. By 1862 the dispute was represented by pro-Removal Stand Watie, the Confederate general, and Chief John Ross who left the Cherokee Nation for Washington with federal troops in 1862 to prove his loyalty to the United States. The United States and the CSA provided the means for renewed war in Indian Territory. The stage was set for chaos within the Indian nations. As the tide of war ebbed and flowed across the region, the current victors sought revenge for long-standing grudges. Much of the destruction of Indian property was carried out by other Indians. So the Indians lost doubly.

The last three years of the war caused unbelievable hardship for residents. Most of the region descended into a state of anarchy as troops nominally under orders from the two national military commands moved through. In addition, the area's fluid authority attracted guerillas and outlaws. A few organized battles were fought. Honey Springs, on July 17, 1863, was the largest engagement of the war in

Cherokee chief John Ross struggled to protect his nation from the challenges of Removal, the Civil War, and white settlement. (Library of Congress)

Indian Territory, but in many ways it reflected the overall state of the war there as it was marked by mistaken troop movements and faulty weaponry. Most of the violence came in more random outbursts.

This level of disorganization created terrible uncertainty for civilians. As most of the men joined one side or the other or hid out to avoid conscription, only women, children, and the elderly remained at home. Women without male protection had to expect the arrival of armed men at any time. There were few reported cases of physical abuse but immense property destruction from the valuable to the silly. Men stole horses, livestock, chickens, plates, utensils, and pretty much anything else they could use. They also took women's dresses and staged fights with feather beds. It was not funny if they were your possessions which could not be replaced. Nothing could be replaced in wartime. As mills burned people had nowhere to grind grain. Stolen oxen meant no plowing; ransacked corncribs left no seed corn for next year. As the destruction spread, women found themselves increasingly isolated with no access to schools, doctors, or eventually friends and family. Many ended up as refugees in the Choctaw and Chickasaw nations or even Texas. The social dislocation of the communities of the Indian nations was nearly complete by 1865 and would take decades to heal. By then the forces of American expansion would have rolled across the Territory and the Creek, Cherokee, Choctaw, Chickasaw,

Chief Ross' niece and her husband George Murrell often hosted influential Cherokees at their Greek Revival-style Hunter's Home in the antebellum period. It is one of the few fine homes in the area to escape destruction during the war. (Library of Congress)

and Seminole nations would have lost their sovereign status and became citizens of the new state of Oklahoma.

The southeastern nations relocated to Indian Territory learned the painful reality that west of the Mississippi River was not far enough for whites in the mid-19th century. The lure of land and perceived opportunities hastened the flood of white immigrants. The whites' fascination with the shiny rock they called gold foretold hardship for the indigenous people who lived anywhere near it. Although California had the earliest and most famous gold rush, the allure of the mineral sparked rushes all over the West. Where gold was discovered Indian people suffered. They saw their lands invaded, resources wasted, and people impoverished. In the 1860s the Rocky Mountains and American Southwest became the latest target of miners.

SOUTHERN CHEYENNE

The Southern Cheyenne and Arapaho people shared the same culture as their kin to the north, but as the 19th century wore on they divided geographically so that they followed distinct social and economic patterns. Both northern and southern divisions of

Arapaho allied closely with the respective Cheyenne of their region. Interestingly, neither tribe learned much of the language of the other despite much cooperation in hunting, trade, and war. They relied on universal sign language which reached a high art on the plains. The southern groups dominated the country between the Platte River to the north and the Arkansas River to the south, central Kansas in the east to the Rockies in the west. The U.S. government even recognized the distinction when it began negotiating separate treaties on the northern and southern plains.

The Southern Cheyenne and Arapaho attracted the attention of the government because they lived and hunted in the high plains east of the Rockies. This put them directly in the path of the hordes rushing to Pike's Peak and the other Colorado gold discoveries. After the announcement of gold in the eastern Rockies, 80,000 immigrants flocked to the Pike's Peak area, south of Denver. Nothing could be allowed to retard the pursuit of wealth so the Indians would have to stay out of the way. With that goal the government negotiated the Treaty of Fort Wise in 1861. As with so many other treaties the government and the Indians did not understand what the other was asking for and the few signatures on the document did not represent the important tribal leaders. The Cheyenne certainly did not expect railroads to cross their hunting lands or to be forced onto an arid reservation south of the Arkansas River. The idea of whites that eastern Colorado had been freed of Indian claims was far from the truth. This set the course for bloody confrontations.

Colorado Territory formed quickly and with few attributes of civilization. Mining was a hard life and attracted rough individuals. The future of statehood, and with it the political aspirations of the territorial governor, John Evans, depended on the increase of a more settled white population. That would not happen unless the "wild" Indians were removed. In Evans' view the Cheyenne and Arapaho who thwarted his vision for the future by remaining free had to go. His opportunity for action came in 1864 when he heard rumors of impending Indian War and was predisposed to believe them.

Political Divisions

In fact, the major chiefs remained at peace with the whites. There had certainly been skirmishes between warriors and whites, many of which involved alcohol, but overall the tribe sought to avoid conflict. The Cheyenne leaders had a difficult choice to make. The arrival of whites had drastically altered their lives; on that everyone could agree. The question was how best to deal with the white threat to the Cheyenne people—to fight or to appease. Younger men, including the members of the legendary Cheyenne warrior group the Dog Soldiers, generally favored war to protect their lives. Other chiefs, particularly men entrusted with the safety of women and children, sought to accommodate whites to spare their people the hardships of war. Black Kettle and White Antelope were two major leaders among the chiefs who pursued the accommodation strategy. They had signed the Treaty of Fort Wise in 1861, but no one had pushed them toward a reservation so their bands continued to roam in the traditional patterns.

The upheavals of the Civil War unsettled everyone in eastern Colorado but still Indians and whites remained at peace. Governor Evans expected an Indian War and the military commander of the Colorado Volunteers raised for Civil War service needed one to occupy his troops. Colonel John Chivington, a Methodist minister dubbed the "fighting parson," had pushed back the only Confederate foray into the Union West and his career would stagnate without further military glory. When spring brought the usual raiding by young Cheyenne men, Chivington was prepared to respond quickly and harshly. The order to "burn villages and kill Cheyenne whenever and wherever found" went out to the troops.[2] Chivington would create an Indian War where none existed.

Native Warfare

Unfortunately, no one told the Cheyenne leaders that war was to be waged on their people. In the spring of 1864 Black Kettle and Chief Lean Bear led their bands northward from a winter village near Fort Larned, Kansas, to hunt bison. When Chivington's men challenged the Cheyenne along the Smoky Hill River they did not worry. Chief Lean Bear had just been to Washington, D.C. to see President Lincoln and carried papers with the Great White Father's signature. As he rode forward unarmed but with the papers, his presidential peace medal on his chest, Lean Bear took a bullet and fell in the dirt. The soldiers continued firing into Lean Bear's fallen body. The orders to "kill Cheyenne whenever" resulted in 28 deaths. Colorado had its Indian War.

White Colorado churned with turmoil over the issue of statehood and panic over the inflated reports of an Indian uprising. Warriors did steal livestock, and kill over two dozens whites that summer. Evans requested another cavalry regiment, the Third Colorado, raised solely to fight Indians. The Cheyenne were similarly upset by the unprovoked killing of Lean Bear. His brother Bull Bear—who led the aggressive Dog Soldier division of Cheyenne—still spoke for peace, but could not hold his young warriors for long in the face of continued white brutality. Chivington was about to drive the Dog Soldiers on the warpath.

Sand Creek Massacre

Chief Black Kettle still sought accommodation. The latest hostilities had cost his people so—despite opposition—the old chief met with Major Edward Wynkoop, commander of Fort Lyons, and came to terms. When Wynkoop jubilantly brought the Cheyenne chiefs to Denver for peace talks he did not foresee a chilly reception, but Governor Evans had not planned on this new twist. The Third Colorado had been raised to fight an Indian threat at Evans' insistence and now the threat was here to *talk*. Colorado could not maintain national attention if there was no Indian threat and military resources went to neighboring Kansas to fight Confederates. Chivington was equally thrown off by this idea of peace. His superior, General Samuel Curtis, declared that he wanted "no peace till the Indians suffer more." Chivington gained nothing from peace, so he blustered that he would fight the Indians until they lay down their arms which they could do at Fort Lyons.

Black Kettle had risked both violence from whites and opposition from some Cheyenne in making peace overtures. He remained committed to the harmony he believed could only come from such accommodation, so he moved quickly to fulfill the army's demand. Little Raven brought 113 Arapaho lodges to Fort Lyon and Black Kettle came to say his 115 lodges were 35 miles away. When Black Kettle arrived he found his counterpart Major Wynkoop had been summoned to the East. The fort could not feed the Indians that Chivington said could secure peace there so they were told to remain nearby and hunt to feed themselves.

The Cheyenne thus remained at Sand Creek in November 1864. While they were there the settled village offered a tempting target for those who wanted an Indian War. Colonel Chivington had been derided as the leader of the "Bloodless Third" since his new unit had seen no action. With their 100-day enlistment slipping by, Chivington had few opportunities left for a grand engagement. Chivington secretly moved his force to Fort Lyon whose new commander had no sympathy for the Cheyenne as Wynkoop had and so supported the plan to attack the village. To those officers who protested that the Cheyenne were under the protection of the U.S. government Chivington replied "damn any man that was in sympathy with the Indians."[3]

Black Kettle's encampment on the small creek had about 100 lodges or 500 people, which gave them about 200 warriors, not the 700 that Chivington claimed. Left Hand had eight or nine Arapaho lodges nearby. After all the hostilities and confusion of the summer the people were on edge. But they had to eat, so most of the men went out to hunt, leaving the village short of warriors. At dawn on November 29, 1864, Chivington ordered his 700 cavalry troopers to attack the sleeping village. According to eyewitness George Bent, the attack caused utter confusion. He describes people rushing out of their lodges partially dressed, women and children screaming, men going back to tipis to grab weapons while others sprinted to get to the pony herd. In the chaos Black Kettle tried to calm people, calling out that the soldiers would not hurt them. The chief "ran this American flag up to the top of his lodge, with a small white flag tied right under it, as he had been advised to do in case he should meet with any troops out on the prairies."[4] Then the troops opened fire from their positions surrounding the village. Chief White Antelope, who had signed the Fort Wise Treaty and repeatedly told his people that whites were good, stood in front of his tipi and sang his death song until the soldiers' bullets found their mark and he fell dead.

What unfolded next can only be described as a massacre. George Bent, a half-blood Cheyenne, remembers running up a dry creek bed to escape the soldiers. As they ran the cavalry fired down on them from both sides. "The dry bed of the creek was now a terrible sight: men, women, and children lying thickly scattered on the sand, some dead and the rest too badly injured to move."[5] The wounded dug shallow pits for protection from the constant firing that continued all day. Black Kettle snuck back to where his wife had fallen and found she was not dead but alive with nine separate wounds. As the undisciplined volunteers headed back to the Indian camp for the night they killed, scalped, and mutilated the wounded.

They were terribly mutilated, lying there in the water and sand; most of them in the bed of the creek, dead and dying, making many struggles. They were so badly mutilated and covered with sand and water that it was very hard for me to tell one from another. I saw the bodies of those lying there cut all to pieces, worse mutilated than any I ever saw before;

the women cut all to pieces. With knives; scalped; their brains knocked out; children two or three months old; all ages lying there, from sucking infants up to warriors.

John Smith[6]

The survivors spent a terrifying night. The temperature dropped and a bitter wind swept the plains. Most people were half-naked and injured. Those who could move gathered grass for small fires in an attempt to warm the wounded. They called out into the night so anyone who fled the battle and wandered on the plains could find them. Others continued the grim task of creeping down to the streambed in search of relatives, occasionally staggering back with a wounded person. The closest respite was the Indian camps on Smoky Hill, over fifty miles away. They started the journey before daybreak and were soon met by relief parties who provided food and horses for the trip. The Indians feared they would be followed by the army, but Chivington's men had already turned toward Denver to celebrate their victory.

As the Cheyenne faced the loss of all of their possessions and almost 150 of their people, the Third Colorado rode into Denver to a heroes' welcome. They carried bison robes, blankets, and clothing looted from the Cheyenne camp. The scalps they took were displayed at a local theater to public acclaim and some soldiers sported tobacco pouches made of flesh from Cheyenne women. The behavior of men wearing U.S. insignia at Sand Creek may have been acceptable on the frontier, but when reports came in to Washington many easterners were outraged at the barbarity that shocked even during wartime. Investigations were launched, but Chivington and his officers had since mustered out and thus escaped sanctions. In the meantime, their actions sparked a southern plains war that would cost the government dearly.

But for that hostile butchery it is a fair presumption that all subsequent wars with the Cheyennes and Araphoes and their kindred tribes might possibly have been averted.

General Nelson Miles[7]

The Cheyenne who escaped the slaughter at Sand Creek quickly spread the news of the massacre. Outraged warriors from both Northern and Southern Cheyennes and Arapaho, Lakota, Comanche, and Kiowa nations sought revenge. Even the three half-Cheyenne sons of trader William Bent rejected their father's people now and rode with their mother's Cheyenne relatives. Chivington's attack had destroyed the lives and power of the chiefs who favored peace with whites. That strategy had clearly failed. The Dog Soldier band of Cheyenne who had refused to go to Sand Creek with the accommodationist chiefs now gained ascendency in councils and prepared for war.

The white man has taken our country, killed all of our game; was not satisfied with that, but killed our wives and children. Now no peace. . . . We loved the whites until we found out they lied to us, and robbed us of what we had. We have raised the battle ax until death.

Chief Leg-in-the-Water[8]

The Indian revenge struck the southern plains hard. Warriors attacked wagon trains, military outposts, and settlements. They ripped up miles of telegraph wire, plundered food supplies, and killed whites. The mutual desire for revenge helped unite the southern and northern wings of the Cheyenne tribe as they camped and raided together with common cause. In July 1865, the Cheyenne cooperated with Red Cloud's Oglala Lakota in a punishing attack of 3,000 warriors on the army's post at North Platte after which the Lakota returned to their home country, satisfied the whites had been taught a lesson.

The army did regret the cost of the Cheyenne War, which had reached $40 million. In order to buy a return of peace, the army offered apologies and reparations for Chivington's destruction at Sand Creek. They also insisted that the Cheyenne and Arapaho remove to the south of the Arkansas River. Black Kettle replied that "It will be a very hard thing to leave the country that God gave us. Our friends are buried there and we hate to leave these grounds."[9] However, eventually the Southern Cheyenne leaders—mostly old, peaceful chiefs—agreed to accept lands in Kansas and Indian Territory intended to keep them out of the way of whites and thus reduce opportunities for conflict. The government had finally driven the Cheyenne and Arapaho out of Colorado. Or so they thought.

Black Kettle of the Cheyenne and Little Raven of the Arapaho remained respected chiefs. But they could not control the younger warriors, especially Cheyenne Dog Soldiers who pledged undying resistance to the whites after Sand Creek. Those bands moved onto their traditional bison hunting territory in 1866, ignoring any piece of paper they did not sign which said the Cheyenne could no longer use their ancestral lands. The United States would not tolerate defiance of its scheme to rid the plains of Indians, so General Winfield Scott Hancock arrived to force Cheyenne cooperation. The Civil War hero had little patience for Indians. When warriors arrived to council wearing U.S. military overcoats that they had captured, he was not amused. Blustering, demanding, and threatening, Hancock earned the Cheyenne name "Old Man of the Thunder." His intent to march his troops to the Cheyenne camp brought memories of Sand Creek and stiff resistance from leader Roman Nose. Hancock's troops found only an abandoned Cheyenne camp which he promptly inventoried and burned—251 tipis, 962 bison robes, 436 saddles—everything the people owned. Furious at this latest attack the Dog Soldiers exploded onto the plains in a flurry of violence against whites. Hancock's approach had been a disaster so the army would try another council.

The Southern Cheyenne and Arapaho had lost a great deal of their power and wealth in the past five years but remained a force to be reckoned with. The United States planned a commission which met at Medicine Lodge Creek in 1867 to forge a lasting peace for the southern plains. The gathering included 4,000 Arapaho, Kiowa, and Comanche, but without the Cheyenne Dog Soldiers the meeting would mean little. Roman Nose and his 500 warriors finally made a triumphant entrance displaying all the power of a mounted force that had few rivals in the world. Despite their display of power, the Cheyenne could not force the government to allow them to remain in their homeland. By the terms of the treaty, which Roman Nose did not sign, all Cheyenne had to move south of the Arkansas River. Chief Black Kettle led his people south, establishing a village on the Washita River in Indian Territory.

Native Warfare

None of the government promises of food and supplies were honored during the winter of 1867–1868 so the Cheyenne went hungry. Restless groups of young men drifted northward to find food. A new commander in Kansas, General Phil Sheridan, was eager to engage any Indians his men could find. He created an irregular force of scouts to seek out Indian camps. In September 1868, the scouts were spotted along the Arikaree Fork of the Republican River by a mixed group of Lakota and Cheyenne. Over 500 warriors prepared to hit the soldiers in one coordinated attack. As happened to similar plans so many times, a few young men disobeyed the plan, attacked early, and alerted the whites. Now the warriors had lost the element of surprise while the army scouts holed up on an island they named Beecher's. Roman Nose arrived to take command even though his powerful medicine which kept him safe from bullets had been compromised earlier. Roman Nose was shot in the hip and died that night. Another great resistance leader had fallen. The attacking force kept the scouts pinned down for eight days, then abandoned the "Fight When Roman Nose Was Killed" (also known as the Battle of Beecher's Island).

Washita Massacre

After the loss of the charismatic leader Roman Nose, many young warriors drifted south to reunite with relatives in Black Kettle's camp. Black Kettle knew their raiding brought danger to the rest of the people, but could not compel the actions of individual Cheyenne. He was, however, ever on the alert to new threats and vowed never to be caught by surprise as he had been at Sand Creek. The old chief could not know that Generals Sherman and Sheridan had planned a war on the Cheyenne and cared little which ones had abided by treaty obligations. However, Black Kettle had heard rumors of troops in the area so he traveled over 100 miles to ask the commander of Fort Cobb for permission to move his village to the protection of the fort or to camp near the Kiowa and Comanche—he was refused. Commanding General Hazen assured the chief that he would not be attacked in his village. Dissatisfied with this response, Black Kettle was determined to ride out to meet the troops the next day and proclaim his peaceful intentions. Black Kettle never got the chance.

On November 27, 1868, the old chief awoke to hear a woman wailing, "soldiers, soldiers!" This could not happen to his people twice! Yet, here was Lieutenant Colonel George Custer's Seventh Cavalry band playing their signature song "Garry Owen" as they charged the sleeping village from four sides. Black Kettle grabbed his pony and swung his wife up behind him. She had been left for dead at Sand Creek, but had miraculously survived and now they endured the nightmare together again. As the pony approached the river ford Black Kettle held up his hand in a peace gesture to the advancing soldiers. Both the chief and his wife fell in a hail of bullets before the troopers rode over their bodies in the mud.

The old peace chief had not survived the second massacre of his people by the U.S. Cavalry. Women in camp sang death songs as warriors tried to hold off the attack and buy some time for escape. Custer's men finished their work quickly. They pursued those who fled, killing 103 and capturing 53, almost all women and children. They also shot the entire Cheyenne pony herd, all 900 animals, and burned tipis, robes, food, and weapons. The rapid destruction only ended because warriors from nearby camps arrived to contest the slaughter and Custer feared a real fight. The slaughter at Washita continued the effort begun at Sand Creek. The Southern Cheyenne lost the resources, leadership, and ability to live as free people and resist U.S. expansion into their homelands.

KIOWA AND COMANCHE

I don't want to settle. I love to roam over the prairies. There I feel free and happy, but when we settle down we grow pale and die.

Satanta, Kiowa war chief [10]

The U.S. Army under the direction of General Sheridan was not about to rest on its "successes." Cavalry would comb the southern plains until all those Indians deemed "hostiles," which meant everyone who was not unarmed and immobile on a reservation, surrendered their freedom. The next targets were the Kiowa and Comanche. Representatives of these nations had signed the Medicine Lodge Treaty in 1867, which pledged them to reservations in Indian Territory where the government would provide the tools for a new lifestyle. However, these supreme horsemen did not want a new sedentary life: farming was not for them. They steadfastly resisted government efforts to change them.

The Kiowa's reputation for resistance thrived on the leadership of bold, talented chiefs Lone Wolf, Satanta (Set-t'ainte), and Satank. These men offered an option for those Indians who sought to remain free. Traditionals saw little incentive to sacrifice their ancestral ways. It had become obvious that, if tribes followed government directives and went to reservations and lived quietly, they soon died of starvation and neglect. Satanta observed that bad Indians got the most while those who submitted to the white road got nothing. He decided that he liked the breech-loading guns of the white man's road, but not the corn. As the chiefs told the government, the only way to get attention and thus presents was to kill whites. Every time officials came to negotiate with "problem"

Indians they distributed goods. Once peacefully on the reservation the same Indians received little attention.

As Quaker Indian agents struggled to carry out the planned transformation of hunters into farmers, the Kiowa men looked on with scorn. What could mighty Kiowa warriors learn from pacifist men doing women's work? Kiowa men had no intention of giving up hunting and raiding. When one agent begged them to stop raiding into Texas a chief replied that if the Great White Father did not want young men to raid in Texas, then he must move Texas farther away where they could not find it. Raids into Texas yielded captives which could be ransomed. Occasionally, there were greater prizes.

In 1871, Satanta led a Texas raid to a place known as Salt Creek Prairie. The hidden warriors allowed a small wagon train to pass unscathed, but hit the next larger train hard, killing 7 whites and taking 41 government mules. The so-called Salt Creek Prairie Massacre outraged one of the members of the first, spared train—the commander-in-chief of the U.S. Army, General Sherman. The fact that Sherman had traveled to the region to appraise the situation shows the power of the Kiowa. Satanta remained unimpressed by the show of army brass, proudly taking credit for the Salt Creek raid. But the Kiowa chief had met his match in power. Sherman ordered the arrest of chiefs Satanta, Satank, and Big Tree. After chaotic scuffling when the chiefs tried to shoot Sherman all three were on wagons to be taken to Texas for trial. Old Satank had no intention of submitting to the white justice system. In the wagon he shouted that he would die the first day and that his people could find his bones alongside the road. Under his blanket Satank struggled to free his manacled hands. When he got his hands loose he seized a concealed knife, rose up, and stabbed a soldier. As Satank grabbed a carbine and tried to fire guards poured in bullets. The old chief died quickly and his body was tossed to the road where it was soon scalped by Tonkawa scouts. Satank had chosen to die in the warrior tradition, exhibiting bravery and resistance to the end. Satanta and Big Tree were tried and convicted of murder and given a death sentence, which was quickly commuted to life imprisonment for fear of an Indian War. Two years later Lone Wolf secured their release under conditions that prevented them from acting as Kiowa warriors and leaders. When the Kiowa went to war in 1874 Satanta did resign his position as war chief and passed on his medicine lance and shield. However, the government returned him to prison because he did not remain peacefully on the reservation as ordered. Back in prison in Texas, Satanta saw little reason to live—his life as a free Kiowa was over. He slashed his own wrists, then died after jumping out of a window at the prison hospital. One by one, the Kiowa lost their best resistance leaders.

Red River War

The violence that landed Satanta back in a white man's prison has been named the Red River War. The Red River divides Indian Territory and Texas. It marked the boundary for the many tribes banished to the catchall of Indian Territory. Indian hunters could not follow their main food source, the bison, across the arbitrary line. However, white traders from Kansas set up trading posts in Texas to profit from the indiscriminate market hunting of the remaining bison herds. The endless slaughter of the central animal in their life infuriated the southern Plains Indians. By some estimates whites destroyed over 95 percent of the 3.7 million bison killed from 1872–1874. The Comanche tribe which had shared many of the Kiowa's experiences became really enraged. At their Sun Dance the medicine man Isatai called for a war to stop the slaughter and save the bison. His power was impressive, as it was said that he could stop white men's bullets. Soon 700 warriors following mixed-blood Comanche chief Quanah Parker targeted the hunters' camp at Adobe Walls, north of the Canadian River in Texas. On June 27, 1864, the assembled Comanche, Kiowa, and Cheyenne force attacked the settlement's buildings sheltering about two dozen whites. The hunters' long-range buffalo rifles allowed them to hold off the warriors until they finally retired with a handful of dead. Frustrated at their inability to make progress against this enemy, the fighters dispersed to take revenge on any whites they encountered. The government reacted quickly to this latest attempt of the Indians to assert their freedom. Just as they had on the northern plains, the government declared that all Indians not enrolled on reservations by August 3, 1874, would be attacked as hostiles. Five columns of infantry and cavalry prepared to enforce the order.

Just as their northern brethren found in 1876, the nomadic people of the southern plains found they had run out of room by 1874. Their beloved landscape was now slashed by telegraph lines, railroads, roads, and settlements. The whites had even penetrated the hunting grounds where the last of the great bison herds roamed. It was a desperate time for everyone as leaders struggled to imagine how to feed, clothe, and protect their people. Some took their depressed followers into the dreaded reservations in the hopes of surviving on the government's promises. Others, knowing the government would strip them of arms and horses and force them to farm on reservations, chose to resist the order.

Lone Wolf's Kiowas, along with some Comanches and Cheyennes, sought out Palo Duro Canyon. This spot, little known to whites, provided an oasis for both people and the beleaguered bison. Here the people killed the animals they needed and prepared meat, hides, utensils, and other supplies. The few hundred Indians and their 2,000 ponies settled in for the coming winter. On September 26, 1874, this idyll was shattered by the assault of the cavalry under the command of Ranald Mackenzie. The warriors held off the charge long enough for women and children to escape. Mackenzie's men did not pursue the fleeing civilians—there were other military columns to do that. Instead they rounded up the Indians' prized possession—their pony herd—and after awarding the best to their Indian scouts, shot 1,048 animals. The horror, the sense of loss, and the sheer waste of the action devastated the Indians.

The non-reservation Indians had been deprived of anything they needed for existence. There was no way to survive the winter without transport, food, or shelter. One by one the chiefs led their people into the forts to surrender. Lone Wolf brought in 252 followers, while Quanah Parker came in with 407 people. This humiliation was not the end for the great leaders of the plains. Lone Wolf was among 34 warriors sent into captivity at Fort Marion in Florida. As the leaders sickened and died in prison their people suffered on the reservations. The bison also suffered the fate of the people whose lives were so tightly intertwined with the animals'. Within a decade of the Kiowa's and Comanche's surrender fewer than 1,000 bison remained as remnants of the once mighty herds of 30 million that had darkened the plains. To the Kiowa this truly meant the end of their world.

The buffalo saw that their day was over. They could protect their people no longer. Sadly, the last remnant of the great herd gathered in council, and decided what they would do. . . . the face of the mountain opened. . . . inside the world was fresh and green. . . . Into this world of beauty the buffalo walked, never to be seen again.

Old Lady Horse, Kiowa[11]

NAVAJO LONG WALK

Not all people in the southern portion of the United States relied on the bison. The native peoples of the American Southwest lived in distinctly different lifestyles. The ancient pueblo cultures of settled

This 1874 *Harper's Weekly* illustration shows the business of hide hunters who ravaged the natives' food supply for profit. (Library of Congress)

agricultural villages had been devastated by the violence and disease of the white explorers and settlers since the 16th century. The nomadic and semi-nomadic Athapaskan speakers, the Navajo and Apache, had not been as severely impacted by the invasions. Their lives had continued on relatively unchanged, even enhanced by the arrival of European horses and livestock. All that was about to change in the late 19th century.

A traditional Navajo medicine man wearing a blanket and turquoise jewelry. (Library of Congress)

The Navajo (or *Dinè*) followed a semi-nomadic pattern of livestock raising and orchard cultivation. They dominated a large territory of northern Arizona and New Mexico. The high desert they occupied held little appeal for American farmers so the Navajo had felt little of the land pressure that annihilated tribes in more hospitable climates. The Navajo coexisted in mutual distrust with the New Mexican settlers, each side raiding the other regularly, but the weak Spanish and then Mexican governments did not carry out a concerted effort to be rid of the Navajo problem. However, in 1846 Stephen Watts Kearny led an American army into New Mexico to claim the region for the United States. The Navajo now had a new white father and things would change quickly. The arrival of the United States would throw off the harmony that was critical to Navajo life.

Social Organization

The Navajo world focused on harmony. This meant careful understanding of the powers in the world—animal, spirit, weather, land, gender, geography—and strict adherence to the rules created to ensure balance between powers. Navajo children grew up with a strong sense of their place within their kin groups and within the Dinè territory. Girls in this matrilineal society trained for their future roles as wives, mothers, farmers, potters, and weavers. Young boys learned early to ride, run, shoot, and endure hardships in order to be stronger warriors in the constant fight against their traditional enemies the Ute. The Ute and Navajo engaged in nearly continuous low-scale warfare that rewarded victors with the spoils of well-conducted raids. The impending conflict with the U.S. Army would be a very different sort of winner-take-all contest that would shake the Navajo world to its roots.

The Navajo had little reason to care which white people flew a flag and claimed their land. They knew that the gods had sent the Navajo to live between the four sacred mountains and there they would stay. No new flag could end the hatred that years of livestock raiding and slave capturing had created between the Mexican settlers and the Indians. The Navajo excelled at living in Navajoland and could see no reason to change anything. The United States had other plans. A confident, expanding culture emboldened by the ideas of spreading civilization looked with horror at the semi-nomadic lifestyle of the Navajo. Clearly these Indians now under the jurisdiction of the United States would have to change.

Political Organization

The first attempts at changing the Navajo were traditional treaties which accomplished little. The Navajo had no organized, central government that could speak for or require anything of the people. Kin groups followed skilled headmen who gained power through action. If the United States wanted to coerce Navajo behavior it would need a new tactic. By the Civil War in the 1860s the new approach arrived with new management. General James Carleton came to Arizona from California where the United States had herded the remaining indigenous people onto agriculturally focused reservations. He planned to apply the same "solution" to the Navajo problem.

The Navajo leaders like Manuelito had taken advantage of the United States' distraction in the 1860s. It certainly looked as though the Indians had won the struggle with the U.S. forces in the region. Since 1858, the Navajo and the army had been engaged in nearly constant conflict. The warriors sought revenge for the slaughter of their people by army troops at Fort Fauntleroy at Bear Spring,

Navajo chief Manuelito waged an ongoing battle to keep whites out of Navajo territory. (Library of Congress)

New Mexico. Then, in 1861, the blue-coated troopers abandoned the forts. The power vacuum created by the United States' need for soldiers in the East to fight the Confederates offered the Navajo a perfect opportunity to raid unchecked. The Navajo stole more than 30,000 sheep and killed hundreds of New Mexicans in 1862. The settlers demanded an all-out, retaliatory war. James Carleton would give it to them.

Carleton had strong ideas about the proper way to deal with the Navajo. One author described Carleton's entrance into the region as one of the most tragic collisions in the U.S. government's long, sorry relationship with Native Americans. A New Englander, Carleton blamed New Mexico's backwardness on the Navajo conflict. He set out to "cure this great evil from which the territory has been so long a prey."[12] Remove the Navajo and the territory would flourish. So with little government consultation or oversight, Carleton set out to remove 12,000 Navajo people from their homelands. He demanded that these semi-nomadic, livestock-rearing people move to a desolate reservation and become farmers.

The future home of the Navajo was to be Bosque Redondo, a broad valley of the Pecos River in southwestern New Mexico. Carleton clung to the idea of the site as an oasis despite all reports to the contrary. An army report pointed out that the bitter, alkaline Pecos River made the location unsuitable for a fort or reservation. Undeterred, Carleton crafted plans to force the Navajo to Bosque Redondo—"entire subjugation or destruction . . . are the alternatives." The plan required all the Navajo—men, women, children, and elderly—to walk 400 miles to reach the new site. The general admitted it would be difficult to wrench people from their homes but decided that "severity would be the most humane course." The roundup and movement, enshrined in history as the *Long Walk*, was extremely severe.

The Navajo knew what the army wanted and were determined to resist it with all their strength. The people had spent generations fighting both indigenous and invading enemies. Hundreds of years of conflict against the Spanish and Mexicans created clever techniques that could be used against the U.S. Army. The Navajo knew their land intimately and had great confidence that they would prevail.

The U.S. Army came in the form of 1,000 men under the command of legendary mountain man Kit Carson. Previously married to Arapaho and Cheyenne women, Carson had years of experience among Indians as a trapper and scout. Now, in a blue uniform, he took orders from General Carleton. Those orders were to round up the Navajo and compel their removal to Bosque Redondo. The only problem was that when the enlisted soldiers and New Mexican volunteers arrived there were no Navajo to fight. The Navajo used their traditional skills in stealth and endurance to disappear into their vast, rugged homeland. The Indians obviously would not offer themselves up as an easy military target so Carson had to adjust his strategy. This would not be a quick raid but a slow methodical war of attrition. Carson employed a scorched earth policy in order to drive the Navajo out of hiding. If his men could not find people to attack, they would attack what they could find in a guerilla war. They set out to burn orchards, slaughter livestock, and destroy homes. Thus the army began a campaign of harassment aimed at demoralizing the Navajo by harassing them constantly.

This was a new experience for the Navajo. Like most other Indian groups they excelled at fast, hit-and-run raids with limited objectives. They usually fought for short periods in specific seasons, away from their living places. Now the people could not get away from war. The soldiers waited to strike anyone they found. People could not gather fruit, tend herds, or engage in important spiritual rituals because of the constant danger. The Ute Indian scouts who rode with Carson guarded every known water supply, every salt gathering place. The U.S. troops destroyed wheat fields, cornfields, and melon patches. They dug up food caches, took or killed livestock, and even destroyed pots and baskets so people could not carry food. Carson figured that he burned two million pounds of food. Naturally, he expected this to "cause actual starvation and oblige them to come in and accept emigration to the Bosque Redondo."[13]

The plan was harsh but effective and by the winter of 1863 many people were suffering. There was little incentive to surrender, however, once a small group of leaders went to Fort Canby in peace only to be imprisoned, forced to bury dead dogs, and eventually shot. The stupidity of the regular army frustrated Carson,

Kit Carson invaded beautiful Canyon de Chelly, striking a blow at the heart of the Navajo nation. (National Archives & Records Administration/ Double Delta)

who realized he had not yet come close to breaking the will of the Navajo. That would require an invasion he had been avoiding.

Despite all their destruction, Carson's men had not entered the tribal stronghold, Canyon de Chelly. This impressive canyon is actually made up of four main gorges and numerous side ravines. It had provided shelter and sustenance for humans for thousands of years as the Anasazi ruins along its walls attest. Canyon de Chelly provided all the Navajo needed to survive—fresh water, flat lands for 3,000 peach trees, grasses for herds of sheep. The Navajo viewed it as the heart of their people, as a sanctuary. Several gods, including the powerful Spider Woman, lived in the canyon. Surely the spirits would not allow whites to enter this sacred space.

But the Navajo did not trust their fate entirely to the gods. Where two large gorges met, Fortress Rock rose up 800 feet from the desert floor. Ancient Indians had carved footholds up the towering spire. There was space for hundreds to camp on top, as well as caves for protection and pockets in the rock that held water. Here the Indians stockpiled food like smoked mutton, piñon nuts, berries, dried grain, and peaches, and cached blankets and water carriers. After improving the old toeholds, the men bridged the last gap in the climb with trees brought from 25 miles away. One cold day in December 1863 the people started up to the hideout prepared to wait for months.

Carson had delayed the difficult task of invading the canyon, but Carleton drove him on, so on January 12, 1864, Carson led most of his 500 men through six inches of snow to the western mouth of Canyon de Chelly at present-day Chinle, Arizona. A detachment of 100 soldiers entered the eastern end of the canyon, passing directly under the 300 refugees huddled on Fortress Rock, while Carson led his men into the western end. As the soldiers sought out the enemy it became apparent that the Navajo had been elusive but not immune to the army's efforts. The eastern invasion captured eight scared and hungry women and children. The commander described them as "in an almost famished condition, half-starved and naked."[14] The scorched earth policy had clearly caused much suffering among the Navajo. Now that the army had invaded their most sacred area the people struck back in any way they could. Soldiers reported that Indians on the rim threw down rocks and sticks trying to stop the march through the canyon. Sticks and stones were no match for rifle fire and many Navajo were shot, others captured.

The hundreds huddled on Fortress Rock remained safe from rifle fire but risked dying from dehydration. As the snows had melted the rock crevices dried up and the people had no access to water. The army engaged in a brief skirmish that killed or wounded 20 warriors and then camped at the creek to deny the refugees access to water. Navajo leaders on Fortress Rock could either watch their people die or come up with a risky plan to obtain water. On a dark night the people formed a long line along the treacherous path all the way down to Tsalie Creek. While the soldiers slept, Navajo warriors lowered gourds on yucca ropes from a twenty-foot ledge over the stream. All night they passed the filled gourds up along the chain to the top. This daring act, recorded only by Navajo oral history, ensured the freedom of the 300 refugees who were never captured by Carson.

Most other Navajo were not so lucky. They could not hold out without the food and supplies the army had destroyed. When 60 Indians surrendered to Carson they told the tale of their people.

Because of what your soldiers have done we are all starving. Many of our women and children have already died of hunger. We would have come in a long time ago, but we believed this was a war of extermination.[15]

This declaration convinced Carson of his approaching success and he ordered his men to lay waste to everything in Canyon de Chelly. They were to burn every home, every field, kill all the animals, and shoot any Navajo who resisted or tried to escape. As a final insult to the Navajo, Carson ordered every one of the 3,000 peach trees to be cut down even though they bore no fruit in winter. The destruction of their precious, well-tended orchards came as a sharp psychological blow to the Navajo. The army truly ripped out the heart of the Navajo nation.

Carson's unremitting violence finally paid off. Freezing, starving, homeless Navajo began surrendering. By mid-February 1864, 2,500 Indians camped around Fort Canby awaiting Carleton's orders which came soon enough. Carleton followed his grand plan to place all the Navajo on a reservation in New Mexico where they would recreate themselves as Christian farmers. But first they would have to get there. The trip, the *Long Walk*, would cost the people dearly.

Groups of several thousand Navajo began the journey throughout March 1864. The harsh winter weather magnified the suffering of the nearly naked people. They had already lost hundreds of relatives during Carson's war and then hundreds more at the fort. Now the hardships of travel and the emotional cost of leaving their homeland killed many more. Of a group of 2,400 who walked out of Fort Canby, 197 died en route. This pattern repeated in all the units on the forced march. Numbers only tell part of the story; it is hard to calculate the effect of removal on the Navajo. They understood their homeland to be the center of the world. They had always been told never to leave the four sacred mountains or their medicine; their spiritual harmony would not operate. So now they truly walked into the unknown as the sacred mountains receded into the distance.

The physical toll of the journey was devastating. Most Navajo had been weakened and sickened by the year of losses to Carson. The food the army provided on the march was often worse than nothing. The rancid bacon made them retch, while coffee beans without grinders were useless. The army issued wheat flour which most Navajo had never seen so they stuffed uncooked flour into their mouths and got sick. The army also abused their captives. Soldiers raped women, shot elders who fell behind, and allowed traditional enemies to steal Navajo children along the route. People drowned crossing rivers, dropped from exhaustion and starvation. All those bodies of loved ones had to be left behind. The army allowed no retrieval of bodies.

Some chiefs held out as long as they could. Manuelito—whose people had been slaughtered at Fort Fauntleroy—remained wary of the whites. He did not see why he had to move.

Why must we go to the Bosque? We have never stolen or murdered, and have at all times kept the peace we promised General Canby. . . . I am doing no harm to anyone. I will not leave my country. I intend to die here.

Manuelito[16]

Navajo who escaped returned to Arizona with terrible stories about the new reservation that strengthened the resolve of those still free, although most would eventually surrender.

After the tortuous journey marred by hundreds of trail deaths, the survivors arrived at Fort Sumner, the army headquarters at Bosque Redondo. They found a wasteland. The poor, arid region could never support the 8,000 Indians crammed onto it. All the trees had been cut so no firewood existed. The army had not provided housing so people dug crude pits for shelter. These formerly successful native ranchers now "lived like prairie dogs." Then Carleton tried to force these semi-nomadic people, used to thousand of acres of room, to live in apartment-style dwellings. Navajo men had to dig a seven-mile irrigation ditch to water the fields that Carleton envisioned feeding the Indians. But each year the crops failed and Carleton was forced to feed the captive Indians which he did by providing food condemned for army use. The whole grand plan had produced nothing but misery. Slowly, the army realized the disaster Carleton had created.

Would any sensible man select a spot for a reservation for 8,000 Indians where the water is scarcely bearable, where the soil is poor and cold, and where the muskite [mesquite] roots 12 miles distance are the only wood for the Indians to use?

A. B. Norton[17]

After seemingly endless visits and evaluations by government officials the United States decided that Bosque Redondo had been a mistake. In May 1868, General William Tecumseh Sherman traveled to New Mexico to assess the situation for himself. Sherman found the Navajo "sunk into a condition of absolute poverty and despair." He met with Navajo leader Barboncito who told him that "we know that this land does not like us. It seems that whatever we do causes death."[18] Faced with radically reduced army funding in the post–Civil War period, Sherman had no interest in paying to feed Indians who used to be self-sufficient. He would send the Navajo back to their homes. The Navajo had to surrender much of their homeland to go back. They lost the rights to the four sacred mountains, but still they returned to a huge territory and it included Canyon de Chelly. Many nations had fared far worse in their struggle with the U.S. Army. However, the experience of warfare, forced removal, and captivity in New Mexico remained buried deep in the Navajo psyche. For over a century, Navajo have carried stones from their homeland to the site of Bosque Redondo to provide those who perished there with a connection to home. The Navajo never forgot the war waged against the people by the bluecoats.

APACHE WARS

The Navajo were not the only Indians incarcerated at Bosque Redondo. In their midst the government thrust a small unwilling band of Mescalero Apache. These unhappy people represented just a portion of the group 19th-century whites came to fear above all others—the Apache. The U.S. fascination and obsession with the Apache arose because they were the last major native group to be forced onto reservations by the army, and because they excelled at skills of warfare which American culture admired. Feared, admired, respected, and hated, the Apache presented the last military challenge to U.S. domination of the American continent.

Economic Life

They call themselves N'de, or Dènè, "the people," but are best known to history as Apache. Anthropologists place the Apache people with the Navajo in the linguistic group Athapaskans, explaining their residence in the Southwest as a result of migration. However, the Apache people know that their god Usen gave them homes in the West and taught them how to thrive there with skills in healing, hunting, and fighting. The men adapted well to the region, hunting deer, mountain lion, and antelope while women collected cactus fruit, nuts, and berries. The people did not farm but could trade with or raid those who did. The arrival of Europeans brought new types of food such as beef, and the acquisition of Spanish horses provided a new form of transportation. Horses allowed the Apache to roam vast territories of the Southwest in pursuit of the nomadic hunting and raiding lifestyle at which they excelled. Everything in their lives, from brush shelters known as wickiups to women's intricately woven baskets, was geared toward a mobile lifestyle.

Social Organization

This fully nomadic lifestyle did not promote unity among large groups of people. Although they shared a common language, the group never resembled a nation in the common sense of the concept. They thought of themselves as members of distinct bands led by capable men to which they owed allegiance. Most observers recognized six major groups by the mid-18th century—the Western, Chiricahua, Mescalero, Jicarilla, Lipan, and Kiowa Apaches, with many sub-groups. The groups might intermarry, occasionally fight or raid together, but were not bound by any common leadership. These people lived a uniquely free life that would be severely challenged by the arrival of U.S. forces in their region in the 19th century.

The idea of a people without borders, without fixed residence, did not fit into the U.S. scheme for the land it acquired from Mexico in 1848. As with the rest of the West, the natives had to make room for the influx of miners, speculators, and settlers soon to arrive. The forerunner of U.S. intentions was the arrival of the U.S. Army. The military intended to guard trails, protect whites, and curtail

Apache raiding over the border to Mexico. The Mexicans and Apache had been raiding each other for years and a thriving trade in enemy captives existed. The U.S. government's representatives had little understanding of either culture or the deep-seated hatred they were about to encounter.

One of the first bloody incidents that set the stage for the long conflict known as the Apache Wars involved captives. In 1861, a foolish young army officer named George Bascomb created a volatile situation. He invited respected Chiricahua leader Cochise to a meeting where he accused the chief of stealing a former captive's runaway son and a quantity of cattle. Despite the insult, the Apache leader calmly denied any involvement and offered to help secure the return of the boy. Bascomb ignored the offer and activated his plan to capture Cochise and hold him captive. As soldiers obeyed pre-arranged orders to surround the tent, Cochise realized the treachery, grabbed a knife, and cut his way out of the tent. He fled through a barrage of bullets still holding his coffee cup, a symbol of white hospitality. Cochise gained his freedom but the army held his family captive. Over the next weeks the chief pled for the return of his relatives—offering to exchange white captives for their release—to no avail. Bascomb eventually freed his wife and children but hung Cochise's nephews. The army had gained nothing by their actions, but had earned the hatred of a talented Apache warrior. The injustice of the so-called Bascomb Affair drove Cochise to spend the rest of his life fighting the Americans.

The ensuing conflict between the army and the various Apache groups simmered throughout the American Civil War. While U.S. troops focused on defeating the Confederacy, Cochise led raid after raid on white settlements. His energy seemed to know no bounds when engaged in revenge attacks, and it seemed to pay off as whites abandoned Arizona. Cochise was joined in his vendetta against whites by other gifted Apache leaders. Mangas Coloradas, chief of the *Chihenne*, whom whites called Warm Springs Apache or lumped in with the Chiricahua, was a tactical genius. He gained a deserved reputation for personal bravery, ruthless torturing of victims, and intertribal diplomacy. Under Mangas' dynamic leadership, related Apaches began to act together to drive the "White Eyes" from their lands. In 1862, Cochise and Mangas led nearly 200 warriors—a large force for the Apache—against the army at Apache Pass, Arizona. Nearly certain Apache victory was prevented by the timely use of the army's howitzers. Cannon would prove to be successful against lance and bow wielding Indians.

The leadership of Mangas Coloradas energized Apaches to defend the southwest against all invaders. (Legends of America)

The United States captured and kept the spring at Apache Pass, an important feature in an arid region.

Now both the Confederate and U.S. governments officially planned to destroy the Apache. The CSA's governor of New Mexico ordered Indians lured into army camps, the men killed, and the children sold as captives to "defray the expense of killing Indians." James Carleton, the mastermind of the campaign to force the Navajo into Bosque Redondo, included the Mescalero Apache in his purge of native peoples. The men were to be "killed whenever and wherever you can find them" while women and children would just be imprisoned.[19] The Chiricahua Apache were well aware of the price whites had placed on their heads so it seems odd that Mangas Coloradas soon walked into a trap. The old chief may have harbored some idea that peace with the whites was still possible. In January 1863, Mangas engaged in a poorly translated negotiation for supplies with a group of miners. The miners seized the old chief and turned him over to a detachment of Carleton's command. As Mangas slept under guard beside the fire that night soldiers burned his feet and legs with heated bayonets. When Mangas sat up to complain he was shot six times. The great leader of the Warm Springs Apache was scalped, then his head was severed, boiled, and the skull sent east for examination. Mangas' death had a great effect on his people. Apaches highly valued honesty, and it was becoming clear that the whites they dealt with displayed little of it. For people who believe the deceased carry their physical condition with them to the afterworld the beheading was particularly horrible. Geronimo later described Mangas Coloradas' murder as "perhaps the greatest wrong ever done to the Indians."[20] Some Apache date the increase in Apache mutilation of white victims to the period after Mangas' beheading. At the very least the martyrdom of a popular chief hardened many hearts toward the invasion of whites.

Camp Grant Massacre

The United States seemed determined to play into the growing Apache distrust and fear of whites. Officials and civilians continued to commit horrendous crimes against the Apache people that drove revenge killings. The army did not carry out all the violence, but nor did they act to stop miners and settlers driven by racial hatred from unspeakable acts. As the 1860s wore on violence on both sides never ceased, but more and more Apache went to collect food and supplies at military camps. The influx of whites made it harder and harder to find food to support families. The Aravaipa Apache band had been decimated by starvation and disease and numbered only 150 people by the time they gathered around the U.S. Army's Camp Grant. Indian hating civilians were enraged at the idea of the government feeding the Apache and decided to take action on their own. On April 30, 1871, a vigilante mob of Americans, Mexicans, and Papago Indians, the Apache's traditional enemies, charged the unsuspecting Apache camp. It did not take long to kill over 120 Apache; all but eight were women and children. An officer called to the scene after the massacre reported finding the dead and wounded with "their brains beaten out with clubs or stones, while some were shot full of arrows after having been mortally wounded by gunshot. The bodies were all stripped." Other witnesses reported numerous mutilations and rapes. Dozens of babies were carried off to be sold as slaves in Mexico, never to be seen again. The Apache were devastated. As a chief said, "I no longer want to live; my women

Apache women and children remained in camp while the men and boys fought to protect their territory. (Library of Congress)

and children have been killed before my face, and I have been unable to defend them."[21]

Incidents like Camp Grant affected all the Apache who heard of it, and faith in whites eroded daily. Yet, moments of trust still occurred. Cochise was now an aging chief who needed to protect his people. Meeting unarmed with a white man named Tom Jeffords, Cochise agreed to take his band to a reservation carved out of the Chiricahua homeland including his beloved Dragoon Mountains. True to his word once given, Cochise kept his people on the reservation until his death in 1874. His son Taza, who became the Chiricahua leader, did not have the same control of his people. The army used the Chiricahuas' resumed raiding as an excuse to close their reservation and move them to San Carlos reservation. Here, far from their homeland, they would be confined in tight quarters with rival Apache bands. The conditions were terrible and hundreds of Chiricahua men would not go. The warriors who refused to bow to the army's ever-changing plans for them came together under the leadership of the brilliant Apache leader, Geronimo.

Geronimo

Geronimo was not the only Apache leader to resist the whites, but he did for so long, with such flair, that he became the symbol of Apache resistance. Contemporary whites preferred to blame the failure of their plans to subdue the Apache on one almost superhuman individual. Historians routinely credit him with being the leader of the last armed Indian resistance. As a traditional Apache man, Geronimo participated in warfare for years before he came to the attention of Americans. His autobiography tells of his acceptance into full manhood at age 17, which meant he could ride with the warriors and marry. This first marriage shaped the path Geronimo's life would take. Mexicans attacked an Apache camp of women and children and slaughtered Geronimo's mother, wife, and three young children. The devastated young man sought revenge against the Mexicans, riding with his band alongside Mangas Coloradas and Cochise. Geronimo outlived both the older chiefs but learned much from their leadership.

By the late 1870s, many Apache had fallen or surrendered to the relentless army pressure. U.S. officials now focused on the relatively small bands that remained free. Geronimo and Victorio led two of these. In April 1877, both men found themselves on their way to San Carlos reservation with their people. Victorio had inexplicably agreed to the move while Geronimo found himself a prisoner in leg irons after an encounter at Ojo Caliente of which we have no clear account. Even the government should have realized how unlikely it was that these Apache would accept reservation life quietly. Two rival Apache groups, the White Mountain and the Chiricahua, shared a reservation with terrible hunting, inadequate rations, and widespread disease. Victorio left first, breaking out with his people and heading to their homeland around Ojo Caliente. The band enjoyed relative freedom for nearly a year before the government applied its resources to forcing them back onto the reservation. The unfairness of what the government asked of him pushed Victorio to total resistance, and he led his followers in an unending bid to remain free. The small Apache groups which never numbered more than 400 people successfully evaded the pursuit of 4,000 soldiers. The Indians relied on their superior knowledge of the land, horsemanship, and toughness. Victorio's sister Lozen rode as a warrior with the group, performing hazardous roles in combat. In the end, all the effort was not enough to survive a war of attrition. Exhausted and desperate for ammunition Victorio led his survivors into Mexico. In October 1880, a Mexican force attacked the Apache, killing Victorio and collecting the government bounty for his life.

While Victorio led his band out on their desperate bid for freedom, Geronimo chafed under the restrictions of reservation life.

His desire for freedom was as strong as any Apache leader's, but he appreciated the advantages reservation life offered in the changed world. The food and blankets the government provided could not be easily replaced anymore. Yet, the Apache felt like helpless targets as cavalry swarmed the reservation, and no one wanted to die without a fight. A year after Mexicans ended Victorio's bid for freedom, Geronimo made one of his own. He and his brother-in-law Juh led their band to a place known as the Stronghold in the Sierra Madre mountains. No one knew this area as the Chiricahua did. Remnants of Victorio's band, led by Nana and Lozen, joined the renegades here. Geronimo then led a small group to San Carlos reservation and forcefully brought the remaining members of that band to the Stronghold. For a brief time, it seemed that the old Apache world was back—they had strong leaders in a powerful place.

Native Warfare

The free Chiricahua had over 600 people in the Sierra Madre. They raided at will in Mexico, secure in the belief that the United States would leave them alone. The U.S. government had 5,600 Apaches on reservations, but the freedom of the 600 tortured army leaders. General Crook focused his attention on a way to get to these renegades. His plan was devious, but practical. Crook paid Apache to spy on other Apaches while he planned an attack into Mexican territory. From one spy Crook learned of the Stronghold, the key to free Chiricahua resistance, and crossed into Mexico in pursuit of the Apaches in 1883. The endless hunt wore down the Apache prompting many to reconsider reservation life. Slowly the bands returned to San Carlos. Geronimo delayed the longest, finally arriving in style in 1884 with 350 rustled Mexican cattle for his people to eat. The army immediately confiscated the animals.

The stolen animals were not just a show of Apache bravado and defiance. The people sorely needed the meat. Everything was in short supply on the reservation except heat. San Carlos was dubbed "Hell's Forty Acres" by the soldiers stationed there.

Almost continuously dry, hot, dust- and gravel-laden winds swept the plain, denuding it of every vestige of vegetation. . . . Everywhere the naked, dirty, frightened little Indian children. . . . Everywhere the sullen, stolid, hopeless, suspicious faces of the older Indians . . .[22]

The Apache, once self-sufficient, free and proud, had been reduced to desperate poverty. Leaders hated to see their people suffer.

Tensions on the reservations ran high all year. Geronimo later complained that although he was living quietly the whites kept saying he was a bad man. Worse than the negative attitude of whites was the rumor Geronimo heard that he was to be arrested. The warrior did not wait to see if it was true—he left the reservation on May 17, 1885, with 42 warriors and their families. The group included 90 to 103 women and children so it was not a war party, but it was led by great warriors including Lozen, Cochise's son Naiche, and Nana, and their expertise was impressive. The Apache had learned years before that the telegraph was a powerful weapon of white troops so cutting it became standard practice. Broken telegraph wires could be easily located and repaired, however. This time, Nana directed young boys to climb the poles to splice in buckskin in place of a stretch of wire. It took the army weeks to find the problem areas. Their cunning gave the breakout group a head start, but it would take all their knowledge, skill, and luck to evade their pursuers. Soon the United States had 2,000 troops in the field chasing a group less than one-tenth that size. However, the odds were not as uneven as they would seem. The Apache killed all the whites they encountered, including soldiers, and ran off 150 horses without losing a singe band member. The reports of violence terrorized the white residents of Arizona who lost all perspective as they imagined themselves "surrounded by Apaches" and clamored for federal assistance.

Within a few months Geronimo's band was across the Mexican border being pursued by both American and Mexican troops. Slowly the army made progress, capturing or killing a few dozen Apache. In this summer of exaggerated reports and overblown charges, Geronimo really earned some of his reputation. He led his band, including women and children, for 500 miles over ground so rough it wore out the U.S. Cavalry. By moving fast, turning frequently, and making excellent use of the terrain Geronimo left the soldiers in the dust. Then he and four companions rode across the heavily guarded U.S. border and onto the grounds of Fort Apache where they liberated Geronimo's wife and three-year-old daughter and slipped away. The victories were real and meaningful but staying free took a huge toll on the people. Constant flight prevented any sense of normal life, and everyone was exhausted. Several warriors longed to see their family members who remained captives of the United States. Other Apaches already scouted for the army, and now the renegades began to divide among themselves. Looking into the future the Apache saw little hope that they could maintain their traditional way of life with such small numbers and under such intense pressure from the army. So Geronimo agreed to talks with General Crook in March 1886.

The Apache leaders wanted a chance to start again. They did not want to rot in white man's jails for their actions, better to die fighting. "There are very few of my men left now. They have done some bad things but I want them all rubbed out now and let us never speak of them again" said Geronimo. Crook understood this sentiment and gained the warriors' surrender on the promise that they would only be locked up in the East for two years and then would return home. One by one Chihuhua, Naiche, and Geronimo agreed to go to San Carlos with Crook. "Once I moved about like the wind. Now I surrender to you and that is all."[23] Geronimo was the most uneasy about what they had done. He would later write that it was hard for him to believe Crook, and that he then knew that what Crook had said was untrue.

The uneasiness persisted after the Apache returned to camp and began to drink. Geronimo summed it up this way, "I feared treachery and decided to remain in Mexico." Naiche was more descriptive. "I was afraid I was going to be taken off somewhere I didn't like, to some place I didn't know. I thought all who were taken away would die."[24] Acting on their instincts and all their cultural traditions that valued freedom, Naiche, Geronimo, and 37 others fled camp rather than head north to certain imprisonment. As the army geared up to pursue these last holdouts, the surrendering Apaches walked into Fort Bowie. General Crook had made promises in the field that neither his commander Phil Sheridan nor President Cleveland intended to honor. Geronimo's escape provided the perfect cover to disavow Crook's agreement with the Apache leaders. When Chihuahua and his 76 followers boarded a train in April 1886 they believed they would be held in the East in "slavery and degradation" for two years; they remained prisoners for 27 years. As Chihuahua's son said, "It would have been a good day to die."[25]

Now the army turned its attention to Geronimo. Amazingly, it would take five months and remarkable resources to capture the 37 Apache who traveled under the leadership of Geronimo, Naiche, and Lozen. Their journey through the Southwest has been described as "the most remarkable campaign of guerrilla warfare ever witnessed on the North American continent."[26] The story of the Apache odyssey has captured the American imagination for over a hundred years and made Geronimo a living legend. For the

The famous "Geronimo band" feared by U.S. citizens amounted to less than 40 people at the end. (Library of Congress)

Apaches on the journey it was simply a desperate shot at survival with little hope of success.

> We were reckless of our lives, because we felt every man's hand was against us. If we returned to the reservation we would be put in prison and killed; if we stayed in Mexico they would continue to send soldiers to fight us; so we gave no quarter to anyone and asked no favors.

Geronimo[27]

The Apaches understood that they were at war with the U.S. Army. They probably could not have conceived of the size of that army. With Crook disgraced by the loss of Geronimo, General Miles took command of the recapture effort. By the summer of 1866, Miles sent 5,000 U.S. soldiers—one-quarter of the entire U.S. Army—to join 3,000 Mexican soldiers hunting Apaches. Amazingly, about 9,000 armed men chased 18 warriors, 13 women, and 6 children. And they did not catch them for months. The soldiers had orders to guard every ranch, every water hole, and every pass near the Mexican border. One hundred hand-picked, best-of-the-best soldiers marched into the wilds after the Apaches. After traveling over 3,000 miles and suffering intense physical hardship, the command only struck the fugitives' camp once. Geronimo had lost only three people during the campaign. Since this overwhelming show of force was not working, the desperate Miles finally tried the only approach that had ever worked—using Apaches to catch Apaches.

Unfortunately, no one in the army had any idea where Geronimo was in August 1866. Finally, Lieutenant Charles Gatewood with a small party that included two young Chiricahuas known to Geronimo, contacted the band. Geronimo's people had been fugitives for a long, hot, dry summer. They were constantly on guard, on the move, seeking food and ammunition to stay alive. They would at least hear what their relatives and the young officer had to say. Geronimo remained determined to surrender only if his people could return to their families on the reservation, not be imprisoned. But the news Gatewood brought struck at the heart of the Apache resistance. He blurted out that all the Apaches from the reservation had been removed to Florida. (In fact Miles would not carry out his plan of making 434 Chiricahua Apaches prisoners of war until September 5th, but Gatewood thought it had already happened.) This revelation seemed to take the fight out of Geronimo who visibly shook when he heard. Everyone in his band had relatives they thought were safely on the reservation but who were now headed for some distant place called Florida. What was the point of resistance if their families were gone? One by one the warriors made their own choices to surrender. Geronimo spoke last, noting that he could not fight without his warriors so he too would give up.

The official surrender came on September 4, 1886, in Skeleton Canyon. Geronimo noted that it was his fourth surrender. Miles had promised that the band would be reunited with their families within a week; it took eight months. Part of the delay was the ongoing debate between General Miles—who had given his word to Geronimo—and President Cleveland—who wanted the Apache warriors turned over to civilian authorities in Arizona that guaranteed speedy trials and deaths. The telegram "I hope nothing will be done with Geronimo which will prevent our keeping him as a prisoner of war if we cannot hang him which I would much prefer" expressed Cleveland's intentions. While the President dithered, Miles confiscated Geronimo's rifle and spurs, and packed him with his surviving band into a train headed east. Geronimo would never see his homeland again. After eight years in Florida the Chiricahua were transferred to Fort Sill, Oklahoma, where they spent another 19 years as prisoners of war. There, away from his beloved mountains, Geronimo died in 1909. The surviving 261

The survivors of the U.S.-Apache wars faced deportation and imprisonment: Most would never go home again. (National Archives & Records
Administration/Double Delta)

Chiricahua were finally deemed to be no threat to the United
States and were set free in 1913, 27 years after they held off one-
quarter of the U.S. Army.

The final resistance of the Apache people brought an end to the
official army-Indian violence that had defined the American Southwest for decades. It did not seem glorious, locking up a small ragtag band of Apache resisters, but the symbolism was powerful.
Geronimo had come to serve as the face of Apache, and even native
resistance to white civilization. With the old warrior behind bars
the western settlers believed they could breathe easier and push
harder toward the development of the West unhindered by fears of
Indian Wars. The Apache, as well as all the other native nations in
the region, had to adjust to the new, and often cruel, world of reservation life. Some of their traditional ways, particularly those
centered on hunting and warfare, were gone forever like the vast
herds of bison. Other practices, beliefs, and values would persist only
through the fierce commitment of native peoples to their culture.

NOTES

1. Clarissa Confer, *The Cherokee Nation in the Civil War*. Norman: University of Oklahoma Press, 2007, 146.

2. Utley, *Indian Frontier*, 87.

3. Jerome Greene, *Lakota and Cheyenne: Indian Views of the Great Sioux War, 1876–1877*. Norman: University of Oklahoma Press, 1994, 17.

4. Testimony of John Smith, March 14, 1865, http://www.pbs.org/weta/thewest/resources/archives/four/sandcrk.htm#smith.

5. George E. Hyde, and Savoie Lottinville, eds., *Life of George Bent, Written from His Letters*. Norman: University of Oklahoma Press, 1983, 153.

6. Testimony of John Smith, March 14, 1865, http://www.pbs.org/weta/thewest/resources/archives/four/sandcrk.htm#smith.

7. William H. Leckie, *The Military Conquest of the Southern Plains*. Norman: University of Oklahoma Press, 1963, 24.

8. Brown, 94.

9. Brown, 100.

10. Brown, 241.

11. Calloway, *Our Hearts*, 129–130.

12. Hampton Sides, *Blood and Thunder: An Epic of the American West*. New York: Doubleday, 2006, 326.

13. Sides, 342.

13. Sides, 342.

14. Sides, 352.

15. Sides, 355.

16. Brown, 29, 31.

17. Brown, 33.

18. Sides, 401.

19. David Roberts, *Once They Moved Like the Wind: Cochise, Geronimo, and the Apache Wars*. New York: Simon & Shuster, 1994, 39; President Jefferson Davis rescinded the order and removed the governor.

20. Roberts, 42.

21. Report of Lieutenant Royal Whitman, July 20, 1871, *New York Times*, http://query.nytimes.com/gst/abstract.html?res=9A04E0D7103EEE34BC4851DFB166838A669FDE, accessed 9/23/09.

22. Britton Davis, *The Truth About Geronimo*. Lincoln: University of Nebraska Press, 1976; reprint), 48.

23. Roberts, 272.

24. S. M., Barrett, ed., *Geronimo's Story of His Life*. New York: Duffield, 1915, 139; Roberts, 274.

25. Roberts, 277.

26. Roberts, 280.

27. Barrett, 141.

6

EPILOGUE: WOUNDED KNEE—THE FINAL INDIAN WAR?

The surrender of Apache leader Geronimo in 1886 is often regarded as the end of the Indian Wars. The United States could take pride in the idea that they had finally made "peace on the plains" come true. All meaningful native armed resistance was at an end. Or was it? Certainly, Geronimo remained behind bars; Crazy Horse, Captain Jack, John Ross, Little Crow, and so many other Indian leaders were dead. Other former adversaries languished on reservations with the remnants of their people. After more than a century of warfare against American Indians, the army could finally turn its attention and resources elsewhere. Except there was one more chapter to play out in this long dramatic struggle.

Hundreds of thousands of Indians had become virtual prisoners by 1890. Some like Geronimo's band, were actually behind bars, while most others remained on reservations. A few reservations coincided with tribal homelands but many people had been relocated away from their birthplaces, sacred areas, and hunting grounds. The U.S. government had given little value to natives' connection to place and had mostly relegated reservations to the most undesirable land where the occupants would be the least trouble. The reservation lands were usually isolated and desolate. Almost none would support the government's idea of farming, nor would warriors condescend to do women's work, so hunger, boredom, and despair stalked the residents. The Bureau of Indian Affairs had to provide supplies to their unwilling charges, and the process of purchasing and delivering the goods was one of the most fraudulent and corrupt in U.S. history. The system for selecting Indian agents to supervise the reservations was equally flawed, so unqualified, unsympathetic, and sometimes pathological men had absolute power over the people.

Since many Indian agents joined the service to get rich, they could devise ways to earn profits that always came at the Indians' expense. This system of abuse created resentment and anger. Many agents believed the only way to contain that hostility was through repressive measures that afforded no power to the residents. Warriors were deprived of weapons, ponies, and authority. Every opportunity was taken to humiliate former leaders and make them aware of their now subservient status. Some agents disregarded the worth of their Indian charges while others feared these alien people so recently defeated. Either way, the atmosphere on most reservations was very tense and only a small provocation would create a storm.

One of the hardest fought sections of the Indian Wars had been the northern plains. Fourteen years after the spectacular victory at Little Big Horn everyone still remembered it. Whites had elevated Custer to heroic status and still thought of revenging his noble death. Lakota warriors remembered their glory days and chafed at their total loss of power. Many friends and relatives had died for the cause of freedom and it now seemed in vain. Conditions on the Lakota reservations were depressing and everyone longed for their previous life.

The Standing Rock Lakota Agency had one thing that most reservations did not. It had a surviving great leader—Sitting Bull. He was the last resister of the government sweep of the Plains Tribes onto reservations. Sitting Bull had led his people to Canada in 1877 rather than surrender with his contemporaries Crazy Horse, Dull Knife, and Little Wolf. The years in the Great Mother's country had been a struggle against starvation as the bison herds dwindled and the U.S. Army harassed the Lakota near the international border. Finally, in 1881, Sitting Bull had agreed to come into U.S. custody. It was a hard decision that reflected the desperation of his people. The great man composed a song that reflected the significance of this move. "A warrior I have been. Now it is all over. A hard time I have."[1] However, even if he could not live as a free-roaming Lakota, Sitting Bull did not intend to slip quietly into oblivion. He possessed both great spiritual power and the corresponding respect of the Lakota people. Sitting Bull did make concessions to his new life, learning to farm, sending his children to white schools, and traveling with Buffalo Bill's Wild West Show to major American cities.

However, the chief remained committed to the Lakota way of life. "I would rather die an Indian than live a white man."[2] As an honored man who remained staunchly traditional, the great Sitting Bull posed a challenge to the authority of the agent at Standing Rock. James McLoughlin was an experienced agent who believed in the future of the Indian, but on his terms. That vision required massive change of native society and had no room for an arrogant, stubborn old leader who insisted on being treated with respect. When the government stripped nine million acres from the Lakota and stuffed them onto six separate reservation sites, Sitting Bull proved to be a vocal opponent. The bitterness at the loss of so much land festered throughout 1889 and many Lakota looked to religious leader Sitting Bull for hope. McLoughlin kept a close eye on the chief, expecting trouble.

GHOST DANCE

The Lakota were a people ripe for a change, a conversion, a way out of their current conditions. The opportunity came in the form of a new religious movement known as the Ghost Dance. The hope that buoyed the hearts of many Lakotas in the hard spring of 1890 came not from the traditional spirituality of their ancestors but from a new holy man. A Paiute named Wovoka preached a message which combined elements of traditional native spirituality with Christianity to offer the hope of a better life. Wovoka spoke of the destruction of the current world and the creation of a fresh, abundant world for Indians to live in *by themselves*. The creator would wipe away the evils of this life and replace it with a new reality that contained all the tribes had lost—deceased loved ones, abundant game, health, and peace. Not surprisingly, the new world would not contain whites. The mechanism to trigger this great experience was a traditional circle dance. As so many Indians found themselves facing a rapidly changing world where the old ways they knew and valued slipped quickly away, they took comfort in a message that affirmed the return of better days. Wovoka's message spread from his home in Nevada and by spring 1890 came to the Lakota.

Sitting Bull remained confident in the power of Lakota spirituality. He did not need a new vision, but he did not stop others who might find strength in a new way. Two Lakotas, Short Bull—a medicine man, and Kicking Bear—a warrior who fought at Little Big Horn with his friend Crazy Horse, traveled to Nevada to hear Wovoka's message first-hand. When they returned to the Lakota reservations in April 1890, Kicking Bear set out to tell everyone who would listen about the new religion which offered a renewed future. To a people who had no hope the message was very appealing. Kicking Bear seems to have added a more militant focus to Wovoka's essentially peaceful message. The Lakota version of the message emphasized the violent end of the current, white-inhabited world, and the Lakota dancers wore "ghost shirts" which looked much like their traditional war shirts and had the power to repel bullets.

Drought plagued the reservations during the summer of 1890 which created more hungry, desperate people to listen to the only good news they had—the Ghost Dance. People began gathering in remote locations to dance and share their excitement about the future. As more Indians became energized and confidant white officials got nervous. Reservation Indians were much easier to control when they were demoralized. Now the Ghost Dance had spread to 12 states and more than 30 tribes. It seemed that a dangerous epidemic had swept Native America and had to be stopped.

The Lakota took up the Ghost Dance in the hopes of bringing on a new world free of the evils of this life. (© CORBIS)

Federal officials ordered an end to the dancing. Indian agents tried to break up dance camps and restore authority. Lakota reservation agents sent worried messages to the government predicting an "outbreak." No agent appeared more terrified of his charges than Pine Ridge agent Daniel Royer. The Indians had derisively named him "Man-Afraid-of-his-Lakota." This former druggist told the federal government he needed troops to prevent an outbreak and he got them. In November 1890, the army arrived at Pine Ridge reservation. The troops' presence frightened the Indians who had all lost relatives to army violence over the decades. The military threat made some dancers more determined to ignore the agents' demand that they quit dancing and come to agency headquarters.

Agent McLoughlin at Standing Rock viewed the orders from Washington as an opportunity to rid himself of the powerful Sitting Bull. He falsely claimed that Sitting Bull was the "high priest and leading apostle" of the movement. McLoughlin allowed his true motivation to show as he accused the chief of being "a habitual liar, active obstructionist, and great obstacle to the civilization of these people."[3] On the basis of this accusation General Miles assumed Sitting Bull to be the instigator of the Lakota resistance. Several thousand Lakota from Pine Ridge and Rosebud reservations remained defiantly in a remote camp, waiting for the arrival of the new world. Sitting Bull was not with them, but when he requested permission to travel to Pine Ridge the government ordered his arrest.

Sitting Bull's Murder

The ultimate insult to Sitting Bull was to be his arrest by his own people, not the army. The reservations had created police forces, recruiting Indians to the service of government enforcement. The position brought better food and supplies as well as a measure of power so there were many recruits. On December 15, 1890, 43 Indian policemen gathered at Sitting Bull's home on Standing Rock reservation to arrest him. The men who followed Agent McLoughlin's order to arrest the great Sitting Bull were Lakotas. Lieutenant Bull Head had fought at Rosebud and Little Big Horn. Other policemen had fled to Canada with Sitting Bull rather than surrender in 1877. Now they came at the order of whites to capture one of the last traditional leaders of their people. The Lakota world had surely changed.

When the policemen burst into Sitting Bull's home he was asleep with his family. Shocked awake he agreed to go with them as the household scattered in confusion. The physically rough treatment he received at the hands of his own people in front of his family aggravated the great man. When his son derided his surrender and the people gathered outside shouted their resistance Sitting Bull stopped cooperating in his arrest. The policemen became increasingly nervous as tensions rose. Suddenly, Catch-the-Bear, Sitting Bull's bodyguard, shot his mortal enemy Bull Head. As Bull Head fell he shot Sitting Bull in the chest with his revolver while another policeman shot him in the head. Catch-the-Bear fell dead from a shot and the scene descended into chaos. Sitting Bull's followers and the Indian police fought a vicious, close quarter battle with guns, clubs, and knives. When it was over, the prophesy that Sitting Bull received when he came to the reservation had come true—he was killed by his own people.

Sitting Bull's murder created panic. His followers scattered as the army arrived with artillery. Most of them intended to head south and seek refuge with the Ghost Dancers led by Hump on the Cheyenne River reservation. It was hard for the wounded to travel and many of the healthy had only the clothes they wore. Fear and desperation drove them on as they sought refuge from the chaos at Standing Rock. The ninety-mile journey took three days and drained their energy. A harder blow was the news that Hump had surrendered to the army and was now in uniform helping to track down dancers. This left the refugees with few alternatives so some chose to seek out Chief Big Foot (who had been called Spotted Elk when he fought in the wars of the 1870s) and his band. Big Foot's people also danced through the summer and now needed supplies. They informed the nearest army officer of the Eighth Cavalry that they were headed to Fort Bennett to pick up their annuities. After that they intended to head to Pine Ridge where Red Cloud's people requested Big Foot's assistance as a mediator. As they began the journey the army ordered Big Foot arrested as a Ghost Dance troublemaker. The band now traveled with an unknown arrest warrant over their heads.

The arrival of the survivors of Sitting Bull's band created confusion for Big Foot's group. The world seemed to be changing so rapidly that the Lakotas could not keep up. Sitting Bull was dead, murdered by government police, yet other Lakota leaders urged obedience to the government. It was hard to know what to do and the promise of a new world never seemed more appealing, so the people danced the Ghost Dance and mourned the loss of a great chief. Meanwhile, the army caught up to the band and, in the face of superior forces, Big Foot agreed to come to Fort Bennett to surrender. As the Lakotas huddled in the cold December weather, events conspired against them. Big Foot caught the influenza that had stalked his people and felt too weak to travel. The army sent waves of troopers out to put down the "uprising," including Custer's former command, the Seventh Cavalry. The sight of so many of their former enemies convinced the Lakotas that the army had come for the final kill. The weakened chief and his followers chose to flee south to Pine Ridge where they hoped to gain protection. The journey was hard in the bitter cold but the people made good time. By December 28th the group was on the Pine Ridge reservation and had only a day's journey to the agency. News had come to them of troops on Wounded Knee Creek, but Big Foot was too ill to endure the extra travel it would take to avoid them. By noon on the 28th, Lakota scouts had captured four soldiers. The commander, Major Samuel Whitside, insisted that the Indians come to the army camp and Big Foot, who had to travel by army ambulance, agreed.

The Lakota men, women, and children were scared. The Seventh Cavalry assumed battle position and then flanked the Indians all the way into camp. Women hurried in the growing December darkness to get camps set up under the watchful eyes of the army. Whitside positioned two Hotchkiss guns, the army's new repeating artillery weapon which could fire one shell per second, on the heights aimed directly at the Indian camp. The officers welcomed the arrival of additional cavalry and artillery, then celebrated the "capture" of the "hostile" Indians. The camp settled in for the night with 350 exhausted, scared Indians surrounded by 462 exuberant troops and four Hotchkiss guns.

The Indian camp awoke with a clear plan. After breakfast they would pack their belongings and be accompanied by the army to the Pine Ridge Agency where they looked forward to visiting with friends. Despite the apparent compliance of the Lakotas the commander of the Seventh Cavalry, Colonel James Forsyth, insisted that the Indians first be disarmed. This order was bound to cause problems. Plains Indian men had weapons as both means of survival and measures of pride and were not likely to part with them easily. Everyone had heard terrible stories of what the army had done to unarmed Indians. Self-preservation, pride, and defiance kicked in and caused Big Foot, now prostrate and bleeding from the nose, to deny that the men had guns. At this refusal Forsyth ordered a search of the camp. The soldiers unloaded wagons, dumped out packs, and searched the women. They confiscated guns as well as knives, axes, hatchets, and even women's quilling needles. The women accepted this invasion of their homes, possessions, and persons with little complaint. However, the men gathered at the center of the camp watched with growing unease. It went against their sense of themselves as warriors, providers, and protectors to allow strangers to take family possessions, especially their weapons. When the soldiers insisted on searching the men as well the tension escalated. It did not take much to spark the unrest that the Lakota men felt. Their medicine man urged them to resist saying, "Do not fear, but let your hearts be strong. Many soldiers are about us and have many bullets, but I am assured their bullets cannot penetrate us. The prairie is large, and their bullets will fly over the prairies and will not come toward us. If they do come toward us, they will float away like dust in the air."[4] One young warrior boldly brandished his weapon. Both sides could feel this situation heading out of control.

Within minutes firing had broken out in the camp. Chief Big Foot and many around him died sitting down. The center of the camp was chaotic with smoke shrouding the hand-to-hand fighting. The poorly armed Indians fell back to their camp where the women and children looked on in shock. Then the army opened up with the artillery, exploding 50 shells per minute into the tipis. The camp became a death trap as shells tore through everything. Women and children fled to the ravines outside the camp, desperately seeking protection. The Hotchkiss guns found them there and it too became a killing ground ". . . . it seemed to me only a few seconds until there was not a living thing before us; warriors, squaws, children, ponies, dogs . . . went down before that unaimed fire," remembered one officer.[5] Still, the killing did not stop until Colonel Forsyth finally yelled "For God's sake! Stop shooting them!"[6]

When the shooting ended bodies covered the ground—84 Indian men, 44 women, and 18 children. The army loaded the wounded and their dead for transport to Pine Ridge, but left the Indian dead where they lay. As the temperature dropped the bodies froze in grotesque shapes. Perhaps 40 more died of their wounds or exposure after fleeing the massacre.

Fully three miles from the scene of the massacre we found the body of a woman completely covered with snow. . . . we found them scattered along as they had been relentlessly hunted down and slaughtered while fleeing

Dead bodies and burned tipis were all that remained of Big Foot's camp after the 7th Cavalry attacked. (Library of Congress)

for their lives. . . . where the Indian camp had stood . . . we saw the frozen bodies lying close together or piled one upon another.

Charles Eastman[7]

All the Indian dead were dumped in a mass grave on the hill where the Hotchkiss guns sat. The site has become an informal memorial, testifying to the horror and loss of the last engagement of the Indian Wars.

The slaughter of the men, women, and children at Wounded Knee Creek in December 1890 cannot be considered a war in the true sense of the word. But then many of the engagements between the U.S. Army and the Native Americans did not resemble conventional war. Too many—Slim Buttes, Big Hole, Washita, Camp Grant—were eerily similar to Wounded Knee, when a professional military force fired on civilian women and children. Of course there were armed warriors present at these engagements on the native side, but no unarmed civilians on the army side. This points out the fundamental problem in the Indian Wars. The U.S. Army brought the war to Indian peoples, to their villages, their camps.

The mass burial site of the Wounded Knee Massacre victims remains a powerful symbol of the treatment of native people. (Courtesy of Clarissa W. Confer)

The Indian men did not often fight in places of their choosing but rather in defense of their homes and families. There was no way to escape daily life in the Indian Wars because it was simply daily life at that time.

NOTES

1. Utley, *Lance and Shield*, 233.
2. Utley, *Lance and Shield*, 269.
3. Jack Utter, ed., *Wounded Knee & the Ghost Dance Tragedy*. Lake Ann, MI: National Woodlands Publishing Company, 1991, 14, 125.
4. Smith, 187.
5. Smith, 193.
6. Utter, 24.
7. Utter, 25.

BIBLIOGRAPHY

Ambrose, Stephen. *Crazy Horse and Custer: The Parallel Lives of Two American Warriors.* New York: Doubleday, 1975.

Anderson, Fred. *The War That Made America: A Short History of the French and Indian War.* New York: Viking, 2005.

Anderson, Gary Clayton, and Alan R. Woolworth, eds. *Through Dakota Eyes: Narrative Accounts of the Minnesota Indian War of 1862.* St. Paul: Minnesota Historical Society Press, 1988.

Barr, Daniel, ed. *The Boundaries between Us: Natives and Newcomers along the Frontiers of the Old Northwest Territory, 1750–1850.* Kent, Ohio: Kent State University Press, 2006.

Barr, Daniel, ed. *Unconquered: The Iroquois League at War in Colonial America.* Westport, CT: Greenwood Press, 2006.

Barrett, S. M., ed. *Geronimo's Story of His Life.* New York: Duffield, 1915.

Braund, Kathryn. *Deerskins and Duffels: The Creek Indian Trade with Anglo-America, 1685–1815.* Lincoln: University of Nebraska Press, 1993.

Brown, Dee. *Bury My Heart at Wounded Knee.* New York: Henry Holt & Company, 1991.

Calloway, Colin. *The American Revolution in Indian Country: Crisis and Diversity in Native American Communities.* New York: Cambridge University Press, 1995.

Calloway, Colin. *New Worlds for All: Indians, Europeans, and the Remaking of Early America.* Baltimore: Johns Hopkins University Press, 1997.

Calloway, Colin. *Our Hearts Fell to the Ground: Plains Indian Views of How the West Was Lost.* New York: Bedford/St. Martin's, 1996.

Calloway, Colin. *The Scratch of a Pen: 1763 and the Transformation of North America*. New York: Oxford University Press, 2006.

Calloway, Colin G., ed. *The World Turned Upside Down: Indian Voices from Early America*. New York: Bedford/St. Martins, 1994.

Carter, Harvey Lewis. *The Life and Times of Little Turtle: First Sagamore of the Wabash*. Urbana: University of Illinois Press, 1987.

Cronon, William. *Changes in the Land: Indians, Colonists, and the Ecology of New England*. New York: Hill & Wang, 1983.

Davis, Britton. *The Truth About Geronimo*. Lincoln: University of Nebraska Press, 1976; reprint.

Dillon, Richard. *Burnt-out Fires: California's Modoc Indian War*. Englewood Cliffs, NJ: Prentice Hall Inc., 1973.

Dixon, David. *Never Come to Peace Again: Pontiac's Uprising and the Fate of the British Empire in North America*. Norman: University of Oklahoma Press, 2005.

Dowd, Gregory Evans. *A Spirited Resistance: The North American Indian Struggle for Unity, 1745–1815*. Baltimore: Johns Hopkins University Press, 1992.

Dowd, Gregory Evans. *War under Heaven: Pontiac, the Indian Nations & the British Empire*. Baltimore: Johns Hopkins University Press, 2002.

Edel, Wilbur. *Kekionga!: The Worst Defeat in the History of the U.S. Army*. Westport, CT: Praeger Publishers, 1997.

Faulk, Odie B. *Crimson Desert: Indian Wars of the American Southwest*. New York: Oxford University Press, 1974.

Faulk, Odie B. *The Geronimo Campaign*. New York: Oxford University Press, 1969.

Glatthaar, Joseph T., and James Kirby Martin. *Forgotten Allies: The Oneida Indians and the American Revolution*. New York: Hill & Wang, 2006.

Greene, Jerome. *Lakota and Cheyenne: Indian Views of the Great Sioux War, 1876–1877*. Norman: University of Oklahoma Press, 1994.

Greene, Jerome A., and Douglas D. Scott. *Finding Sand Creek: History, Archeology, and the 1864 Massacre Site*. Norman: University of Oklahoma Press, 2004.

Grinnell, George Bird. *The Fighting Cheyenne*. Norman: University of Oklahoma Press, 1956.

Grinnell, George B. "An Indian Perspective on the Wagon Box Fight." *Midwest Review* 9. February and March (1928): 1–7.

Hampton, Bruce. *Children of Grace: The Nez Perce War of 1877*. New York: Avon Books, 1994.

Hauptman, Laurence M., and James Wherry, eds. *The Pequots in Southern New England: The Fall and Rise of an American Indian Nation*. Norman: University of Oklahoma Press, 1990.

Hurt, R. Douglas. *The Indian Frontier: 1763–1846*. Albuquerque: University of New Mexico Press, 2002.

Hyde, George E., and Savoie Lottinville, eds. *Life of George Bent, Written from His Letters*. Norman: University of Oklahoma Press, 1983.

Jackson, Donald, ed. *Black Hawk: An Autobiography.* Urbana: University of Illinois Press, 1955.

Joseph. "An Indian's View of Indian Affairs." *North American Review,* April (1879): 412–433.

Josephy, Alvin, Jr. *500 Nations: An Illustrated History of North American Indians.* New York: Alfred Knopf, 1994.

Josephy, Alvin, Jr. *The Nez Perce Indians and the Opening of the Northwest.* Abridged ed. Lincoln: University of Nebraska Press, 1965.

Larson, Robert W. *Red Cloud: Warrior-Statesman of the Lakota Sioux.* Norman: University of Oklahoma Press, 1997.

Lavender, David. *Let Me Be Free: The Nez Perce Tragedy.* New York: Harper-Collins, 1992.

Leckie, William H. *The Military Conquest of the Southern Plains.* Norman: University of Oklahoma Press, 1963.

Mahon, John K. *History of the Second Seminole War: 1835–1842.* Gainesville: University of Florida Press, 1967.

Marquis, Thomas B., interpreter. *Wooden Leg: A Warrior Who Fought Custer.* Lincoln: University of Nebraska Press, 1931.

Marshall, Joseph. *The Day the World Ended at Little Bighorn: A Lakota History.* New York: Viking, 2007.

Mattes, Merrill J. *The Great Platte River Road.* Lincoln: University of Nebraska Press, 1987.

McConnell, Michael N. *A Country Between: The Upper Ohio Valley and Its Peoples, 1724–1774.* Lincoln: University of Nebraska Press, 1992.

McWhorter, Lucullus Virgil. *Yellow Wolf: His Own Story.* Caldwell, ID: The Caxton Printers, 1948.

Middleton, Richard. *Colonial America: A History, 1565–1776.* New York: Wiley-Blackwell, 1991.

Monnett, John. *Tell Them We Are Going Home: The Odyssey of the Northern Cheyennes.* Norman: University of Oklahoma Press, 2004.

Monnett, John. *Where a Hundred Soldiers Were Killed: The Struggle for the Powder River Country in 1866 and the Making of the Fetterman Myth.* Albuquerque: University of New Mexico Press, 2008.

Murray, Keith. *The Modocs and Their War.* Norman: University of Oklahoma Press, 1958.

Roberts, David. *Once They Moved Like the Wind: Cochise, Geronimo, and the Apache Wars.* New York: Simon & Shuster, 1993.

Rountree, Helen. *Pocahontas's People: The Powhatan Indians of Virginia through Four Centuries.* Norman: University of Oklahoma Press, 1990.

Rountree, Helen. *The Powhatan Indians of Virginia: Their Traditional Culture.* Norman: University of Oklahoma Press, 1989.

Schofield, Brian. *Selling Your Father's Bones: America's 140 Year War against the Nez Perce Tribe.* New York: Simon & Shuster, 2009.

Schultz, Duane. *Over the Earth I Come: The Great Sioux Uprising of 1862.* New York: St. Martin's Press, 1992.

Sides, Hampton. *Blood and Thunder: An Epic of the American West*. New York: Doubleday, 2006.

Smith, Rex Alan. *Moon of Popping Trees: The Tragedy at Wounded Knee and the End of the Indian Wars*. Lincoln: University of Nebraska Press, 1975.

Starita, Joe. *The Dull Knifes of Pine Ridge: A Lakota Odyssey*. Lincoln: University of Nebraska Press, 1995.

Steele, Ian. *Warpaths: Invasions of North America*. New York: Oxford University Press, 1994.

Sugden, John. *Tecumseh: A Life*. New York: Henry Holt and Company, 1998.

Sword, Wiley. *President Washington's Indian War: The Struggle for the Old Northwest, 1790–1795*. Norman: University of Oklahoma Press, 1985.

Tanner, Helen Hornbeck. "The Glaize in 1792: A Composite Indian Community." *Ethnohistory* 25, no. 1 (Winter 1978): 15–39.

Taylor, Colin. *The Plains Indians*. London: Salamander Books, 1994.

Utley, Robert. *Bluecoats and Redskins: United States Army and the Indian, 1866–91*. London: Cassell, 1975.

Utley, Robert. *Cavalier in Buckskin: George Armstrong Custer and the Western Military Frontier*. Norman: University of Oklahoma Press, 1988.

Utley, Robert. *Frontiersmen in Blue: The United States Army and the Indian 1848–1865*. Lincoln: University of Nebraska Press, 1981.

Utley, Robert. *The Indian Frontier of the American West, 1846–1890*. Albuquerque: University of New Mexico Press, 1984.

Utley, Robert. *The Lance and the Shield: The Life and Times of Sitting Bull*. New York: Henry Holt and Co., 1993.

Utley, Robert M., and Wilcomb E. Washburn. *Indian Wars*. Boston: Houghton Mifflin, 1977.

Utter, Jack, ed. *Wounded Knee & the Ghost Dance Tragedy*. Lake Ann, MI: National Woodlands Publishing Company, 1991.

Nonprint Sources:

Pequot War

http://www.forttours.com/pages/pequotwar.asp
accessed June 9, 2010

Pontiac War

http://www.forttours.com/pages/pontiac.asp
accessed June 9, 2010

French and Indian War

The War That Made America: The Story of the French and Indian War, PBS, 2006

http://www.earlyamerica.com/review/1998/scalping.html
accessed June 9, 2010

Sullivan Raid

http://sullivanclinton.com/
accessed June 9, 2010

Fallen Timbers

http://www.fallentimbersbattlefield.com/
accessed June 9, 2010

Prophetstown

http://www.prophetstown.org/settlement.html
accessed June 9, 2010
We Shall Remain, PBS, May 2009
http://www.nps.gov/libi/indian-memorial-at-little-bighorn.htm
accessed June 9, 2010
http://www.eyewitnesstohistory.com/custer.htm
accessed June 9, 2010

Plains Wars

The Way West: How the West Was Lost & Won 1845–1893, PBS Home Video,
      2006
http://www.pbs.org/weta/thewest/resources/archives/six/bighorn.htm
accessed June 9, 2010
http://www.sittingbull.org/
accessed June 9, 2010
http://www.us7thcavcof.com/GCompany.html
accessed June 9, 2010
http://www.us7thcavcof.com/Forts.html
accessed June 9, 2010
The History Of Warfare: The Battle Of The Little Bighorn, War File DVD, 2006

Nez Perce War

http://www.nps.gov/nepe/historyculture/nez-perce-stories.htm
accessed June 9, 2010

Chief Joseph

http://www.pbs.org/weta/thewest/people/a_c/chiefjoseph.htm
accessed June 9, 2010

Big Hole Battle

http://www.nezperce.com/bholebf.html
accessed June 9, 2010
http://www.fs.fed.us/npnht/quotes/bighole.shtml
accessed June 9, 2010

Wounded Knee

http://www.woundedkneemuseum.org/index.htm
accessed June 9, 2010
http://www.bgsu.edu/departments/acs/1890s/woundedknee/
    WKIntro.html
accessed June 9, 2010
http://www.nmai.si.edu/education/codetalkers/
accessed June 9, 2010

INDEX

About the Author

CLARISSA W. CONFER graduated from Pennsylvania State University with a Ph.D. in American History. She is currently the Director of the American Indian Institute at California University of Pennsylvania. Her previous books include *The Cherokee Nation in the Civil War* and *Daily Life in Pre-Columbian Native America*.